The Political Economy
of Inflation

The Political Economy
of Inflation

*edited by Fred Hirsch and
John H. Goldthorpe*

Harvard University Press

CAMBRIDGE · MASSACHUSETTS

Second printing, 1979

Printed in the United States of America

Library of Congress Cataloging in Publication Data

Main entry under title:

The Political economy of inflation.

  Bibliography
  1. Inflation (Finance)   I. Hirsch, Fred.
II. Goldthorpe, John H.
HG229.P64   332.4'1   : 77-26195
ISBN 0-674-68583-0

Contents

Acknowledgments

The Warwick Conference on The Political Economy of Inflation was sponsored by the International Political Economy Group and the Money Study Group, with financial assistance from the Social Science Research Council. We would like to express our appreciation for this support and its contribution to the present work. Organisation of the conference and of contacts between the editors and authors was largely in the hands of Ruth Hirsch. In preparing the papers for press we received valuable secretarial assistance from Audrey Skeats and Joy Gardner. The bibliography and the index were prepared by Donald Hirsch.

Fred Hirsch
John H. Goldthorpe

Note: Billion is used throughout as thousand millions (or milliards), and not million millions, which was the old European usage.

Shortly after correcting the proofs of this book, on 11 January 1978, Fred Hirsch died at the age of 46. We wish here to record the sadness we feel at his loss, as colleague and friend, but also our good fortune in having had the opportunity to work with him in the last months before his death. Through the sharpness of his intelligence and the range of his knowledge and interests he extended our minds; and through the manner in which he faced great personal adversity—with unfailing courage, wit and style—he enhanced our lives.

In its conception and inspiration, this is Fred Hirsch's book: to help realise it was our privilege.

M.A.	J.H.G.	D.P.
S.B.	C.S.M.	R.P.
C.C.	M.P.	M.R.
J.S.F.	A.T.P.	

Contributors

MALCOLM ANDERSON, Professor and Chairman of Department of Politics, University of Warwick. Previously Lecturer in Department of Government, University of Manchester and Research Fellow, Fondation Nationale des Sciences Politiques, Paris. Joint author of *The Right in France 1890–1919* (1962), author of *Government in France: an Introduction to the Executive Power* (1970), *Conservative Politics in France* (1974), and articles mainly in the fields of French and European politics.

SAMUEL BRITTAN, principal economic commentator of the *Financial Times* and Visiting Fellow, Nuffield College, Oxford. Author of *Steering the Economy* (1971), *Capitalism and the Permissive Society* (1973), (with Peter Lilley) *The Delusion of Incomes Policy* (1977), *The Economic Consequences of Democracy* (1977), and of numerous articles on political economy.

COLIN CROUCH, Lecturer in Sociology, London School of Economics. Author of *The Student Revolt* (1970), *Class Conflict and the Industrial Relations Crisis* (1977) and of articles and Fabian Society pamphlets in the fields of social stratification, industrial relations and social policy. Editor (with L. Lindberg and others) of *Stress and Contradiction in Modern Capitalism* (1975) and (with A. Pizzorno) *The Resurgence of Class Conflict in Western Europe since 1968* (1978).

JOHN S. FLEMMING, Official Fellow and Investment Bursar, Nuffield College, Oxford. At various times has worked for, or advised, the Board of Trade, the Bank of England and the Treasury. Author of *Inflation* (1976) and of articles on macro-economics, capital theory, public finance and social economics.

JOHN H. GOLDTHORPE, Official Fellow, Nuffield College, Oxford. Previously Lecturer in the Faculty of Economics and Politics and Fellow of King's College, Cambridge. Publications include (with David Lockwood and others) *The Affluent Worker* series (1968–9), (with Keith Hope) *The Social Grading of Occupations* (1974) and other monographs and articles in the fields of industrial sociology, social stratification and social theory.

FRED HIRSCII, late Professor of International Studies, University of Warwick. Previously a senior adviser at the International Monetary Fund and Financial Editor of *The Economist*. Publications include *Money International* (1967), (with David Gordon) *Newspaper Money* (1975), *Social Limits to Growth* (Harvard, 1977) and other books and articles mainly in the field of international finance.

CHARLES S. MAIER, Associate Professor of History, Duke University and currently co-director of a study group on The Politics and Sociology of Global Inflation for the Brookings Institution. Previously Assistant Professor of History, Harvard University and Visiting Professor, University of Bielefeld. Author of *Recasting Bourgeois Europe: Stabilization in France, Germany and Italy in the Decade after World War I* (1975) and of articles on twentieth century European history and recent American diplomatic history.

MILIVOJE (MIĆA) PANIĆ, Adviser, Bank of England. Previously Chief Economist, National Economic Development Office. Editor and contributor, *The UK and West German Manufacturing Industry 1954–72* (1975) and author of monographs and articles in the fields of international economics, industrial economics and economic growth.

ALAN T. PEACOCK, Principal-Elect and Professor of Economics, University College at Buckingham. Previously Professor of Economics, University of York and Chief Adviser to Departments of Trade and Industry, and Prices and Consumer Protection. Author (with G. K. Shaw) of *Economic Theory of Fiscal Policy* (1971, 1976), (with Jack Wiseman) of *Growth of Public Expenditure in UK, 1890–1955* (1962, 1967) and of monographs and articles on the economics of public finance, fiscal policy, social policy and the Arts.

DAVID PIACHAUD, Lecturer in Social Administration, London School of Economics. Adviser on social policy to the Prime

Minister's Policy Unit, 1974–76. Author of articles on poverty, prices, low incomes and social security.

RICHARD PORTES, Professor of Economics, Birkbeck College, University of London and, for 1977–8, Guggenheim Fellow and Visiting Professor of Economics, Harvard University. Previously Official Fellow, Balliol College, Oxford and Assistant Professor of Economics and International Affairs, Princeton University. Author of articles on centrally planned economies, economic theory and East-West economic relations.

MARTIN RICKETTS, Lecturer in Economics, University College at Buckingham. Previously Research Fellow, Institute of Social and Economic Research, University of York. Author or co-author of articles on economic stabilization, housing and environmental policy and the history of economic thought.

Prologue

Fred Hirsch and John H. Goldthorpe

At a conference of monetary economists a few years ago, Professor Richard Cooper, who is currently Undersecretary in the U.S. State Department, and a man not given to facetious comment, cut through a theological wrangle on the sources of inflation with a neatly synthesizing complaint. 'I have never been able to understand the impasse between the monetarist and the sociological explanations of inflation. I have always assumed the money supply to be sociologically determined.' The remark provides a fitting text for this volume.

In the past decade, the problem of inflation has escalated from a continuing irritant to a blight on the stability and efficient performance of the leading economies and to a potential threat to the preservation of democratic societies. Both the defenders and the opponents of modern capitalist society now see inflation as its great unsolved issue. In fine irony, it is only in the communist states, which reject the centrality of the market mechanism, that money, the essence of that mechanism, now retains its value over time. The problem is worldwide, but has become most prominent in troubled economies such as those of Britain and Italy.

Inflation has traditionally been seen as an economic problem and has been studied by economists. Such studies have been intensified in recent years, and our understanding of the economic mechanisms involved has been broadened and deepened. Yet these studies themselves have emphasized that inflation of the kind now endemic in the non-communist world is more than an economic problem. It pervades the political and social structures of society and may become embedded in those structures. So while most discussions of the inflation problem have focussed on technical issues such as the extent to which inflation is

1

a purely monetary phenomenon or connected with other economic forces, the larger issue is the extent to which inflation is now rooted in political and social forces, and their connection with the economic mechanism: inflation as a problem of political economy.

There is widespread agreement that to understand the role of inflation in our society, it has to be considered in this larger context. Yet few attempts to do so have been made. Economists themselves have been shy to venture outside their established field of professional expertise. Confronted by political and social disturbances, economists in this stance have slid easily and often unthinkingly into the assumption-cum-conclusion that the non-economic factors are the extraneous variables that can be expected in the end to adapt to an overriding and objective economic reality. Technical remedies are available and adequate; all that is necessary is for them to be accepted at the political and popular levels. An approach of this kind in the basically reassuring report of the McCracken group of economists on the feasibility of a return to full employment and reasonable price stability in the industrial market economies (McCracken, 1977), has been tellingly criticised by a political scientist for its methodological naivity and ideological prejudgement (Keohane, 1977). Yet political scientists and sociologists have felt uncomfortable in economic territory and have been slow to step into the breach. The ensuing lacuna in analysis has resulted in a continuing underestimation of the depth of the inflation problem in contemporary society.

The present work was designed as a contribution to a more broad-based study of inflation. This necessarily required an interdisciplinary group, which in turn risks two familiar pitfalls. One is a multi-disciplinary (or worse, non-disciplinary) mishmash. The second is a dialogue of the deaf. We sought to steer our way through by first selecting contributors who were firmly based in their own discipline of economics, sociology or politics, and yet willing to become actively engaged in cross-disciplinary discussion. We wanted also to cover as wide a range of the ideological spectrum as seemed consistent with effective communication. The latter constraint entailed omission of a full blown Marxist analysis as well as a hard-line or purist monetarism, but still allowed us to cover a range spreading well beyond the bounds of the liberal consensus. Finally, while we asked all contributors to respect the overriding policy interest of the project, and not retreat into scholasticism, we urged that the links should be shown between policy analysis and the related theory. We have therefore attempted to achieve integration or at least confrontation in three respects: between disciplines and their differing methodologies, between different ideological positions, and between theory and practice.

In pursuit of this objective, we proceeded as follows. The content of the contributions to the book was finalized by the authors jointly at a meeting held in January, 1977. First drafts of the chapters were then discussed at a conference held at Warwick University on 26 May, 1977, which brought together some seventy social scientists under the auspices of the International Political Economy Group and the Money Study Group. These drafts were then revised in the light of the conference discussion and of further interchanges among authors that were prompted in part by the assignment of each author to act as critic of another's contribution, in most cases in a different discipline. By these means, the several chapters of the book were brought into closer relation with each other and, as will be seen, an encouraging amount of cross-referencing occurs.

Largely on this account, the most appropriate ordering of the chapters was not easy to decide upon. Because their inter-connections are multiple, they cannot be placed one after another in a strictly logical sequence. We have aimed to provide a balance of continuity and contrast that we hope will stimulate but not bewilder readers; many will no doubt select an order for themselves.

The objective of the first chapter, contributed by Flemming, is to give an account of inflation as an economic—and indeed, as Flemming would argue, an essentially monetary—phenomenon. However, it is important to note that Flemming's monetarism, while lacking nothing in rigour, is of a distinctively latitudinarian kind. As Michael Posner observed, as a discussant at the Warwick conference, 'Flemming provides a niche for almost everyone': there is no withdrawal of the economist's union card from those adhering to cost-push theories or from other dissenters. To be sure, some will find their niches more comfortable than others, but the extent of Flemming's eclecticism serves to bring out all the more clearly the crucial issues on which economists disagree and on which, moreover, economists and other social scientists must engage with each other, whether in collaboration or conflict. For example, is it or is it not a valid assumption that the 'intensity of . . . feelings and urgency' of labour's demands do not matter, since in fact 'everyone maximizes' all of the time (p. 31)? Or again (and of course relatedly), is it or is it not the case that non-economic influences on the rate of inflation can operate only via government—that is, particularly via monetary policy—and *not* via other channels (p. 36)?

In the second chapter, that by Maier, the perspective on inflation that is offered changes sharply. From the economic analysis of inflation at a relatively high level of generality, and hence of abstraction, we shift to the historical analysis of the course of particular inflations that have occurred within modern economies, mainly capitalist, during the present century. The idealized actors of economists' theories now give way to flesh-and-blood historical figures and to highly specific social groupings. The theories themselves reappear, not just as cognitive enterprises to be judged as true or false but as technical instruments or as ideologies to be assessed in terms of their pragmatic value to their exponents in the complex coalitions and conflicts that are attendant upon inflation. However, Maier does not fall back on the easy option of mere antinomianism—the denial of any possibility of going beyond the description of particular cases. While sensitive to the dangers of over-generalization, excessive formalism and attempts to transcend history, his central concern is none the less to move from the historical record to develop a typology of inflationary situations and of the configurations of socio-political interests that are involved in their creation and resolution.

The third chapter, contributed by Portes, represents another style in the combination of history and theory. The historical fact from which he begins is that over the last two decades the communist states of Eastern Europe have largely avoided inflation (while money incomes and real consumption have grown). His aim is then to explain why and how price stability has been maintained, and also the recent loss of this stability—i.e. the occurrence of some open inflation—in two countries, Poland and Hungary. The student of centrally planned economies, as

Portes makes clear, cannot but be a 'political' economist: 'No important economic problem could be treated purely technocratically in such an economy, any more than Kantorovich could become President of Gosplan. Planning is a political process' (p. 73). Thus, political—and also sociological—considerations are integral to Portes' analysis. But, writing as an economist, he focusses his attention on the techniques of economic management that socialist planners deploy, on the institutional means through which these techniques are implemented, and also on the economic theory that underlies them—for example, in the monetary field, 'a fairly unsophisticated, short-run version of the quantity theory' which, however, 'may not be unreasonable in the CPE context' (p. 78).

The differing approaches of our first three authors give some idea of the range and variety of issues that any adequate political economy of inflation must be able to address. The next trio of papers serves to illustrate how some of these issues might be systematically pursued with empirical methods. For example, analyses of the interest-group politics of inflation, of the kind essayed by Maier in chapter 2, must obviously be founded on knowledge of which groups are likely to gain and which to lose from inflation (or from different policies aimed at stabilization). In chapter 4 Piachaud provides a critical review of evidence on the effects of inflation on the structure of economic inequality, and in particular on the personal distribution of income, in Britain during the last twenty years. As important, perhaps, as the substantive conclusions that he reaches is his demonstration of the complexity of the effects that operate, and his methodological point that these effects must be seen as bearing on those who at any one time are found in particular roles or collectivities—among which, however, individuals will typically move a good deal in the course of their lives.

In the contributions presented in chapters 5 and 6 attention shifts back to the causes rather than the consequences of inflation, and in both cases the procedure of the authors is the classic one of moving from theoretical analysis to specific hypotheses and then to the statistical testing of their hypotheses in as rigorous a way as possible. Peacock and Ricketts, drawing on an economic theory of politics as well as on economic theory of a more conventional kind, develop an argument that implies that the size and rate of growth of the public sector of a national economy should be positively associated with the rate of inflation. From a combination of economic and sociological theory Panić, derives hypotheses that relate the rate of inflation inversely to the levels of income and consumption that a nation has achieved in comparison with those of other nations, but positively to the degree of inequality in its internal income distribution. In the event, Panić is able to show stronger statistical support for his position than are Peacock and Ricketts. But, as the authors themselves stress, the findings they report should not be regarded as at all conclusive. Rather, they should be seen as representing preliminary results in areas of enquiry where formidable problems arise—in securing reliable data, in choosing appropriate indicators, in locating the direction of causation in complex interrelated processes, and above all, perhaps, in making *ceteris paribus* assumptions when relationships are being tested across countries that differ widely in their political institutions, social structures and cultural traditions.

In chapters 7, 8 and 9, written by Brittan, Goldthorpe and Crouch, we again have a set of three closely interrelated papers. They are alike in raising questions of method that are, however, of more than philosophical significance alone, since they connect directly with questions of the most immediate socio-political interest; questions, no less, of the viability of liberal democracy. Brittan's contribution may be read as in effect a continuation of that of Flemming. It is an attempt to go beyond the recognition of inflation as a 'monetary disease' and to examine 'the forces which lie behind excessive injections of money into the economic system' (p. 161), while retaining a consistently 'economic' mode of analysis. It is, in other words, a sustained essay in the economic theory of politics (as earlier utilized by Peacock and Ricketts) in which political actors—voters, bureaucrats, politicians—are also included in the conceptual world in which 'everyone maximizes' or at least tries their best to do so. However, in this case the result is no celebration of an inherently self-regulating system. On the contrary, the question to which Brittan's analysis ultimately leads him is that of whether or not an interaction of economic time-lags and imperfections in the political process will serve as the engine of a 'doomsday machine' that, through the generation of ever higher rates of inflation, will destroy liberal-democratic institutions. And rather than giving any direct answer to this question, Brittan adds to its complexity by recognizing that, while the problem of runaway inflation may be overcome, this could in turn lead to the abiding tensions within liberal democracy being revealed in some still more uncongenial fashion.

The starting point of Goldthorpe's paper is with the 'residual categories' of economists' theories of inflation (including those that seek to encompass political influences), through which, he argues, the attempt is made to deal with modes of social action that cannot, in terms of these theories, be accounted for as rational. What Goldthorpe then attempts to show is that such action can in fact be rendered intelligible in the context of a sociological account of inflation, the basic supposition of which is that a free market economy will tend always to create divisions and conflict within the society in which it operates unless its disruptive potential is offset by exogenous factors. Inflation is then to be regarded as one particular manifestation of conflict in capitalist society between groupings with different market and work situations; and the current high rates of inflation may be seen as reflecting recent changes in the form of social stratification within capitalism, through which such conflict has been rendered both more intense *and* more equally matched.

In this way, then, there arises an interesting convergence of view between Goldthorpe and Brittan. Although beginning with different questions and pursuing different, indeed contrasting, styles of analysis, they end in substantial agreement on the point that inflation is not just a technical economic problem, to be resolved by technical expertise, but is rather itself a 'solution', of sorts, to more fundamental problems of a socio-political character. In Crouch's contribution this same point is in fact accepted at the outset. Inflation is treated as one of a set of problems of 'interest regulation' that, Crouch argues, must in any society be handled by some combination of economic, moral and political sanctions. He then outlines how in modern capitalist society various processes of change, but most crucially the progressive organization of economic interests, have led directly to a growth in the importance of regulation via political means, and hence in the functions and institutions of the state.

It follows, therefore, that if a solution to the problem of inflation is to be found, it cannot be, as monetarist analyses would often imply, in economic policy alone. Solutions advocated as 'non-interventionist' are by no means non-political; and their implementation in the present context is indeed difficult to envisage without some still further considerable increase in the coercive power of the state. For Crouch, the key to the control of inflation and to the more successful regulation of organized interests generally must lie in a continuation of institutional development leading to the more effective political integration of these interests. What is needed, over and above economic technique, is political creativity.

In the analyses presented in each of this last set of papers, the concepts of power and power relations play a crucial role. Yet these are concepts of notorious difficulty, the use of which often conceals as many questions as it resolves. In the first part of his contribution in chapter 10, which may be read as a coda to the preceding papers (and to that of Maier), Anderson reviews the central issues that have arisen in recent debates on 'power' among political scientists, and points to two possible ways forward. One is to accept that in treating power relations one is, willy-nilly, forced to take up a political and not just a theoretical stance, since power is 'an essentially contested concept' (Lukes, 1974). The other way—seemingly less indulgent—which Anderson himself favours, is to attempt analyses of specific types of power relation which, while limited in scope are still susceptible to criticism on the basis of empirical enquiry rather than resting solely on their authors' political predilections. Thus, in the second part of his paper Anderson follows the lead of more sophisticated exponents of the economic theory of politics to develop a model of the exercise of power in the form of 'inducement/coercion'. This, he then seeks to show, is a model appropriate to relations between governments and organized economic interests and, in particular, to understanding the pattern of events in major confrontations and their eventual *dénouements*.

The concluding chapter of the collection, written by Hirsch, is then an attempt to present an integrated view of inflation as a problem of political economy. It draws sustenance and inspiration from the preceding contributions, without claiming or seeking to synthesize them into a coherent whole. It considers inflation as the joint product of technical monetary factors and of socio-political and broad economic influences, working as correlates. The release of paper money from its earlier gold base is seen as the basic permissive factor in twentieth-century inflation; universalist political legitimacy as its driving impulse. The major theme is that this latter impulse has operated indirectly through the irresolution of group or ideological conflicts, with inflation resulting from the blocking of non-inflationary or less inflationary alternative policies that appear ideologically threatening. In this approach, the socio-political framework in which monetary policy operates is brought inside the analysis as an interacting variable, rather than being taken as an unchanging or idealized fixture. Assessment of alternative financial policies needs to be broadened correspondingly. Thus, rather than Keynesian policies appearing as a fundamental cause of inflation, both Keynesian policies and inflation are seen as defensive responses to the common politico-economic imperatives of a democratic age. The limitation of this broadened analysis is that at the present stage it can be no more than suggestive, pending its further development and refinement.

Our main hope for the book as a whole is that it will spur the fuller integration of different methodologies and fields of interest in the social sciences that is needed to deal with major policy issues, of which inflation is merely the most prominent current example. We have found our own excursion into the inter-disciplinary badlands encouraging, despite initial difficulties in coaxing potential contributors to leave their familiar pastures. The engagement of the different approaches produced a special intellectual stimulus, both in the authors' group and in the wider circle of the Warwick conference. To give a flavour of that conference discussion, we append, on page 215 following Goldthorpe's contribution, an extract of a poignant exchange on the role of the social scientist. But the value of such exchanges must lie ultimately in the degree to which they influence subsequent thinking and writing. This book is the outcome of one attempt by social scientists in different disciplines to speak to each other. The most important measure of its success will be the extent to which it prompts others to carry on the dialogue.

Fred Hirsch and John H. Goldthorpe

STATISTICAL BACKGROUND

TABLE 1   *Inflation Since World War II: Consumer Prices 1948–76*
(annual averages; 1970 = 100)

	Germany	Japan	UK	US	Total OECD
1948	–	32.7	44.8	61.4	
49	68.5	41.0	46.1	62.9	
50	64.3	38.1	47.3	61.9	
51	69.2	44.2	51.9	66.9	
52	70.7	46.0	56.4	68.4	
53	69.4	49.5	57.3	68.9	
54	69.6	52.2	58.3	69.2	
55	70.7	51.5	60.3	69.0	64.0
56	72.5	51.9	62.9	70.0	65.4
57	74.0	53.5	65.0	72.4	67.5
58	75.6	54.0	66.8	74.4	69.8
59	76.4	54.8	67.2	75.1	70.7
60	77.4	56.7	67.9	76.3	72.0
61	79.2	59.7	69.8	77.0	73.4
62	81.6	63.7	72.5	77.9	75.2
63	84.0	68.7	73.9	78.8	77.3
64	85.9	71.5	76.3	79.9	79.2
65	88.7	76.7	79.9	81.2	81.6
66	91.9	80.5	83.0	83.7	84.4
67	93.4	83.7	85.2	86.0	86.9
68	94.9	88.4	89.2	89.6	90.3
69	96.7	93.3	94.0	94.4	94.7
70	100.0	100.0	100.0	100.0	100.0
71	105.3	106.3	109.4	104.3	105.3
72	111.1	111.5	117.5	107.7	110.2
73	118.8	124.5	127.9	114.4	118.8
74	127.1	152.7	148.4	127.0	134.9
75	134.7	171.2	184.4	138.6	150.3
76	147.0	187.7	215.0	146.6	163.2

Sources: Germany, Japan, UK, US: IMF, *International Financial Statistics.* Total OECD: 'OECD Growth Triangles', OECD mimeograph. Weights are based on private final consumption expenditure in 1970.

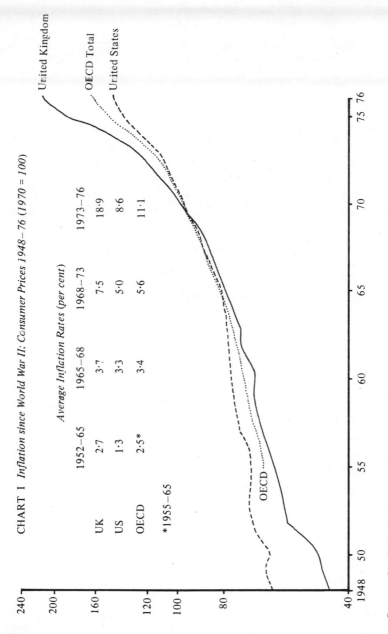

CHART 1 *Inflation since World War II: Consumer Prices 1948–76 (1970 = 100)*

Average Inflation Rates (per cent)

	1952–65	1965–68	1968–73	1973–76
UK	2·7	3·7	7·5	18·9
US	1·3	3·3	5·0	8·6
OECD	2·5*	3·4	5·6	11·1

*1955–65

Sources: See Table 1

CHAPTER 1

The Economic Explanation of Inflation*

J. S. Flemming

Introduction

This chapter presents an economic account of the inflationary process and a brief economic analysis of counter-inflationary policies. It examines the influence of exchange rate policies, changes in the terms of trade, the behaviour of trade unions, public expenditure and other elements that are commonly cited as factors in the recent inflationary process independently of monetary policy. But it is important first to have a working definition of inflation and useful, as a reference point, to have a sketch of how it might occur in a competitive, isolated, unregulated economy.

The rate of inflation is commonly defined as the rate at which the general level of prices is changing. By 'the general level of prices' is meant the amount of money required to buy a representative bundle of goods—it is the relative price at which goods in general (a composite commodity) and money are exchanged for one another. In a competitive economy relative prices are determined by supply and demand. If, at a given price, demand for a particular commodity exceeds supply, a price rise is called for in response to which output will rise, and consumption fall, bringing supply and demand into line. Changing relative prices are due to factors causing changes

*This essay draws substantially on my book *Inflation* (Oxford University Press, 1976). Certain sections are reproduced verbatim by kind permission of OUP. The reader is referred to the book for amplification of several of the themes of this essay as well as a discussion of other aspects of inflation and fuller references.

13

either in relative demands (tastes, incomes etc.) or in relative supplies (climate, technology etc.).

On this basis we might conclude that the general price level is determined, for given tastes and stocks of assets, by the quantity of money (stock) relative to the available quantity (flow) of the composite commodity. If so, a change in the general price level (inflation) must stem either from a change in tastes affecting money holdings, or a change in the quantity of money (or some other asset) relative to the quantity of the composite commodity.

The demand for money depends on the money value of the transactions people expect to be undertaking, the cost of holding money rather than non-money assets, and the ease with which non-money assets can be converted into money. The supply of money is subject to the influence of the government, which may issue money to cover a budget deficit when it spends more, either on goods (such as school furniture), services (such as teachers render), or transfers (such as old-age pensions), than it raises in taxation, or for the purchase of financial assets, notably its own debt or foreign currency.

The Effects of an Increase in the Money Supply on Prices and Output. The money supply may be increased for a number of reasons—as an objective in itself, or to reduce interest rates, or to prevent them from rising. Whatever the motive, the money supply is increased by the government buying in some of its outstanding debt in exchange for which the sellers will receive cheques which when presented and cleared, will increase not only their own bank deposits but their banks' deposits at the central bank. As these are an important part of the banks' reserves of liquid assets, both the sellers of securities and the banks are more liquid than otherwise. At an unchanged interest rate the banks would want to convert some of this extra liquidity into less liquid, and more profitable, investments such as advances to customers. An increase in the money supply thus tends to reduce interest rates. There are several reasons why a reduction in interest rates should increase demand for output: not only does it encourage investment by raising the present value of future profits relative to present costs, but also, with higher prices for all claims on future income (stocks, shares, houses etc.), people will be wealthier and likely to spend more of their income.

If then, it is accepted that monetary expansion will increase the level of aggregate demand, in money terms, in this way, we still have to allocate the change in the money value of demand between a quantity change and a price change. Hicks (1965; 1974) has introduced the terms 'fix-price' and 'flex-price' to characterize markets that respond to demand changes by changing quantities and prices respectively.

In a market in which each week's output was auctioned off on Fridays, an unanticipated increase in the money value of demand would be reflected entirely in price changes because supply would be fixed. This is the flex-price case. In practice most industrial products are sold at advertised prices by stock-holding outlets. In this case the initial impact of an increase in demand falls on retailers' stocks. Since retailers tend to work to conventional margins they are unlikely to raise their prices as long as they can obtain supplies from manufacturers at unchanged prices. Manufacturers also hold stocks and, even if their costs of production rise with output, they may not raise output at once, preferring to meet the extra demand by running down stocks; even when they do raise output, it is quite likely that if they can buy materials and hire labour, at unchanged prices and wages, their costs will not rise significantly. Indeed, as for retailers, an increased throughput at fixed margins increases the return on fixed capital unless capacity is a binding constraint. Thus, manufactured products tend to fit the fix-price model, at least in the short run.

In the long run the price of the output of fix-price manufacturers cannot be independent of the prices of raw materials that, like agricultural commodities, are traded on flex-price markets. The long-run response of industrial prices also depends on what happens in the market for their labour input. In the absence of general involuntary unemployment, employers will not typically be able to increase their work force in a competitive labour market without offering higher wages, if only as an overtime premium. If, however, trade unions have negotiated wages in particular industries at which firms face an excess supply of labour, and if only the unemployed actively seek these jobs, an increase in the number of jobs offered by employers will reduce unemployment in the fix-price manner.

Thus the system responds initially to an increase in demand by increasing the sales and output of manufactures at unchanged prices; employment rises at unchanged wage schedules but the prices of flex-price commodities rise. Because these are volatile anyway, manufacturers will tend to iron out fluctuations in commodity prices when deciding on prices for their own products, so that even the commodity-price rises are unlikely to be passed on in full at once.

However this situation is unsustainable; ultimately three things will undermine it. The increased level of output implies a higher level of money income, even at unchanged prices; this will increase the demand for money, tending to make interest rates rise again and thus dampening the initial stimulus to demand. The increased commodity prices will, if maintained, eventually be reflected in product prices. Finally the sectors of the economy employing workers at a competitive market-clearing wage will tend to lose labour to the premium employers in the general process of labour turnover. This loss of labour can be made good only by bidding up the competitive wage, which should anyway have risen in line with any increase in prices.

The Scope for Speculation. The important point about this story is that an increase in monetary demand is likely to be met initially by an increased volume of output and only later by increased prices, which stay up even when output reverts to its original trend level. Moreover, as the length of the story suggests, the process may be long drawn out and the possibilities of speculative anticipation may make the delay rather erratic.

Speculative anticipation would tend to accelerate this process but, depending as it does on expectations, it is unlikely to operate very systematically as far as timing is concerned. The interest rate relevant for most real investment decisions is an interest rate adjusted for the expected rate of inflation—the *real* rate of interest. If the price of bricks, or tinned salmon, is confidently expected to rise by 10 per cent over the next year, one can make a profit of 10 per cent, less storage costs, merely by holding them for resale, or use, at the end of the year. Thus at a given nominal interest rate, a higher expected rate of increase of prices stimulates demands for durable goods with low storage costs, and probably fixed investment as well. Thus a monetary expansion, which both lowers nominal interest rates and raises the price level expected to rule in two years' time, is a double stimulus to demand, which tends to make the price increase occur sooner. The working of this mechanism depends on people's consciousness of the link between current monetary changes and future price changes; this consciousness probably varies from time to time, tending to rise with experience of inflation. Thus the delays in the process are initially long, but, if a series of inflationary episodes follow one another fairly rapidly, the process by which monetary expansion is translated into price increases is likely to be less drawn out each time. Hence Friedman's dictum (1968) that the lags in the process are not only long but variable. Indeed inflation may even be caused by the mere expectation of inflationary expansion; this possibility indicates the difficulty of testing the monetary theory of inflation sketched here by finding out statistically whether changes in money supply typically precede, or follow, changes in real output, money income, and prices. Even if income changes first the subsequent monetary change may not reflect passive accommodation by the authorities, but be an autonomous change on their part already correctly anticipated by the market.

International Aspects

Exchange Rate Regimes. Under fixed exchange rates it is clear that the rates of inflation in different countries can diverge only to the extent that goods entering the price index are not freely traded—whether as a result of their natural or artificial protection. The existence of such a system depends on the respective monetary authorities committing themselves to exchanging foreign currency for their own at fixed rates. This means that the commitment to a fixed exchange rate involves a restriction on the ability to increase the domestic money supply.

If a small country (A), with a fixed exchange rate, increases its money supply more rapidly than its neighbours (after allowing for differences in real growth rates) the open-market purchases

will in effect be from foreigners since nothing has changed
the domestic demand for either money or bonds. As A's currency
thus accumulates in the hands of foreigners, their confidence
in the exchange rate is weakened by the growth of their potential
claims on A's unchanged reserves of foreign exchange. If they
demand that A's authorities honour their pledge to maintain
the exchange rate, by giving foreign currency in exchange for
their holdings of A's currency, then A's authorities' reserves
of foreign currency will be depleted and their ability to sustain
their commitment jeopardized. Thus a real commitment to maintaining its exchange rate requires that no country expand its
money supply too fast.

The situation of a large country in such a system is rather
different. If one country does half the world's trade it is natural
that other countries should choose to ⸝hold about half their
foreign exchange reserves in that country's currency as long
as it is assumed to be stable. If every country has holdings
of this currency it is likely to be used to finance trade with
third countries and the demand for it may well rise above
50 per cent of total exchange reserves. In this situation a devaluation of the major currency is unlikely to be a matter of indifference
to its trading partners for three reasons. First it reduces the
value of their reserves in terms of the quantities of third-country
imports they command; secondly it is likely to accelerate inflation
in the large country, thus reducing the purchasing power there
of holdings of its currency; and thirdly it represents an increase
in the competitiveness of an important rival and thus jeopardizes
the other countries' own surplus positions. The minor countries
are therefore likely to be ambivalent in their attitude to the
major country's exchange rate and this may make them reluctant
to press for conversion of their holdings for fear of precipitating
a devaluation.

This fear and this reluctance present the dominant country
with an opportunity to enrich itself at the expense of its neighbours. If it expands its money supply it will run a trade deficit,
i.e. it will be able to consume more than it produces, which
implies that other countries produce more than they consume.
They can avoid the payment of this tribute only by revaluing
their currencies or demanding conversion of their reserves, either
of which would precipitate a capital loss. In this situation,

the authorities in the dominant country may well at some stage attempt to exploit their position (possibly accidentally, e.g. the United States in the face of the Vietnam war) which, for a while, will involve their domestic inflationary policy generating a worldwide inflation. In the longer run, this behaviour will probably bring the fixed exchange rate regime to an end. This, at any rate, is what happened in the period culminating in 1971–3.

Flexible Exchange Rates. At the other extreme from commitment to fixed rates, with the necessity that countries hold official reserves of foreign exchange, is a system of freely floating rates which, in its purest form, implies that countries hold no *official* reserves at all, though some private people may hold foreign currency for speculative reasons or to balance their portfolios. If this demand is small, the floating-rate system approximates to the closed-economy case with two provisos. The first of these is that expected real interest rates will tend to be equated in all countries if capital markets are free. In this situation a country's exchange rate will tend to change at the rate at which its inflation rate differs from that of other countries, while its inflation rate will be related to the rate of domestic monetary expansion as in the closed-economy case. The second qualification is that in an open floating economy the time pattern of responses may, as we shall see, be very different from a closed one.

Between these extremes of exchange-rate system lie the 'adjustable peg' fixed-rate system established at the postwar Bretton Woods conference and the 'managed floating' rate system into which it was transformed between 1971 and 1973. Both of these systems allow for exchange-rate changes but at the initiative of the authorities rather than that of the market. Under the 'adjustable peg' system each country commits itself to maintaining its exchange rate within a small margin on either side of a par value fixed in terms of some other currency, or mix of currencies, for the time being, but is able to vary its par value from time to time. Since these changes are infrequent they take the form of discrete steps. Under a 'managed float', by contrast, the authorities are not committed to maintaining any particular exchange rate, even in the short run, but choose to hold reserves so as to be able to influence the market rate day by day.

Thus, under the adjustable peg, devaluation is not unthinkable and countries may be willing to risk that consequence of an expansionary monetary policy. A more interesting question is whether, if most countries are inflating, any one country can resist the impact of world inflation by revaluation of its currency. Under the adjustable peg system such revaluations would have to be relatively infrequent; this has two unfortunate consequences for the country (e.g., Germany in the 1960s) trying to pursue a stable price policy in defiance of the trend of world prices. First, the periodic revaluations are liable to become anticipated and lead to currency speculation with a consequent disruption of the whole system. Secondly, the discrete adjustments, when they occur, involve a temporary loss of profitability in export industries and import-competing industries. Naturally this gives rise to lobbies and pressure groups which will try to make the authorities delay the revaluation. The longer this is delayed the greater the upward pressure on prices and the more nearly the country's inflation rate will be brought into line with world rates.

Price and Quantity Responses Under Floating Exchange Rates. Although lip-service was given to price stability as an objective of economic management throughout the postwar period of quasi-fixed exchange rates, the effective constraint on expansionary policies, which it was hoped would raise the rate of economic growth—'going for growth'—was seen, at least in Britain, in terms of the balance of payments. One reason for the balance of payments playing this constraining role, and thus displacing price stability as even a secondary objective of policy, follows from the preceding analysis of the consequences of monetary expansion. There it was argued that quantity effects would precede price effects in a closed economy. In an open economy with a fixed exchange rate, much of the initial increase in demand following a monetary expansion would be met from increased imports and reduced exports. These combine to worsen the balance of payments on current account even if negligible price changes occur. Thus the balance of payments can be seen as a constraint on the expansion of demand without any reference to intervening effects on prices.

Under freely floating rates the effect of expansion is very different; apart from deficits which may be covered by private capital movements, the current account must balance under a 'clean', unmanaged, float. In this situation demand expansion affects the price level by inducing a fall in the exchange rate and this effect is likely, for two reasons, to be much quicker than in the closed-economy case discussed above. First the foreign-exchange market is just the kind of flex-price market referred to there; and now when the initial increase in demand for goods spills over into increased demand for imports, and reduced supply of exports, it is translated into a change in the balance of supply and demand for foreign exchange, and hence in the exchange rate. This effect will quickly lead to an increase in the prices of all tradeable goods if the exchange devaluation is not considered transitory.

This brings us to the second reason for a quick price response; exchange-rate changes are unlikely to be regarded as transitory by importers and exporters because in their experience speculators successfully even out most predictable fluctuations. These speculators are well advised professionals who are fully aware of the connection between domestic demand and the exchange rate; they are therefore quite capable of moving the exchange rate down not only in immediate response to expansionary monetary or fiscal policies but even on the basis of their judgement that such policies are imminent.

External Disturbances: The Terms of Trade and Real Income. We noted at the outset that inflation might be caused by falls in the supply of the representative consumption commodities. Barring war, earthquake, revolutions and plague, supply disturbances are unlikely in closed industrial economies. An open economy is, however more exposed to disturbances in the form off discrete changes in the world prices the country faces, perhaps the result of natural or political disasters elsewhere. A deterioration in the terms of trade is equivalent to a reduction of supply. This is most clearly to be seen in the case of a country producing only one good, some of which is exchanged for some imports. A rise in the relative price of imports reduces the real purchasing power of the country's full employment output. Real income is reduced and if equilibrium is to be restored real wages must fall. Inflation *need* not occur if the foreign currency price of imports rises, since an appropriate appreciation of the currency will reduce the domestic currency increase in the price of imports and make the price of the domestic product actually fall.

The establishment of this equilibrium is not a simple matter if domestic wages are not flexible in a downward direction. It is important to distinguish three theoretically relevant cases: flexibility of both real and money wages, flexibility of real but not of money wages, and inflexibility of the real wage (in which case there is no question of cutting the money wage). If both real and money wages were flexible, equilibrium would be achieved by both falling by the amount by which real income has fallen—say, 5 per cent.

If the authorities restrict the money supply and appreciate the currency when real, but not money, wages are flexible, domestic producers will find their profit margins squeezed and are likely to respond by cutting employment. The reduction of the real wage to its equilibrium level could, given its flexibility, be achieved by allowing the domestic price level to rise by 5 per cent, and leaving the money supply and exchange rate unchanged. The domestic price of the exportable good and money wages are also unchanged. What falls is the volume of domestic absorption—it falls in line with the fall in real income. In this case inflation is being used to facilitate adjustment to a lower real income; any attempt to 'shield' people from the 'threat' to their living standards, represented by the tendency of the price level to rise relative to domestic wages at the unchanged exchange rate, would add unemployment and a balance-of-payments deficit to the 'imported' inflation.

If the authorities believe that real wages are inflexible, or that it would be very costly in terms of unemployment, social distress, and output forgone to reduce them, they may choose to borrow from abroad, against the security (if any) of the economy's growth prospects, in order to sustain current levels of real absorption. This policy clearly involves a deficit on the current account of the balance of payments. What does it imply for inflation? If no reduction in real wages is planned there is no reason to allow any inflation at all. The problem is then one of maintaining employment despite the fall in the profitability of domestic production at the given level of real wages. This problem could be resolved by a transitional wage subsidy or a cut in payroll taxes (such as National Insurance contributions); the consequent government deficit, being the counterpart of the trade deficit, would be financed by foreign borrowing, and would not increase the domestic money supply. Thus in such an economy, with inflexible real wages, the optimal response to a 10 per cent rise in import prices might (if imports accounted for half of domestic absorption) consist of a 5 per cent revaluation of its currency and the introduction of a temporary 5 per cent wage subsidy to be phased out over two or three years if the underlying growth rate is 2 or 3 per cent per annum. As far as the real-income effect of an adverse change in the terms of trade is concerned, we conclude that unemployment and inflation should be used only to the extent that they would ease any necessary reduction of real wages.

Effects on Resource Allocation in the Multi-Product Case. Let us now turn to the effects on resource allocation. These can be introduced by the removal of the assumption of the previous argument that the country in question produces only one good. Suppose instead that it also produces some goods of the type it imports—an import-competing (importable) good—as well as exportable goods and non-tradeables such as retail services, restaurant meals, and construction activity, which together account for one-half of domestic 'absorption'. For simplicity we continue to assume that importables and exportables loom equally large in the country's 'absorption' of goods and services so that a 10 per cent increase in the foreign-currency price of all imports would still have no effect on the domestic price level if the currency appreciated by 5 per cent.

If this appreciation takes place the situation will differ significantly from the previous case: the production of import-competing goods will have become more profitable than the production of exports. If importables and exportables are equally important in the country's absorption, it is clear that exportables must have the larger share of its output. This implies that the 5 per cent fall in the domestic price of exportables affects more producers than does the 5 per cent rise in the price of importables. Sackings, or reduced hirings, by the manufacturers of exportables, whose profits fall, will therefore tend to exceed the extra hirings by producers of importables, whose profits rise. The net effect is that unemployment rises; this reflects the abnormal deviation of the actual distribution of labour, between importable and exportable industries (and related non-tradeable activities), from the new equilibrium, and the consequent need for abnormally large shifts of resources.

If the deterioration in the terms of trade came about through a fall in the foreign-currency price of exportables, instead of a rise in the price of importables, domestic-price stability would still require a fall in the money supply, but in this case it would be accompanied by a devaluation of the domestic currency. In line with the previous example, a 10 per cent fall in the foreign-currency price of exports would require a 5 per cent devaluation which would cause a 5 per cent rise in the domestic price of importables to offset the 5 per cent net fall in the domestic price of exportables. Once the exchange rate has changed the consequences of the fall in export prices and the rise in import prices are identical; in both cases real incomes fall by the same amount and unemployment will rise as resources shift from the production of exportables to importables.

In the face of this additional transitional unemployment the authorities might well choose to inflate the economy, reducing the money supply by less than the fall in real income, and revaluing by less, or devaluing by more, than the amounts suggested above. At least the smaller revaluation and larger devaluation would be necessary if other countries, which must on average experience an improvement in their terms of trade if ours deteriorate, maintain their domestic-price levels. Might they want to inflate too?

In fact they could well choose to inflate since the same *relative* price change, and the consequent need to shift resources, and associated rise in unemployment, affects them as well as us—although they have no problem of reduced real incomes. If the foreign price of a country's exports rises it must revalue its currency if it wants to preserve its domestic-price level. On the other hand, if its imports fall in price it must devalue. But in both cases the money supply should rise in line with the increase in real income. In order to facilitate the necessary shift of resources, from the production of their importables to exportables, they might try to exploit people's tendency to think in money terms by a temporary inflation and thus revalue by less, or devalue by more, than otherwise, increasing the money supply more than the increase in real income. In this way variations in relative prices on a worldwide scale may have a worldwide inflationary bias. As Portes points out (this volume) those Eastern European countries most successful in preventing inflation have used the *Preisausgleich* mechanism to insulate their economies from relative changes in international prices.

Changes in the Terms of Trade and the Causation of Inflation. This analysis raises important questions. Can a government that adopts the policy suggested here in response to a change in its terms of trade be held responsible for the consequent domestic inflation? Could it reasonably claim that the inflation was caused by changes in international prices beyond its control? If we grant this claim we are at least halfway towards the 'cost-push' position that domestic inflation may be the result of external cost pressures independent of monetary factors. Although some of the issues involved may be semantic, or even relate to the ethics of apportioning responsibility, they have attracted considerable attention and are worth analysing.

We saw above that under flexible exchange rates a country should be able to maintain domestic-price stability even though the rest of the world was inflating. We also saw that this was more difficult under the 'adjustable peg' quasi-fixed-rate system. Under the latter system a country's authorities may be able to blame domestic inflation on external events—but only as long as they can justify not floating the currency. Realistically the imported inflation would probably have reached significant proportions before the authorities could screw up the courage to float. All this related to the import of inflation caused by excess monetary expansion in other countries at a time of equilibrium in real magnitudes. What of the terms of trade changes discussed above? Did the 1972 commodity-price boom make some inflation in commodity-importing countries inevitable?

The answer suggested by our analysis is very simple; it is 'No, not inevitable, but possibly wise, if money, but not real wages, were inflexible while price expectations were insensitive.'

Where does this answer leave the *causal* status of import-price increases with respect to domestic inflation, which is the issue raised by the cost-push theory? Since many links in economists' causal chains consist of agents' rational, but freely chosen responses, a commentator must be allowed to say that the import-price rise *caused* the inflation that followed the authorities' response. The authorities themselves, however, cannot make much of this argument since to do so they must deny the conscious wisdom of that response—they cannot claim credit for choosing wisely while denying that they rejected an alternative policy involving more unemployment and less inflation. It may, of course, be argued that the choice was forced on the constitutional 'authorities' by other powers, such as trade unions, who would not stand for the unemployment implied by the alternative strategy. It then becomes a moot point, for both the commentator and the constitutional authorities, whether the inflation was caused by the deterioration in the terms of trade or by the political power of the unions.

To say of an inflationary episode in a particular country that its *ultimate* cause was an import-price increase (the *proximate* cause being the authorities' monetary and exchange-rate policy) does not go very far to meet the cost-push position. We have distinguished two reasons for inflating in response to a change in the terms of trade; first, if the change is adverse, and if money, but not real, wages are inflexible, temporary inflation might facilitate the achievement of the new equilibrium real wage. This argument applies not only to the cost-push case of an import-price rise, but equally to an export-price fall. The second reason for inflating was as a response to the problems of reallocating resources after *any* change in the terms of trade. This argument not only applies symmetrically to an import-price rise and an export-price fall, as above, but it would also apply to an export-price rise or even an import-price fall!

Moreover, from a worldwide viewpoint a change in relative prices cannot be regarded as autonomous. The commodity-price boom of 1972 was associated with an exceptional increase in demand by industrialized countries the economies of which all experienced expansive phases simultaneously—and monetary factors played a large part in these expansions. As mentioned above, commodities typically show a quicker price response to increased monetary demand than do industrial products. International dollar reserves rose by almost 50 per cent in 1971, the dollar price of non-oil commodities by about 25 per cent in 1972, and developed areas' export prices by the same amount the next year. Part of the deterioration of the terms of trade of industrial countries associated with these changes was thus merely the change in relative prices of raw materials and industrial products characteristic of a particular phase in the inflationary process.

The oil-price increase of 1973–4 does look more like a genuinely autonomous disturbance in international prices, if not actually an act of war, but even this had an inflationary background. Oil prices were fixed in U.S. dollars, and as inflation in the United States accelerated, and the U.S. dollar depreciated in relation to other currencies, so the amount of manufactured imports the oil exporters could buy with their oil production diminished. On this view the Arab-Israeli war was merely the catalyst for the crystallization of, and reaction to, the growing discontent of the producers at the erosion of their position by inflation in the industrial West.

The Role of Trade Unions

The argument of the previous section that discrete changes in import prices might justify temporary inflation, though developed from a background of 'monetarist' analysis, involved conceding that 'cost-push' theories contained at least a germ of truth. Their proponents typically lay more stress on the activities of trade unions, which are the subject of this section, than on the changes in the cost of imported goods.

Trade union organization and monopoly power will influence the equilibrium pattern of real wages and the equilibrium allocation of labour. This implies that *changes* in the pattern of union power have to be added to changes in tastes and technology as influences generating the movements which, in the presence of friction, create frictional unemployment. Unions tend to reduce wage flexibility and thus to shift the burden of any necessary adjustment from prices and wages to quantities and employment.

This change is one of degree rather than kind since some wage rigidity, and the consequent reliance on employment adjustment, would characterize capital-intensive industries even if the labour market were perfectly competitive (Flemming, 1976, pp. 44–6).

In these two ways, unions tend to raise the normal/natural level of unemployment; it can, however, be argued that their activities also have the opposite effect by increasing the efficiency of job search in two ways. By collective bargaining they establish uniform wage structures for relatively large categories of jobs. If people bargained individually one could find out what one would earn in a given job only by trying to negotiate a rate for it. Thanks to the activities of unions, the employers' opportunities to discriminate are substantially reduced and the amount of search required falls proportionately. Secondly, by informing their members of the results of their central research on pay in other sectors, on which they may base a wage claim, they disseminate information more widely and cheaply than would the unaided grapevine.

Wage increases occur for at least two distinct reasons. In the face of increased demand for their product, employers may raise wages in order to maintain an appropriate flow of job applicants. Secondly if prices, or wages, elsewhere are rising employees will want to reopen previous agreements in order to maintain their real, or relative, values. Trade unions have very different impacts on these two mechanisms. The first cannot apply to an employer who has conceded higher wages than he would otherwise have done as a result of trade-union pressure. An effect of trade-union monopolies is so to distort relative wages that there is an excess supply of labour to those industries and skills whose wages they have raised. However not all trades are unionized and wage increases in response to increased demand are likely to occur in the less-organized sectors first if price increases do not lead wage rises, i.e. if inflation does not reduce real wages. If, on the other hand, inflation does reduce real wages it is the organized sectors in which the wage response is likely to be most prompt.

These considerations suggest the following theoretical account of the place of trade unions in the inflationary process. An expansion of monetary demand, which might be based on a 'dash for growth,' or be a response to changed terms of trade, leads to a relatively rapid rise in the wages of the unorganized workers in the growth sectors of the economy. As time passes the unions discover that they have slipped behind and succeed in enforcing parity. This leaves the unorganized workers in the declining sectors with substantially lower relative real wages. Some of the union-negotiated wage increases may have been obtained by strikes in essential services with attendant publicity. A natural reaction of the unorganized is to join unions and this further changes the pattern of labour-market monopolies, the equilibrium structure of real wages and the natural rate of unemployment (at least temporarily).

Autonomous Wage Push? This account attributes no role to *autonomous* labour-market disturbances which, as was noted above, are central to a cost-push theory of inflation. The logical possibility of such a disturbance cannot be denied; if ten million workers suddenly banded together and demanded that their money wage be doubled, their employers and the authorities would be in real difficulties and temporary inflation might well ensue. This possibility may be regarded as being of doubtful relevance for three reasons. First, the wage demands we observe are not co-ordinated over a very wide range of workers. If they were, the demand for higher *money* wages would be odd, indeed irrational. Equally, rational demands for higher real wages should then recognize the constraint of available resources; income from employment and self-employment has accounted for over 80 per cent of national income in recent years. The demands of an individual union can, however, present the authorities with a macroeconomic dilemma by virtue of its implications for other unions' demands. Secondly, it is difficult to reconcile any spontaneous wage demand of a novel order of magnitude with the rationality of those concerned, not because the demands are not in their interest, but because the rational pursuit of self-interest leads to discontinuities in behaviour only when circumstances, or the perception of them, change discretely. Finally, and most importantly, most of the instances of allegedly spontaneous upsurges of militancy in individual unions can be fitted quite easily into the theoretical account just given, in which unions appeared as responding to, rather than being responsible for, inflation.

The second argument above can easily be overstated. This

argument from the consistent behaviour of rational agents has
three weaknesses. It overlooks all the well-known problems of
forming a rational collective from rational individuals (Olson,
1965). Secondly, 'consistency' may apply either at a point in
time—in which case it is an aspect of rationality—or over time
in which case it refers to the stability of preferences, possibly
under the influence of habit. While individuals may be fairly
consistent in both senses, a smooth trend of individual preferences
from preference for one faction to preference for another with
a very different policy may lead to a discontinuity in the leadership
which may determine union policy. Thirdly, even if unions were
rational and neither the fickleness of fashionable ideology nor
the power of individual, but changing, leaders had any effect,
there would still be problems associated with inevitable ignorance.

Monetarists sometimes argue that unions are just like other
monopolists and maximize a stable objective function subject
to certain market-imposed constraints. What matters, however,
is their perception of those constraints. What happens if the
union leaders do not know how many of their members will
lose their jobs for each pound by which they raise the real
wage? Other monopolists conduct market research, but that
is difficult when one is confronting one's customers across the
bargaining table. In this state of ignorance it is difficult to
rule out a union deciding, as evidence accumulates, that it
has got the demand elasticity wrong, and that to buy a lot
of information by making a big change is appropriate. Thus
big changes in relative real wages could not be ruled out on
theoretical grounds, even if unions were 'rational' by the criteria
appropriate to individuals. On the other hand, whether such
autonomous changes would occur on a sufficient scale to have
a noticeable impact on macroeconomic variables is very doubtful.

The evidence to the contrary to which British cost-push theorists most frequently point are the major industrial confrontations
and strikes, the occurrence of which was not entirely predictable,
and the consequences of which certainly appear to have been
widespread imitation and accelerating inflation. To reconcile those
in which substantial changes in relative real wages have indeed
occurred with the account given above one should notice three
things about them. The best-publicized strikes, which have been
in the public sector, have taken place when the inflationary

process had already acquired considerable momentum but no inflationary equilibrium had been established. Secondly, they were fought specifically on the basis that public-sector wages had been slipping behind those paid elsewhere, and these claims were substantiated. Thirdly, and most importantly, in several cases (miners and nurses for example, although the first case might have been influenced by increased government 'protection' for the domestic coal industry) they were followed by increased recruitment rather than the cutback which would follow a real-wage-raising initiative of the type associated with the fuller exertion of monopoly power. What had happened was that the government had, as a counter-inflationary strategy, failed to allow wages in these industries to rise despite recruitment difficulties. With such evidence of excess demand any reference to these events as pointing to a wage-push explanation of inflation is clearly misplaced.

The fuller exertion of monopoly power is not a straightforward matter. The reason that economists are so unsympathetic to the appeals to trade union 'militancy' is that it suggests that the intensity of feelings and the urgency of demands matter. This is not possible in the economist's world where everyone maximizes. Trying harder makes no difference; only changes in *relative* intensities of preference matter. In this context increased militancy leads to higher wages only if it reflects either a shift in preferences away from fuller employment and towards higher incomes for the employed or away from submissive quiescence and towards confrontation and strike action.

Non-Monetary Public Policy

Growth and Level of Public Expenditure. It is sometimes suggested that the growth of public expenditure is inherently inflationary. To the extent that the emphasis is on the *growth* rather than the high level of public expenditure, the argument may merely be that a switch in revealed preferences from private to public goods, like a switch from butter to margarine, calls for a redistribution of resources which raises frictional unemployment and may induce the authorities to respond by adopting inflationary monetary policies.

In the case of the *level* of public expenditure it can be argued that the deadweight burden of distortions induced by conventional taxes increases as they rise in proportion to national income. Thus rising public expenditure increases pressure on the authorities not to ignore any potential revenue source. Inflation is such a source, being a tax on the holding of money (and transitionally on the holding of longer-term government debt). For this reason one might expect the rate of inflation to be persistently higher in countries in which both public expenditure and other taxes were also higher. Similarly, countries in which the administration and collection of other taxes was relatively difficult would choose higher rates of inflation for given levels of public expenditure. Empirical evidence on the relationship between inflation and government shares in national income is presented by Peacock and Ricketts, later in this volume.

Expenditure Cuts. The part played by public expenditure in recent British debates on inflation has been less as cause in either of these respects than as a possible remedy in conjunction with monetary restraint. Expenditure cuts are advocated as being less unpalatable, and having less cost-inflationary side effects, than either the higher interest rates associated with an unchanged budget surplus, or the higher taxes associated with a larger budget surplus (or smaller deficit).

That many monetarists have an ideological predilection for this remedy is unquestionable; however, they also have reasons which deserve to be taken seriously. If one has started from an optimal level of public expenditure, one should be indifferent at the margin between public expenditure and the alternative private uses to which the resources could be put. The welfare cost of cutting public expenditure is not the value of the output but the *difference* between the value of the results of public and private use of the resources. At the margin there should be no such difference. Moreover, if public expenditure has been financed by the creation of money, the authorities may have believed that the economy required reflating. In this case they may have indulged in 'make-work' public projects such as the construction of Lansbury's Lido in Hyde Park in 1930. Such projects are often justified by the argument that the opportunity cost of unemployed labour is less than the wage that it is paid. However, if inflation follows such a programme, the level of full employment has been misjudged and the programme should be cut. Alternatively, the authorities may have been determined to undertake certain expenditures although they did not believe that they had adequate public support for non-inflationary tax finance. If they were right that the electorate would not choose to support the expenditure with tax money, then it seems appropriate that the inflation following the monetary expansion should be curbed by cutting the expenditure whose constitutional propriety is in doubt.

Social Benefits. Particular items of public expenditure or other policies may have a big, if indirect, impact on inflation. This is particularly true of welfare measures such as increased paid holidays, shorter working hours, larger retirement pensions and higher unemployment benefits. Each of these tends to reduce the level of output at the natural rate of unemployment, as indeed do other taxes if their disincentive effects encourage people to enjoy more leisure.

Among these policies, that of raising unemployment benefits is peculiarly apt to lead to cumulative inflation. This is because any consequent rise in unemployment not only reduces equilibrium output but also raises an indicator in response to which Pavlovian authorities may expand aggregate demand just when aggregate supply has fallen.

Incomes Policy. Incomes policy is designed to restrain inflation, but it is important to recognize the ways in which it may backfire. These hinge crucially on the unlikelihood that any incomes policy will *permanently* reduce either the velocity of circulation of money or the normal/natural level of unemployment. Under these circumstances such a policy can, at best, offer a breathing-space—an opportunity for relatively painless monetary contraction. However, the temptation is to see such a policy as an alternative to a restrictive monetary/fiscal policy and thus to expand the money supply behind the cover of the incomes policy. If this happens, the exhaustion of the effects of the incomes policy will leave the situation worse than it would otherwise have been.

An incomes policy that successfully restrains nominal labour incomes is likely to tend to raise the level of unemployment for two reasons. It will probably be so designed as to reduce the share of profits in national income even though their share may well already have fallen at the phase of the inflationary process at which the policy is introduced; this threat to profitability reduces investment and employment. Employment is further threatened if the incomes policy is designed to change relative wages, typically raising the relative cost of employing unskilled workers for whose services other factors, and for whose output other goods, are then substituted. Moreover, changes in relative wages change both relative prices and relative incomes, thus causing switches in demand, the response to which in turn generates frictional unemployment.

A short-term wage freeze would not have these consequences and might, suitably combined with restrictive monetary and fiscal policy, contribute to the rapid reduction of inflationary expectations and thus enhance the effectiveness of a counter-inflationary package. However the availability of this option depends crucially on there not having been recent failures with more ambitious policies.

Uncertainty and the Costs of Inflation. This chapter started with an account of the inflationary process and has moved on to consider counter-inflationary policies without first asking why inflation should be countered. Many people attribute recent adverse changes in their real or relative incomes to the inflation that has occurred in recent years without establishing any direct causal link. Inflation has happened; inflation is said to be bad; therefore it is responsible for the bad (but not the good) things that have happened; therefore it is indeed bad.

More careful analysis reveals that the effects of perfectly anticipated inflation could be reduced to a very low level. If interest could be paid on cash, and the tax system suitably reformed, the cost would merely be that of repricing goods. If interest is not paid on money, or if such inflation compensation is taxed, the cost of holding cash balances rises and their use will, at the cost of some little inconvenience, be curtailed. These costs are small, and may even be offset by gains to the government; clearly our troubles lie in the difficulty of anticipating inflation. But why is inflation more difficult to forecast than 'stable prices'? After all, prices have always gone up and down from time to time as harvests were good or bad.

There seem to be three reasons. Reduced dependence on agriculture may reduce the uncertainty of next year's price level, but uncertainty about inflation increases the uncertainty of prices five years hence. Inflation typically implies a failure on the part of the government which neither planned nor expected it. The occurrence of the unexpected and the revelation that the authorities have not been in control are both unsettling. Thirdly, the acceleration of inflation depends on the speed with which experience of inflation is reflected in people's expectations; there are reasons (Flemming, 1976, ch. VII) for this process to occur more rapidly when inflation diverges significantly from price stability. Thus the rate of change of prices may be less predictable at higher levels of inflation.

The effect of higher uncertainty about inflation rates is to undermine confidence in the real value of nominal contracts (including wage agreements). Having settled the money wage does not ensure any particular standard of living. Thus even if living standards do not fall, confidence and peace of mind are lost. Moreover, it is particularly the longer term contracts relating to the finance of investment which become less attractive to both parties as uncertainty about the movement of prices over the next twenty years grows.

It can, of course, be argued that the general feelings of insecurity will lead to increased saving and thus to a higher level of investment despite the reluctance of financiers to sign the relevant contracts. However, a given quantity of resources invested in shorter-lived projects may be of reduced productivity. Moreover, one effect of inflation is to erode, and render uncertain the real value of private pension funds. One response to this is to increase the scale of unfunded public provision for old age. This meets the demand for security without providing for economic growth; inflation thereby brings security and growth into conflict.

Conclusions

Underlying this analysis is a distinction between changes in relative prices and inflationary changes in the *general* price level.

If a society consists of sufficiently heterogeneous groups this distinction may break down (cf. Piachaud, this volume). If the rich consume quite different things from those consumed by the poor, the stability of the price of a basket including both is of interest to nobody. For this reason it may be preferable to revert to the old tradition of defining inflation (as does my 1952 *Concise Oxford Dictionary*) as an 'abnormal increase of the currency.'

A major advantage of this usage is that it would make clear that the contribution of economics is to answer (as I have attempted to do) two questions: what are the effects of monetary expansion? and what (good) *economic* reasons might a government have for monetary expansion? Any government is subject to a variety of pressures and influences relating to its monetary and fiscal policy, pressures deriving from the opinions, preferences and powers of various segments of the population which might lead to inflation; but while there may be an economic element in their analysis economics is unlikely to make a major contribution.

It has been argued that restricting the role of non-economic forces to their influence on government policy—particularly monetary policy—is to miss most of the channels through which social and political forces work. It is certainly true that in the short run an unofficial move for voluntary pay restraint, or against hoarding, will affect the dynamic evolution of prices even given government policy. However, I do not believe that the collective exercise of unofficial will-power will long reduce the velocity of circulation of money. (Such events will be little longer lived than a fakir's reduction of his temperature or pulse.) They can, of course, like a temporary official squeeze, provide an opportunity for a government to change its monetary policy—illustrating the possibility of influence rather than pressure. In the long run, however, non-economic factors will influence inflation only to the extent that they influence monetary policy.

CHAPTER 2

The Politics of Inflation in the Twentieth Century

Charles S. Maier

The Limitations of the Economic Models

Of the more than sixty years since the outbreak of World War I over half have comprised periods of sharply rising prices: 1914 to 1921 or to 1926 (the terminal date depending upon the particular economy), 1938 to 1953 (with 'creeping inflation' still prevailing from 1953 to the late 1960s), and 1967 or so to the present. Nonetheless, political scientists have only recently begun serious analysis of inflation, while historians of politics and society have been even more laggard. Even economic historians strictly speaking have contributed few studies, although this is not surprising. Until recently most economic historians concentrated on questions of development and growth, and above all on industrialization. Inflation, however, presents an urgent problem of welfare and allocation. Sometimes it involves distributing the dividends of economic growth, but often it serves as the mechanism for sharing out the costs of stagnation and decline. All the more central a theme it should be, therefore, for the historian of twentieth-century politics and society. His investigations cannot avoid the political bitterness that has arisen in epochs when growth faltered or fell. In that distributive conflict, inflation has played important roles, either easing or exacerbating the struggle over shares.

The historian can draw only limited assistance from the economic models proposed to understand inflation. (For the most recent see Gordon, 1975.) On one level they provide the raw material for a history of ideas; they indicate how strongly theoretical systems are influenced by refractory problems and policy dilemmas of the day. Quantity theory served economists writing on the inflationary experiences of the 1920s. They might differ as to whether balance-of-payments difficulties or internal budget deficits prodded currency emissions, but they attributed inflation to growing monetary circulation and in France at least tended to define inflation as the increasing volume of currency, not the rise in prices. (Rogers, 1929, pp. 91–128; Aftalion, 1927; Graham, 1930; Ellis, 1934; Bresciani-Turroni, 1937, pp. 79 ff.)

The Keynesian analysis turned from the quantity of money to levels of income and expenditure. But, as interpreted by those whom Coddington (1976) has termed 'hydraulic' Keynesians, the problem presented by potential excess demand was viewed as a mirror image of insufficient demand. An implicit theoretical parity suggested that if the $C+I+G$ streams of demand (consumption, investment and government spending) produced an inflationary gap, macroeconomic adjustments could reduce them easily to a full-employment non-inflationary equilibrium. This extrapolation from a world of depression to one of inflation was too simple, and for the historian of economic ideas, the development of Phillips-curve analysis after World War II can be interpreted as a defensive retreat on the part of the Keynesians. They abandoned the presumed mirror-image symmetry between deflation and inflation and fell back on the more intractable trade-off. Yet even the Phillips-curve redoubt has come under heavy bombardment from Friedmanite critics, and earlier defenders are themselves uncertain of its soundness.

Although the historian can trace these themes as they have developed since the 1930s, they do not offer an effective starting point for his or her own sociopolitical analysis. Monetarism focuses on the keepers of the printing press and summons them to abstinence, but rarely explains what pressures sustain or overcome their resolution (Friedman, 1956; Patinkin, 1969; Teigen, 1972). Keynesian analysis tends to look at consumption decisions on the part of the generality or sometimes postulates the coherence of a class of wage earners. Conservatives, regardless of theoretical camp, postulate gloomy secular changes in a society undermined by 'growthmania,' dark-skinned immigrants or Caucasian egoism. (Mishan, 1974). The point is that the actors posited by the economists are not the agents a historian or social observer will find critical. Each economic model usually implies a particular sociological model, but not all are useful. Refinement of the implicit sociology can make possible decisive advances in economic theory: one of the basic claims of *The General Theory* (1936) was that the group behaviour alleged by classical orthodoxy did not correspond to actual decision-making in the collectivity. A finer breakdown of savers and investors (at least as roles if not as separate individuals) explained why the presumption of full employment was ill-founded. Keynes did not propose an equivalent sociology of inflation, probably because he felt its origins were more centrally determined by war finance (cf. Keynes, 1940; Weintraub, 1960; Trevithick, 1975). Nor do I think that economic models since Keynes have allowed a sufficiently plausible sociology of inflationary propensity, in part because the different class roles vary in different societies, and in part because class alignments themselves evolve in the course of inflation. Social and political structure helps to shape inflation; conversely inflation alters collective social roles. No economic theories, so far as I know, incorporate these reciprocal influences.

Some economic models, however, have begun from assumptions of institutional or class behaviour and not from the postulates of pure competition or marginal-choice rationality. Analyses of cost-plus or other administered pricing go back to Gardner Means, Joan Robinson and Edward Chamberlain in the 1930s, were incorporated by Fred Holzman in his 1950 analysis of inflationary wage–price spirals, and recently have been accredited by William Nordhaus (1975) after being elaborated by French and German economists as well (Koblitz, 1971; Biacabe, 1962, pp. 247–250). Marxist concepts, which link political alignments and economic outcomes even more closely, offer two major theoretical lines of development. James O'Connor (1973) and Ian Gough (1975) stress the contradictory burdens placed upon the public sector in capitalist society—the state's need to bear all the 'externalities' of the profit system, even while it must provide sufficient welfare payments to prevent social upheaval. (Their analysis here converges with many points made by free-market critics of the mixed economy.) This Marxian concentration on the budgetary process derives from Goldscheid's fiscal sociology of the early twentieth century. Goldscheid (1926) did not break down the different class and sectoral claims impinging on the state but emphasized growing public indebtedness *vis-à-vis* private accumulation, and he called upon the state to 'reappropriate' the assets it had allowed capitalists to assemble.

Other Marxian models look less at the state than at the clash of class claims directly in a society where state and economy have largely interpenetrated. Hilferding's concepts of 'organized capitalism' (1915) and the 'political wage' (1927) pointed to the connection betweeen political strength and market power in the raw pluralism of the Weimar Republic. Labour's success in wage negotiations depended upon the German Social Democratic Party preserving the ground-rules for collective bargaining and arbitration; in turn the SPD could remain powerful only so long as its affiliated trade unions retained leverage in the labour market. Similar ideas, of course, have been offered by liberal theorists who stress interest-group rivalry, from Bentley to McConnell (1966) and Lowi (1969). In what Beer terms the collectivist age (1967) and what I have elsewhere (Maier, 1975, pp. 9–15, 580–6) termed corporate pluralism or just corporatism, several developments may facilitate inflation. The state has become 'spongier', more extensive in function and reach but less distinct in administration *vis-à-vis* private interests. The modern economy seems to increase the disruptive possibilities for organized groups—not necessarily because schoolteachers, dustmen and even truck-drivers are more crucial today than railroad workers half a century ago, but because we seem to feel more uncomfortable when they withhold their services, perhaps because the legitimacy of a pluralist system depends precisely upon the appeasement of grievances short of a group's actual walkout. (How else can we explain the potency of student strikes?) In any case, the brokerage of group demands may seem less painful than showdown; as Tobin argues, 'Inflation lets this struggle proceed and blindly, impartially, and nonpolitically scales down all its outcomes. There are worse methods of resolving group rivalries and social conflict' (Tobin, 1972, p. 13).

While this sort of analysis can remain empty or trivial, it does suggest that the state is no longer just an umpire (even a biased one) but a player deeply enmeshed in the game of social and economic bargaining. This player possesses one trump: control of the money supply. But in its control of money and credit (sometimes shared with central bank authorities who achieve genuine independence), the state does not act qualitatively differently from other groups. Each competing interest under inflationary conditions seeks in effect to monetize the assets it controls, whether by means of commodity currency keyed to agricultural products thereby stabilizing the income of farmers, control of interest rates on the part of banks, or index wages that would make labour time the unit of value. Rapid inflation involves the search for constant income shares and thus the attempted coinage of each group's respective scarce goods. Coinage, however, has been a traditional prerogative of sovereignty. Inflation thereby tends to erode sovereignty. Likewise it usually accompanies the devolution of state regulatory capacities upon private interests and, even more generally, dissolves the very sense that an effective public authority exists to enforce the same rules on haves and have-nots together. The loss of commonwealth is, I would argue, one of the severest tolls of inflation, but a cost that the usual welfare functions of economists cannot accommodate.

The analysis of group bargaining thus begins with a tautology, namely that the granting of price and wage claims beyond the given money value of the national product produces inflation. But this recognition, derived from either Marxian or liberal theories of group rivalry, at least assists in demystifying inflation and understanding it as one of the major forms of distributive conflicts in contemporary society. This at least provides the starting point for linking political and social analysis to economic outcomes. For the specification of particular group conflicts and outcomes, case-by-case analysis is required.

Levels of Inflation and the Configuration of Interests

Efforts to infer a sociology or politics of inflation have often foundered on their over-generalization and their formalism. However, inflation is not a uniform phenomenon; it may rather be a syndrome of very different group conflicts. At the risk of over-simplification we can establish a typology of three infla-

Charles S. Maier

tionary plateaus and a deflationary process as well. They are labelled here: 'hyperinflation', 'Latin inflation', 'creeping inflation' and 'the stabilization crisis'. The first three cases are analysed in this section, the stabilization crisis in the following section. Each case, I submit, is characterized by one or two different configurations of interests and group alignments.

Table 1 summarizes the respective inflationary types and their associated socio-political alignments. It is important to note that the differing levels of inflation may be more or less stable. There is no inevitable slide from creeping inflation to Latin inflation or thence to hyperinflation; significant alterations in group attitudes and/or group behaviour are necessary for these step-changes. (On the other hand, hyperinflation involves such a great destruction of the real value of money in circulation that it usually provokes an economic crisis deep enough to regroup political forces and impel currency reform. Hyperinflations are the super novas of the monetary firmament, exploding furiously outward only to collapse into the dark neutron stars of economic contraction. Likewise a stabilization crisis cannot continue indefinitely although deflationary pressures can remain prolonged, as from 1930 to 1933.

It is natural to ask whether the coalitions associated with different levels of inflation actually help cause the inflation or merely result from it. Of course, incipient inflation can encourage the crystallization of groups whose very demands will thereupon aggravate the inflationary pressure. But even beyond this recursive scenario, the alignments themselves appear to me causative in important ways. At the least they help determine the extent and duration of an inflationary experience, even if the initial shock to the system is provided by an exogenous event such as the need to finance a war, the changes in prices of key imports or the sudden cashing in of domestic currency balances held abroad. Thereafter internal coalitions—not always prepared in advance but quickly, if sometimes unwittingly, woven across existing party lines according to patterns of wealth, income and industrial affiliations—themselves generate inflationary impulses of varying intensity. Likewise, the stabilization crisis is often triggered by signals from abroad that the time for 'responsibility' has come. The signals include outflows of reserves (under fixed exchange rates), currency depreciation (under flexible rates)

TABLE 1 *The Coalitions of Inflation*

	Economic characteristics	Coalitions
Hyperinflation (over 1000% year)	Initial economic expansion; crisis of credit and production in final stage.	*De facto* industrialist–trade-union collaboration on basis of wage–price spiral, export premium, hostility to foreign power. Relative expropriation of rentiers, unorganized salaried employees, eventually small businessmen. The inflation of the producers.
Latin inflation (10–1000%/year)	Either real growth and development, or unproductive subsidies of export sector and services. Side-by-side persistence of modern and pre-modern sectors.	Strong interest-group disaggregation and working-class–bourgeois conflict. Redistribution of resources toward working classes, and/or key resistance of middle-class and upper-class elements *qua* consumers and savers. Effort to avoid direct taxes by broad evasion, export of capital. Bourgeois leverage precludes early fiscal redress.
Creeping inflation (up to 10%/year— typically, creeping inflation up to 7%)	Real growth.	General consensus of all classes on high employment and welfare. Remains under control only so long as real increases do not require cutting back any sector in absolute terms.
Stabilization and/or deflation	Initial crisis and recession; then expansion or weak recovery with periodic crises.	Initial collaboration of middle-class *qua* consumers and savers with entrepreneurial spokesmen on basis of capital formation. Can lead to middle-class alienation because of inadequate revaluation of assets, stringent credit, or higher taxes.

or admonitions from the IMF. Nevertheless, while such pressure from guardians abroad is often needed to persuade domestic policy makers to undertake stabilization or to provide politically weak but deflation-minded civil servants with useful symbols of national emergency, the ensuing course of stabilization is still associated with a characteristic domestic structure of interests and classes. Foreign bankers reinforce domestic interests.

Clearly, the classifications proposed here are over-simplified. The initial approach to sorting inflations according to their magnitude represents an effort to rank the 'intensity' of these economic experiences. However, the level of inflation may be less politically relevant than the acceleration of inflation. A rapid slide from an inflation rate of 5 per cent to one of 12 per cent or more, as in the major market economies during 1974, may be more destabilizing than a long period of continuing 50 to 75 per cent inflation as in Brazil. For the hyperinflationary experience, the distinction tends to collapse since only very great accelerations of inflation can produce the astronomic magnitudes that are recorded. Conversely in 'creeping' inflation the rate of change of inflation must be very low or the level of inflation itself would quickly become worrisome. But in the middle range it is possible that what is politically important is the second and not the first derivative of prices with respect to time. Yet the continuing, if stable, high rates of inflation in a country like Brazil do suggest underlying class cleavages of a strong and characteristic type. A society with prolonged but steady Latin inflation has different inner conflicts from a society with prolonged creeping inflation.

Hyperinflation. Hyperinflation is, of course, the most sadly picturesque deterioration of purchasing power. Cagan, who has presented a systematic monetarist treatment (1956), dates the appearance of hyperinflation from the month in which price rises reached 50 per cent. Extended steadily over a year's time this rate would yield 130-fold price increases. Societies in recent times that have lived through hyperinflation by this measure include Austria, Hungary, Germany, Poland and Russia in the wake of World War I; Hungary again, Rumania, Greece and China during and after World War II. The highest rate of inflation was achieved not by Weimar Germany (which stabilized

TABLE 2   *Selected Annual Rates of Inflation*

a.   *Creeping Inflation: the experience of the 1960s*
     Mean annual percentage increases in consumer prices, 1961—71

United States	France	Germany	Britain	All OECD countries
3.1	4.3	3.0	4.6	3.7

b.   *Latin Inflation: some major episodes*
     Percentage increases in consumer prices

	1914—18	1919	1920	1921	1922	1923	1924	1925	1926	1927
France	138.0	21.0	37.7	−21.6	−1.0	17.8	9.6	13.0	27.2	−6.3

	1938—44	1945	1946	1947	1948	1949	1950	1951	1952
France (retail food prices only)	182.0	36.7	71.1	62.2	58.7	9.4	14.3	17.4	8.5
Italy	1120.0	95.9	18.0	62.4	5.7	1.7	−	−	−
Argentina	−	20.7	17.1	12.2	13.0	32.7	24.6	37.2	38.1
Brazil	−	−	27.3	5.8	3.5	6.0	11.4	10.8	20.4

	1958	1959	1960	1961	1962	1963	1964	1965	1966	1967
Argentina	31.4	113.9	27.3	13.5	28.1	24.0	22.1	28.6	31.9	29.2
Brazil	17.3	51.9	23.8	42.9	55.8	80.2	86.6	45.5	41.2	24.1

	1968	1969	1970	1971	1972	1973	1974	1975	1976
France	4.6	6.1	5.9	5.6	5.9	7.4	13.6	11.8	9.6
Italy	1.3	2.7	4.9	5.1	5.4	10.8	19.1	17.2	15.7
Britain	4.7	5.4	6.4	9.5	7.1	9.2	15.9	24.2	16.8
Argentina	16.2	7.6	13.6	34.7	58.5	62.5	23.4	171.2	486.0
Brazil	24.5	24.3	20.9	18.1	14.0	12.6	27.5	29.0	41.7
Chile	27.9	28.9	35.3	20.1	77.9	319.5	586.0	380.0	229.5

c.   *Hyperinflation: two Central European cases*
     Percentage increases in internal prices

	1914—18	1919	1920	1921	1922	1923 (to November)
Germany	140	223	68	144	5,470	75×10^9

Percentage increases in government cost-of-living index

	1914—18	1919	1920	1921	1922 (to October)
Austria	1,226	197	87	797	1,603

Sources: Creeping inflation: OECD, *Economic Outlook*, December 1974.
      Latin inflation: IMF, *International Financial Statistics*, January, 1948;
      January, 1954; October, 1973; and August, 1977. Also Sauvy
      (1965), Wachter (1976) and Skidmore (1976).
      Hyperinflation: Walré de Bordes (1924); Bresciani-Turroni (1937).

CHART 1: *Selected Inflationary Experiences. 1914–76*

Note: The positions show the average annual rate of inflation for the timespan indicated. For simplification, only the maximum annual rates have been used for the hyperinflations. The plottings are approximate only, and are designed to show the relative position of each country within the particular episode.

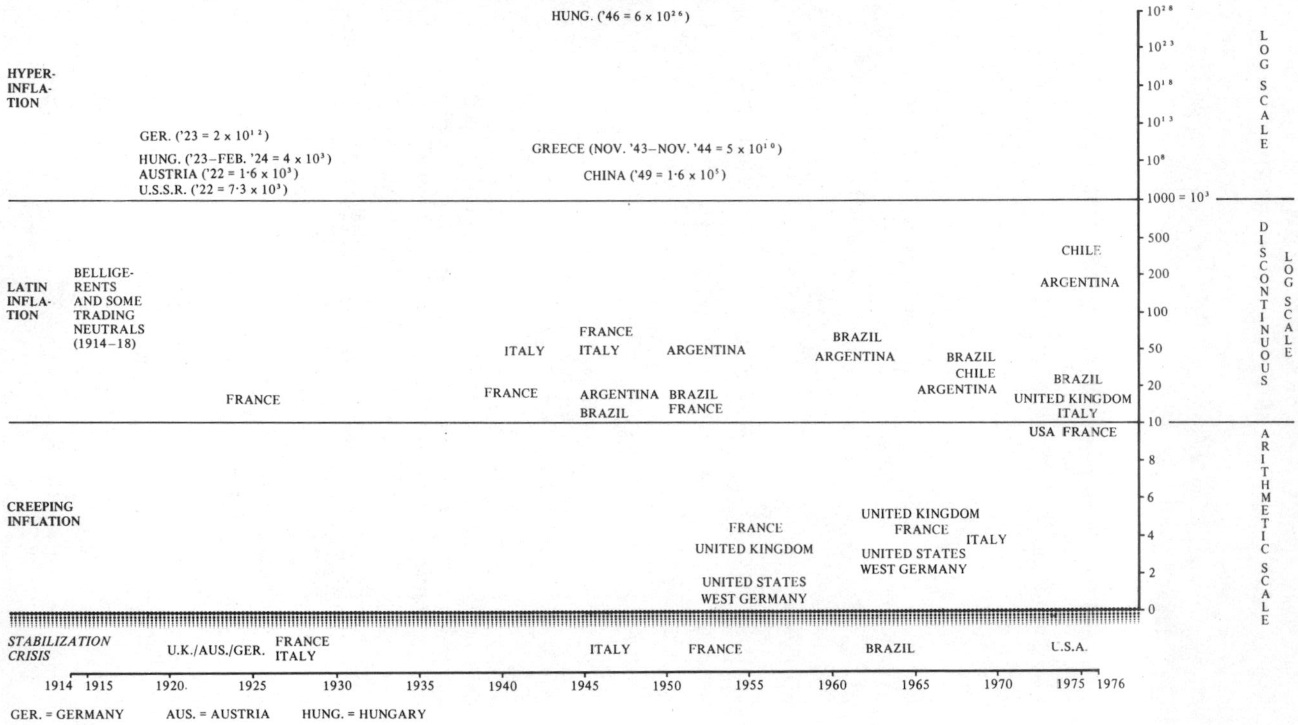

% INFLATION

LOG SCALE
10^{28}
10^{23}
10^{18}
10^{13}
10^{8}

DISCONTINUOUS LOG SCALE
$1000 = 10^{3}$
500
200
100
50
20

ARITHMETIC SCALE
10
8
6
4
2
0

HYPER-INFLATION

HUNG. ('46 = 6 x 10^{24})

GER. ('23 = 2 x 10^{12})
HUNG. ('23–FEB. '24 = 4 x 10^{3})
AUSTRIA ('22 = 1·6 x 10^{3})
U.S.S.R. ('22 = 7·3 x 10^{3})

GREECE (NOV. '43–NOV. '44 = 5 x 10^{10})
CHINA ('49 = 1·6 x 10^{3})

LATIN INFLATION

BELLIGERENTS AND SOME TRADING NEUTRALS (1914–18)

CHILE
ARGENTINA
BRAZIL
UNITED KINGDOM
ITALY
USA FRANCE

BRAZIL
CHILE
ARGENTINA

BRAZIL
ARGENTINA

FRANCE
ITALY
ARGENTINA BRAZIL
FRANCE

ITALY
FRANCE
ARGENTINA BRAZIL

FRANCE

CREEPING INFLATION

UNITED KINGDOM
FRANCE ITALY
UNITED STATES
WEST GERMANY

FRANCE
UNITED KINGDOM
UNITED STATES
WEST GERMANY

STABILIZATION CRISIS

U.K./AUS./GER. FRANCE
ITALY

FRANCE ITALY

BRAZIL

U.S.A.

1914 1915   1920.   1925   1930   1935   1940   1945   1950   1955   1960   1965   1970   1975 1976

GER. = GERMANY   AUS. = AUSTRIA   HUNG. = HUNGARY

its new currency at 10^{-12} prewar marks), but by Hungary between August 1945 and July 1946. After a year of frantic issues of Milpengö (10^6 pengö), bilpengö (10^{12}), then tax pengö based on astronomic index numbers, Budapest finally stabilized a new forint at the rate of 4×10^{29} pengö, or about 400 times a billion cubed. (Falush, 1976; Nogaro, 1948).

Effectively, such a degree of inflation destroys money in circulation and substitutes foreign currencies or book-keeping units. Keynes estimated that a government could double the supply of money every three months without entirely destroying its use in retail transactions; the Germans first exceeded this multiple between September and November 1922 and then vastly accelerated by mid-1923 (Keynes, 1923, p. 55 note). Introduction of a new currency or index-money can in fact accentuate depreciation. The Soviets issued a chervonets in November 1922 and allowed the original rouble and successive heavy roubles to sink until a final conversion ratio was established in early 1924. The German authorities consciously drove down the mark in the last two weeks before stabilization in November 1923 in order to prepare the ground for the forthcoming Rentenmark.

What is the political context of such currency disasters? As in other inflations, weakness of the state is an underlying general condition. But that alone specifies little. In certain circumstances hyperinflation accompanies outright civil war, as in Russia from 1917 to 1921 or China between 1945 and 1949. Austria and Germany after World War I, Hungary after World War II were sharply divided polities. Secondly—and as also is the case in other inflations—an important incentive may exist for major socio-political interests to avoid early stabilization. The Bolsheviks felt they might exploit inflation against their class enemies; the Hungarian Communists in the coalition of 1945–7 could likewise perceive political and economic advantages; German exporters learned about the advantages of dumping, and the German right in general could see that the inflation effectively paralysed the reparations system they hated. Thirdly—and this seems a distinguishing aspect in societies with a cohesively organized working class—common economic advantages of an inflationary policy bind industrialists and labour together, even if politically they remain at daggers drawn.

None of this is to deny that hyperinflation is proximately

generated by massive fiscal dislocations. Hyperinflation is amplified by wage–price spirals, but at any one time the increase in money supply represents in effect a frenzied effort at tax collection. Preobrazhensky pointed this out to the Soviets in 1921 (Erlich, 1967, p. 43 note), and two years later Keynes wittily explained that the diversion of purchasing power to the state amounted to a mode of taxation: 'The income-tax receipts which we in England receive from the Surveyor, we throw into the wastepaper basket; in Germany they call them bank-notes and put them into their pocket-books; in France they are termed Rentes and are locked up in the family safe' (Keynes, 1923, p. 42).

This taxation operates differently, however, according to the rate of inflation. While double-digit inflation under a progressive tax system will increase government revenues by pushing income earners into higher brackets, hyperinflationary conditions destroy the normal tax framework. The delay between levying a tax bill and collection wipes out much of the value of the receipt with the important exception of weekly withholding. By March 1923, 95 per cent of German income taxes derived from those wage-earners and employees subject to withholding—a situation the General Trade Union Federation (ADGB) vigorously protested (Harbeck, ed., 1968, pp. 228–31)[1]. In addition the state cannot usually raise the price of public services quickly enough to avoid a massive subsidy. German freight rates were a noted example. Replacing conventional taxes by currency emissions provides a heady though ultimately self-defeating alternative. In the hyperinflations that Cagan reviews, the tax yield of new currency issues ranged from 3 to 15 per cent of national income, except for the Soviet state which had a return below one per cent. But as the real value of cash balances declines, the yield must fall unless the government can issue paper ever more rapidly; and it is never rapid enough to keep the money supply and tax base from shrinking to a tiny fraction, inadequate for commercial needs or for public revenue (Cagan, 1956, p. 89).

Critical to the unleashing of runaway inflation, therefore, is the failure of the normal fiscal system. Unexpected demands of war finance usually trigger such note issues in some degree, but political factors determine how far the community will thereafter choose direct sacrifice or continued levies through inflation. Soviet finance revealed a situation where an inflationary levy seemed actually purposeful and not just an expedient. After the fact, the Soviets justified their drastic depreciation of the rouble as a way of expropriating the bourgeoisie. During the era of War Communism, Soviet theorists could likewise celebrate a reversion to a moneyless economy characterized by direct requisitioning and provision of goods and services to workers. Even as over 10,000 employees printed roubles (the total value of which by 1921 was no more than a thousandth of the money stock in November 1917), the state pared rents, sought moneyless payments between its agencies and envisaged the elimination of taxes. Still, the monetary collapse remained, it seems, a result of desperation, not calculation in advance.

The advent of the New Economic Policy in the spring of 1921 ended the anti-monetary revery. 'State capitalism' required money and book-keeping criteria of efficiency. Budgeting, which had been largely ignored, was revived, and the expected deficit was reduced from about 85 per cent of government expenditure in 1920 and 1921 to 40 per cent for the first three quarters of 1922. In the same period conventional taxes rose from 1.8 to 14 per cent of government revenue, while the levy derived from the note issue fell from 90 to 56 per cent (with payments in kind making up the remainder). While the old rouble and periodic successors continued to collapse, the chervontsi of November 1922 provided a stable accounting unit until the final currency reform in 1924. In retrospect the Soviet inflation possessed a certain unwitting, costly and ruthless logic for an era of civil war. Ideologists may have made a virtue of necessity when they praised demonetization as an indicator of socialism—a fervour soon after discarded as 'infantile'. But at the price above all of urban–rural exchange, inflation did permit a harsh and coercive control over the allocation of goods and services (Carr, 1952, vol. II, pp. 256–68, 345–59; Katzenellenbaum, 1925; Yurovsky, 1925; Fetter, 1977).

More relevant for other Western countries are the German and the Austrian hyperinflations. Both societies had a cohesive, organized urban working class enjoying critical political influence after the revolutions of 1918–19. At the same time conservative élites were not uprooted and ably resisted incursions into their

real property and prerogatives. To carry on the Weimar Republic
required the appeasement, if not originally of diehard Junkers,
then of the industrialists whose leadership seemed essential for
recovery and to meet reparation demands. Successive governments
in Berlin reflected either a stalemate among different interests—the
Joseph Wirth–Walther Rathenau cabinets of 1921–2 sought to
keep Social Democratic support and business cooperation simultaneously—or else they reflected the conventional wisdom of
the industrial and financial community as under Wilhelm Cuno
(1922–3). The price of industry's toleration was fiscal paralysis.
If in Russia monetary debasement was a weapon of civil war,
in Central Europe it became its surrogate. Moreover, recourse
to the printing press seemed more attractive because of a widely-
shared unwillingness to meet reparation charges from national
income. Until the last months, hyperinflation was virtually welcomed by many business leaders and bureaucrats as providing
a demonstration that without a change of policy in Paris, the
German monetary disaster could only injure British and American
commerce (Maier, 1975, chs. 4 and 6; Witt, 1974; Feldman,
1977).

From May 1921 through to the summer of 1923, the Wirth
and Cuno ministries by and large accepted the view of the
industrial leadership that further increases in the floating debt
represented the only possible fiscal option. When stabilization
came under consideration in the fall of 1922, leading industrialists
such as Hugo Stinnes raised the spectre of serious recession.
Stabilization would indeed impose transitional costs, which might
involve unemployment for the working class and real taxes
for industry and personal income. The question facing the political
system was which group would pay more. Inflation had disguised
the levies and at first had imposed them on middle-class households, although its results later hit labour too. Finally the government and representatives of industry accepted a stabilization
programme once the alternative appeared grave Communist-led
unrest and once depression threatened as credit dried up in
the summer and fall of 1923. In addition, the export premium
that inflation had provided ended in the summer of 1923 as
domestic price increases outran the mark's depreciation in terms
of foreign currency. (In effect all prices became set in terms
of the daily dollar or pound rate plus a hefty mark-up for

the expected depreciation to follow—a self-defeating form of indexation.) Industry still understood how to alleviate its own costs and the liquidity crisis accompanying stabilization by imposing longer working hours and a disadvantageous calculation of stable-money wages upon the unions. The inflation and Ruhr conflict had almost totally undermined their financial and organizational capacity for resistance (Hartwich, 1967, pp. 67, 102; Maier, 1975, pp. 363–64, 445–50)[2].

Still, the trade unions had accepted the inflation with surprisingly little labour unrest, even before the French occupation of the Ruhr imposed a patriotic front. But then, demand remained strong and employment high, and Germany was spared the brief but severe depression of 1920–1. In part, too, business and the government allowed union wages to keep relative pace with rising prices, although there were painful lags in 1921 and 1922 and growing misery as real income for the society dropped sharply in 1923.

The German Social Democrats and the bourgeois left did indeed suggest alternative fiscal policies between 1919 and 1923. The Catholic Centre leader, Matthias Erzberger, then Social Democratic ministers and advisers, proposed mild capital levies. But even when taxes were theoretically stiffened, as with Erzberger's reforms of 1919–20 and the 'tax compromise' of 1922, they came to nought because payment was stipulated in rapidly depreciating paper marks. Instead of winning needed fiscal reform, working-class representatives won relative wage protection, though not without recurring losses of real income. And by the end of 1923 and early 1924, the stabilization crisis that brought winter unemployment to at least two million allowed industry to renegotiate with labour the terms of the social partnership that had been accepted five years earlier only under menace of revolution. The end of inflation meant the end of tacit union–industry partnership.

The Austrian inflation involved another collaboration of trade unions and entrepreneurs through a formalized index-wage scheme. In November 1919 the Social Democratic prime minister, Karl Renner, summoned employers and employees to an economic summit that accepted an indexation scheme to be worked into collective contracts and which provided bimonthly and later monthly wage adjustments. Such a compact was facilitated because Austrian industry was enjoying a surge of export demand. As elsewhere, unskilled workers kept their earnings closest to the 'peace parity'; skilled workers emerged relatively protected; while the Viennese middle classes suffered most drastically. By the end of 1921, in fact, the pace of depreciation taxed workers anew. As in Germany, prosperity was dissipated as the volume of money contracted and a credit crisis loomed. By October 1921, the Social Democrats declared themselves ready to cooperate with stabilization measures even at the price of ending their favoured food subsidies. Ending the subsidies, however, only briefly halted the inflation. By a round-robin of diplomatic negotiations that played on the Western powers' fear of Austria's disappearance as an independent state, Chancellor Ignaz Seipel finally extracted a stabilization loan from the League of Nations. The Geneva Protocols of October 1922 also pledged Austria to remove the government's financial measures from parliamentary scrutiny for two years. Seipel's stabilization thus cost the Austrian Social Democrats their latent coalition role, just as in Germany a year later stabilization was to be carried out at the cost of Social Democratic representation in the cabinet and the eight-hour day (Gulick, 1948, vol. I, pp. 149–71; Walré de Bordes, 1924).

Hyperinflation thus involved an implicit coalition of labour and industry at the expense of rentiers, professionals, the civil service and modest entrepreneurs. Industrialists with access to credit stood to profit greatly and industry in general could benefit by heavy demand. Labour avoided postwar lay-offs and preserved relative wage protection until the final months of the monetary collapse. The cost was intermittent lags in real income, harsh unemployment in the transition to stable currency and a sacrifice of collective political influence.[3] Inflation represented a second-best or perhaps maximin strategy of curtailing predictable losses in a situation where the preferred policy of stabilization at full employment appeared unavailable. For any social group the restraint needed to end the spiral of prices and wages seemed doomed to become just a unilateral and costly renunciation. Confidence that restraint would be fairly distributed disappeared; and thus in a sense the true cost of inflation came to involve the very premises of civil society.

This lesson should be sobering today for those who contend

that setting rigid monetary targets can make unions police their own wage demands by making unemployment the logical price of excessive claims. Most workers, of course, will evade the penalty for claiming too much but will surely pay one if they claim too little.

Latin Inflation. The second class of monetary depreciation comprises severe cases of what is usually called double-digit inflation but can range easily up to 100 per cent and sometimes even to several hundred per cent per annum. I have chosen the more playful designation of 'Latin inflation', for salient experiences have included France in the mid-1920s, France again and Italy in the years after World War II and over more protracted periods, Brazil, Argentina, Chile and other Latin American countries. Inflation rates in Latin America in the last few years have ranged up to 700 per cent. Contemporary Britain and Israel also merit inclusion in terms of percentage range, even if not of ethnic designation.

It would be wrong to impose a false unity on these inflationary experiences. Nonetheless, a certain logic of social disaggregation does seem to mark them all. South American inflations are often described as the 'structural' outcome of societies afflicted with concentrated, quasi-feudal distributions of resources while undergoing rapid development. But as Hirschmann has pointed out, since inflation can be conceived of as a failure of production to respond to expectations, almost any social or economic impediment can be invoked as a cause of structural inflation (Hirschman, 1963, pp. 213–16; Lambert, 1959, pp. 43 ff.). Just this perspective, though, suggests a relationship to the heavy inflationary pressures in the developed European economies. The emergence of powerful group interests with divergent policy priorities characterizes all the Latin cases. Of course, this disaggregation of interests marks hyperinflation as well. What, then, distinguishes the politics of Latin inflation from hyperinflation?

First, in Latin inflation the *de facto* coalition of producers is less important. The latent collaboration of labour and industry does not coalesce, and the socio-economic cleavage tends to run horizontally between classes and not sectorally, uniting unions and management.

Second, the relationship to the international economy is also a different one in the case of Latin inflation, embodying elements of dependence more than defiance. Hyperinflation can gather momentum from the widespread conviction among all classes that a stable fiscal system will primarily benefit foreign exploiters, such as Germany's victors seeking reparations after World War I, or perhaps Hungary's Soviet occupiers in 1945–6. Latin inflations are the expression less of monetary unilateralism than of relative weakness. In Germany and Austria currency depreciation against the dollar was accepted almost fatalistically as a condition for maintaining high export demand and relative social peace. In Latin America devaluation has generally accompanied conservative efforts at stabilization designed to curb wage advances and to redress the balance of payments in order to secure foreign capital. (The Brazilian resort to continual incremental devaluation is more a unilateral recourse but rests simultaneously upon thorough price indexation—and in any case was a relatively late response to inflationary difficulties.) Devaluation, however, has in turn triggered new bouts of inflation led by higher import prices. Thus the susceptible economies have oscillated between phases of high employment, leading to international deficits and shortages of foreign capital, and efforts at stabilization, including currency devaluations that just renew inflation. Argentina's stop–go cycles in the 1950s were an exaggerated version of Britain's similar difficulties (Diaz-Alejandro, 1970, pp. 351–390; cf. Vogel, 1974; Pazos, 1972; Skidmore, 1976).

The Latin cases suggest that middle-class or entrepreneurial elements wager more on foreign capital than upon a continuing high-growth, high-wage industrial economy. Their strategy often reflects economic weaknesses and domestic political strength simultaneously, whereas the German entrepreneurial strategy in the hyperinflation corresponded to underlying economic strength but post-revolutionary political weakness. Fearing a decisive rupture with labour, German industry could rely upon the demand for their advantageously-priced manufactures or industrial semifinished products. In contrast, the export capability of most countries vulnerable to Latin inflation has consisted primarily of price-inelastic minerals or commodities subject to great price oscillations and loss of revenue; or it has involved services ranging from tourism to Britain's banking. The lesser-developed of the Latin' cases reveal the familiar economic dualism that tends to integrate an export-oriented élite into the investing circles of the more economically powerful nations while leaving large backwaters of poverty. The relative factor constraint for the Latin cases is capital, not labour. In fact, once capital became the major constraint in the later stages of the German hyperinflation, the tactic of monetary defiance had to be abandoned.

In a further distinction from the cases of hyperinflation, while the countries afflicted with Latin inflation embark upon stabilization efforts at lower threshholds of depreciation, their attempts seem less likely to stick (Skidmore, 1976). Either a political leadership friendly to labour has secured working-class acquiescence in stabilization—Peron in 1952-3; Britain 1976—or conservatives have resorted to confrontation (army take-overs in Latin America, the Industrial Relations Act in Britain), but the upshot is often just to unleash a new cycle of inflation. Class divisiveness may spare these societies hyperinflation but it seems to condemn them to longer or recurrent periods of double-digit price increases.

The class antagonisms in the Latin cases are often part and parcel of the structural handicaps to real growth: persistent unemployment due to traditional sectors (Italy, Argentina, Brazil, even Britain), or premature expansion of the service class and large bureaucracies (Chile, Uruguay, perhaps Italy). Sometimes the inflationary process itself can help to mobilize savings and to tax incomes on behalf of real development. Brazilian growth seems to have been invigorated by heady price rises in the 1960s, and the French inflation of the mid-1920s may have accelerated reconstruction and stimulated new investment. But the inflation often lingers after growth flags and becomes counterproductive.

Springing as it does from a deeply divided society, Latin inflation can be generated by either of the opposed dichotomous class groupings. In Peronist Argentina, inflation accompanied a redistributive effort on behalf of the urban working-class migrants. But just as significantly a broad defensive reaction on the part of bourgeois holders of money and bonds often plays an important role. Thus middle-class elements end up acting less in their capacity as producers than as savers. In the face of class stalemates, the *de facto* coalition of labour and industry that acquiesces in hyperinflation does not become influential. Therefore, if hyperinflation rests upon a precarious social compact among producers, Latin inflation in Europe has often incorporated the decentralized and sometimes self-defeating choices of savers and rentiers. In seeking to protect their portfolios, middle-class interests, however, often aggravate the very levies they are seeking to avoid.

The French inflation of 1924 to 1926 revealed the capacity of a broad middle-class community to prevent stabilization under the rules of the monetary game. These precluded exchange controls and gave a politicized central bank week-to-week control over advances to the government. From 1919 to 1924 a conservative–centrist parliamentary coalition sanctioned massive credits for reconstruction, which the bourgeois public largely underwrote by subscribing to government bonds. Debt charges accumulating since 1914, however, threw the budget into prolonged deficit. The National Assembly disguised rather than defrayed the deficit by establishing a 'recoverable' budget that would supposedly be covered by German reparations. The governments of the centre and right, which bequeathed an unacknowledged inflationary fiscal policy, were succeeded by those of left and centre, who moved in with inconsistent financial remedies and internal political divisions. The Socialists and left wing of the Radical Socialists around Edouard Herriot advocated a tax on capital of 10 to 12 per cent to be collected over several years. This proposal alienated the votes of the moderates in their own electoral cartel and thus fell short of a majority. The Cartel moderates were willing instead to seek the votes of the conservative opposition to impose further indirect taxes and restore 'confidence' in capital, which amounted to relaxing the controls designed to curtail tax evasion (Goldey, 1961; Schuker, 1976).

The controversies over fiscal policy proved all the more debilitating to the left because of the trumps that monetary policy gave to conservatives. Left as well as right accepted the principle that there should be legal ceilings on the bank notes in circulation and on the advances of the Bank of France to the state. At the same time, however, the bourgeois public held directly large quantities of short-term bonds. When, alarmed by plans for a capital levy, they failed to renew these bills, the Treasury had to draw upon occult Bank of France advances to redeem the volatile public debt, disguising the overdrafts by covering them weekly with overnight private bank loans. The left thus became hostage both to distrustful private banks as well as to the hostile central bank, even while it was unwilling to cease frightening bondholders with talk of 'radical taxes'.

With the final exposure of the concealed overdrafts the Cartel collapsed, to be succeeded by a parade of ministries which introduced alternately left and right financial expedients. Only after dramatic political crises and flights from the franc did Raymond Poincaré form a ministry of national unity in July 1926, which achieved stabilization with no further technical innovations. By finally demonstrating the political exhaustion of the left wing of the Radical Socialists and persuading Herriot to join his cabinet, Poincaré generated the confidence that proved so crucial in the presence of the diffuse pattern of middle-class thrift, the mass of short-term bonds, and the leverage of the Bank of France (Maier, 1975, pp. 494–507; Moreau, 1954).

Inflation probably imposed a burden just as high as the mild capital levy suggested by Blum and Herriot would have done. Fixed-income patrimonies and deposits stood at about half their 1913 value by 1929 (allowing both for appreciation through interest and the toll taken by inflation). An alternative calculation is that a composite portfolio of money savings, bonds and shares would have been producing perhaps 30 per cent less real revenue by the time the franc was stabilized than two years earlier when the centre–left government came to power. (Of course, equity returns would then have grown again.) The Blum–Herriot capital levy would actually have been collected as a twelve-year surtax on income from assets of perhaps 20 per cent per year (assuming a 5 per cent yield on capital).

Post World War II experiences in France and Italy revealed a similar middle-class tendency to accept the indirect taxation of inflation rather than confront the direct levies needed to avoid it. In 1945 de Gaulle rejected the currency reform proposed by Mendés-France and backed away from any radical amputation of private balances (Parodi, 1971, pp. 66ff.; Brown, 1955, pp. 227–48; Grotius, 1949; Gurley, 1953; Dupriez, 1947). The French price index rose from 285 in 1944 (1938 = 100) to 1817 in 1949, stimulated by state deficits and a four-fold expansion of bank reserves through 1946–7. In Italy, the 1945 price index

stood already at 16 times that of 1938 and before stabilization
at the end of 1947 had climbed to 49 (retail) and 55 (wholesale)
times 1938 levels. Government borrowing rose from 11 billion
lire in 1938 to 152 billion for the year 1943 and 572 billion
for 1944–5. At the same time the central bank made liberal
credits available to the banking system as a whole, and reserves
at the Bank of Italy rose from less than half a billion lire
in 1938 to 1,920 billion in 1945. These monetary pressures
occurred, moreover, in societies whose 1945 real national income
was reduced to about 50 per cent of the prewar level (Hildebrand,
1965, chapters 2, 8).

Removal of the Communists from the governing coalition
in 1947, the division of the labour movement, and Washington's
declaration of intent to provide 'Marshall Plan' funds that would
ease the constant external pressure against the lira allowed a
stabilization programme to be launched by the successive governors of the Bank of Italy, Luigi Einaudi and Donato Menichella.
This effort involved principally the severe restriction of central
bank credits. Rome, like Paris, rejected the blocking of accounts
and direct levies that other continental countries such as Belgium
adopted. Nor would either emulate the tax severity imposed
in Britain. Italy resorted to a contractionary monetary policy
rather than a severe fiscal policy. The result included a recession
that bottled up labour in the South and effectively passed much
of the burden of stabilization to the popular classes (De Cecco,
1968; Foa, 1949; European Cooperation Administration, 1950;
Barucci, 1973; Ruffolo, 1974).

Stabilization involved a break with the Communists over wage
policy. The post-Liberation governments had not been prepared
to clamp down on wages. Instead the Communist labour leadership initially pledged an effort at full production and won general
wage indexation—an issue that has recently become crucial once
again. As cost-of-living adjustments dwarfed the base-pay differentials, an inflationary levelling of wages took place. This was
a development Communist unions favoured and over which
they separated from the non-Communists during the 1950s.

When stabilization came in France it was, similarly, under
the conservative leadership of Antoine Pinay. The end of the
Resistance-born coalitions with the Communists was probably
a prerequisite for anti-inflationary efforts. Nevertheless, even

as both French and Italian governments shifted to the centre or right, they could make no drastic attempt to cut back into enlarged wage shares (especially when the Korean war and rearmament created new scarcities and inflationary pressure). The governments of the 1950s in Europe ruled out cooperation with the Communists but launched no bourgeois or business counter-revolution. Thus the political logic of the third major type of inflation we encounter: the persistent incremental price rises of the 1950s and 1960s.

Creeping Inflation. The prerequisite for creeping inflation was the remarkable record of economic growth that avoided a harsh distributional conflict between classes. By the early 1950s, bottled-up demand had spent itself; capital building had brought national incomes back to and beyond 1938 levels; international terms of trade began a long-term shift in favour of commodity importers. Marshall Plan assistance eased foreign-exchange constraints; at the same time, United States enthusiasm for currency convertibility helped maintain fiscal and monetary discipline.

The related factor behind the creeping inflation was the balance of social forces. The 1944–49/51 inflation had been a unique legacy of wartime destruction. But the way in which the governments of postwar Europe had sought to allocate the losses reflected their broad political composition and the coalitions that emerged from the Liberation: wage increases for the working class, tax avoidance for the middle classes, relatively easy credit for business. Even after the Catholic–Communist–Socialist coalitions fractured, the possibilities of real growth and the felt need to prevent a renewed polarization of the working class precluded any drastic renegotiation of the postwar social bargain. Growth, pursued in an effort to reconcile all important social groups, became the objective of postwar governments.

Some differences persisted between coalitions of the centre–right and those of the centre–left. The former stressed capital formation and currency stability whereas the latter emphasized using the new wealth to pay for social insurance schemes. But these were differences of degree. Labour made no serious effort to claim a radically larger allotment of national income, and, in an implicit social contract, Conservative or Christian Democratic ministers made no effort to contest full-employment targets,

even if keeping demand buoyant involved a persistent upward
price trend. (Only when balance-of-payment concerns intervened
did this commitment flag.)

In retrospect this era of creeping inflation may appear unique
and based upon transitory advantages. The significant increase
in agricultural productivity and the continuing exodus from
the farms allowed a funnelling of resources to industry and
services. The terms of trade favoured food and commodity
importers, i.e. Europeans, at the expense of their suppliers.
Old and new middle classes—employees, small entrepreneurs,
bureaucrats—now pressed their own claims effectively through
interest-group bargaining. They did not resort to right-radical
protest to the same degree as in interwar Europe. The absence
of a fascist revival on any significant scale meant in turn that
no major ideological attack was levelled against the class collaboration that was occurring.

The international constellation also made its contribution.
Thanks in part to the Cold War, the United States proved
willing to finance Europe's deficit on current account well into
the 1950s if not longer. The Cold War also led to decisions
to encourage the reconstruction of Germany and Japan as productive centres for the non-Communist world in general. For many
complex reasons, workers in both countries exhibited exemplary
wage restraint. Success confirmed its own rewards, as persistent
growth focused political dispute less upon the division of the
national income than the proper uses of the expected increments.
And in turn this level of bargaining did not open larger issues
about what groups enjoyed basic power or real legitimacy.

The question for the contemporary observer is whether these
conditions were exceptional or potentially durable. The relapse
into double-digit inflation after 1973 had its proximate origins
in contingent developments: the Vietnamese war with its increase
in American deficit financing and its stimulus to international
liquidity, and also new price rises in petroleum and food. But
the pressures may be more long term. The era of rapid agricultural
dividends may be closing; and as growth becomes problematic,
disputes over the allocation of national income raise ugly confrontations or require increased dosages of inflation. The very structures of policy making may also heighten vulnerability. The
growing role of quasi-independent planning agencies and authori-

ties helped depoliticize distributional conflicts after 1945, but they reinforced a trend in which interests win representation not merely in the legislature, but in the executive agencies of the state. The *de facto* corporatism that eases economic bargaining also facilitates inflation.

Redistribution and Coalition

We have sought hitherto to specify deductively the coalitions that help to generate inflation. This essay presupposes that there exist or are called into being relatively coherent interests which foresee (sometimes incorrectly) different outcomes for different fiscal and monetary policies. No group is likely to be an advocate of inflation absolutely; rather it is the costs of stabilization that will seem more or less acceptable.

Even this assumption, however, is problematic. The stakes of inflation are far more ambiguous than they are often presented as being. Consider some of the obvious difficulties. First, individual interests may not mesh with class interests; the worker may find his own real resources declining even while his class increases its share of national income due to higher employment of previously idle labour. Alternatively his individual wages may decline in real terms but his family income may jump as his wife seeks and finds employment. Second, inflation acts consistently only upon types of income and wealth (or economic roles), not upon real individuals. It is clearly better to be a debtor than a creditor when the value of money is eroding, but most members of the middle classes are both. If the state effectively repudiates a quota of the public debt, it likewise spares taxpayers the burden of servicing it. Third, changes in subjective welfare are hard to sort out. Each individual will certainly feel whether he is better or worse off than he was formerly. But will he also take account of the new comparative rankings of salaries across occupational lines? The formerly well-paid civil servant may feel terribly humbled in terms of his old salary but even more bitter about how close he now ranks with the skilled manual labourer. Conversely the poor charwoman may be closer to her boss but thrown from 'decent' poverty into real impoverishment. And even if the community might choose to trade a degree of wealth for an increment of equality, it may never be fully aware of the equality it purchases; for a few well-publicized cases of inflation profiteering will dominate the public consciousness. Finally, the society as a whole may be sufficiently risk-averse that even equal chances of gains or losses would not compensate for the unpleasant wager entailed.

Do these considerations mean that we must abandon efforts at a political sociology of inflation? No, but they impose great caution about imputing simple correspondence between interests and political behaviour, especially since interests are often far from clear. A further complication emerges from the fact that rational behaviour early in an inflationary surge may prove less rational later, especially if one passes to a much higher rate of inflation. (Conversely, as is to be explained below, some groups will be vulnerable both during inflation and stabilization.)

Inflation-sheltered assets are by definition more secure than monetary holdings, but such assets become rarer, more expensive and more exposed. What seems a Noah's Ark at the outset of inflation can become a millstone by the end. Rampant inflation, such as the German one, illustrates that few assets are inflation-proof. Ownership of real property, especially if it was mortgaged, seemed a windfall, unless the property was an apartment building subject to the widespread imposition of rent control. In the wake of World War I, landlords in France as well as Germany were locked into property ownership that was more costly than rewarding. On the other hand, this often helped elderly or other middle-class lodgers. Similarly many public services including transportation and higher education became subsidized. The small businessman seemed well-off at the beginning of the inflation and many middle-class investors sunk savings into enterprises. But by the later stages of hyperinflation such proprietors found themselves squeezed by the shortage of credit and working capital, especially as replenishing inventories became ever more costly. Consequently, without knowing when in the inflationary cycle an enterprise was capitalized, it was difficult to determine its value as a shelter. (Eulenburg, 1924; Bresciani-Turroni, 1937, chaps. V, VIII.)

The effect on wages and salaries is also less simple to determine than initially appears. In Germany real wages periodically fell behind and then spurted forward when the government published new cost-of-living indices and adjustments followed. Organized workers in major industries may have seen their real wages erode as badly in late 1922, when index revisions lagged, as they did at the height of the inflation in the summer and fall of 1923 (Bresciani-Turroni, 1937, pp. 308–13). In Vienna, however, real wages oscillated less but fell behind at the height of the hyperinflation.

Although trade unions may secure relative protection for their memberships (and thereby intensify inflation), there may be greater gains for unorganized workers if inflation accompanies a boom thereby creating new jobs and bidding up low wages (Peretz, 1976, ch. III). In Austria and Germany the fate of civil-service salaries depended upon rank; the real income of the higher grades fell perhaps 70 per cent, but minor clerks were cut much less (Elster, 1928, pp. 444–9). On the other hand, the conditions of employment seemed so secure that the bureaucracy remained a favoured occupational choice (Eulenburg, 1924, p. 775). Levelling of earnings within each occupational group, the shrinking of differentials between the less and more qualified, seems to be universal in periods of increasing inflation. Data from different countries and periods suggest the greater proportional vulnerability of higher salaries even when conscious redistribution is unintended (Ogburn and Jaffé, 1927, p. 164; Routh, 1965, pp. 108ff.; Hildebrand, 1955, pp. 194ff.). On the other hand, the tendency towards equalization—at least when the tempo of inflation is not too drastic—can be offset by differential relative price increases. Researchers have cited British and American experiences where the outlays for poorer families, with their greater share devoted to necessities, have risen more steeply than the consumption costs of wealthier households (Seers, 1949; Brittain, 1960; Muellbauer, 1974; Williamson, 1976a, 1976b; Piachaud, this volume). In wartime emergencies, when rent and food prices are controlled, however, the poor may benefit relatively on the price as well as the earnings side. Even if we assume that income-equalizing tendencies have prevailed in twentieth-century inflation (cf. Nordhaus, 1973, for possible theoretical results), this still might not determine political (or socio-economic) outcomes in its own right. An increase in equality that accompanies a growing national product yields different results from equalization in a stumbling economy. In the former case, a vigorous demand for labour bids up the wages of the unskilled without undue penalties for the more established; while in the latter more painful case, the exposed higher-income positions are reduced more dramatically.

There are other suggestions that inflation promotes a levelling of incomes, but the political consequences are far from clear. Studies of the United States since World War II have suggested that the inflationary trends have transferred income shares to wages and salaries at the expense of unincorporated businesses, farms, rents and net corporate profits (Bach and Stephenson, 1974). These redistributions thus reinforce the longer-term transformations that Kuznets has pulled together for the period from the late nineteenth century, reflecting the concentration of economic units and the move out of agriculture (Kuznets, 1959, pp. 45, 86 ff.). The former major regressive toll of inflation— the erosion of pensions—is now being transformed as social security pensions are increasingly inflation-proofed, while private- sector pensions lag behind. At the same time, tax schedules for nominal income strongly reinforce progressivity under double- digit inflation. Consequently, income effects in the last few years, whether in the United States or more drastically in Britain, have probably been equalitarian. The political implications, how- ever, are far from clear-cut. Levelling has few advocates when GNP falters in its upward course or falls. And a few spectacular speculative windfalls may convey to the public a sense that inequality is rifer and more pernicious, even if aggregate income differences are actually diminishing.

Changes in wealth and assets may be even harder to sort out during the course of inflation. The debates over accounting procedures illustrate the complexity of the issue. To compare the outcomes upon families in the 1920s I have sought to measure the inheritances of the late 1920s in Germany and France against those of 1913. French patrimonies were approxi- mately halved in real terms, and the larger the estate the greater the percentage sacrifice. German wills were apparently cut down to less than two fifths real value. The Germans virtually wrote off their entire public debt and revalued old corporate bonds, mortgages, bank accounts and life insurance policies up to only a 25 per cent maximum. The brunt of the loss may have been borne, however, by the more humble legatees, not the largest. All the more reason for a middle-class reaction.[4]

The role of the corporation adds to the difficulty of calculating redistribution. It has been estimated for the United States that perhaps $500,000 million had been transferred from creditors to debtors in the twenty-five years after World War II, largely at the expense of households and to the benefit of business and government. (Bach and Stephenson, 1974, p. 12; cf. Carré, Dubois and Malinvaud, 1972, pp. 362–70) These long-term transfers reflected the lowering of corporate and national indebtedness in real terms. The incidence in terms of individuals and families, however, is hard to ascertain. Individuals might lose on corporate bonds, but their stock portfolios should have risen as corporate indebtedness was reduced, and their tax bills should have been relatively lighter as government debt service became cheaper.

It is just as hard to ascertain the direct effect of inflation on share prices. While investors may initially bid up equity prices, they learned both in Britain and the United States in 1973–5 that shares could not easily keep up with double-digit inflation. Developments in the German hyperinflation might have provided a forewarning. Share prices in Germany tended to follow the dollar exchange until late 1921 largely as a hedge against inflation. Corporate profits seem to have dropped to about 30 per cent of 1913, although this was disguised by inadequate valuation of depreciation. Nonetheless, firms could cut back dividends and add to their reserves as well as seek their own inflation-proof assets through mergers, acquisition and the general process of vertical integration. By 1922, however, share prices could no longer keep up with depreciation, and in October they represented less than 3 per cent of the 1913 values. The assets of the Daimler works, according to the bourse, were worth only 327 of their own automobiles. By late 1922 the growing liquidity shortage precluded investment in the market. Foreigners were dissuaded from takeover bids by the fact that new shares carried no voting rights. However, with the collapse of the 'support action' of February to April 1923 and Berlin's ever more massive recourse to the printing press, investors returned to the bourse. The parity of shares against gold marks

(1913 = 100) rose from 5.24 in January to 16 in July, and as gold–mark accounting was instituted more broadly from July share prices rose even faster to reach 40 (even 120 when the mark was held artificially high for a few weeks) and to end the year, after stabilization, at 27 (Bresciani-Turroni, 1937, pp. 253–85).

Although Wall Street tended to ignore the lesson during the palmy 1960s, it learned again with a vengeance that share prices cannot easily provide shelter against persistent inflation. The capital base of companies becomes eroded through inventory profits and inadequate depreciation. Of course, share prices become a reflection in part of the cost of holding alternative assets: relative shelter should matter more than intrinsic value. Corporation prosperity, on the other hand, may become divorced from share value and depend upon credit availability. In Germany, in Italy and France after World War II, in the United States until late 1975, access to credit was not seriously limited. The extent to which even high nominal interest rates will inhibit corporate borrowing will depend on how far the market anticipates inflation and on how the monetary authorities respond to it. Fearing a liquidity crisis, guardians of the central bank will often see the continued supply of business needs as vital; for each Einaudi there is a Havenstein—the director of the Reichsbank during the German inflation—who can argue that since advances to the state are so large, further credit to business hardly adds to inflationary pressures.

The cost, if 1975 America was an indication, may well have been at the expense of private housing and of credit availability for mortgages and smaller businesses that did not enjoy privileged relations with their banks. In this sense, inflation taxes households for the sake of corporate expansion. This transfer may help prevent a quick lapse into recession, for the deficiency of private consumption is compensated by vigorous business spending and investment. Office buildings may go up after housing starts to slow down. Ultimately, diminished household resources will dampen industrial expansion.

So long as the economy remains vigorous, however, a trade-off can be expected. If households subsidize corporations, those wage and salary earners tied in to the corporations are generally protected. The corporation may no longer reward its shareholders concomitantly, but it protects the strong unions and management. Hence there emerges an analogue to the effects of a wage–price spiral at the expense of the rentier or small entrepreneur: credit availability and the delayed tightening of money differentially benefit those organized sectors—labour and management—affiliated with large-scale economic units (Cf. Sylos-Labini, 1974, *passim.*).

These results, however, do not necessarily produce clear-cut political alignments. As noted, inflation taxes economic roles in a society and not necessarily real people. If any major division emerges, it should, of course, separate those who enjoy relative inflation leverage and those who do not. Corporations, their executives, and strong unions (if not necessarily shareholders) should square off against the congeries of vulnerable middle-class proprietors, pensioners and savers. (Since pensioners are increasingly granted indexed benefits their vulnerability has recently been reduced.) One can envisage a coalition of filling-station owners, stenographers and insurance salesmen against the executives of Exxon and the United Auto Workers.

But if this latent coalition emerges under inflation, it rarely corresponds to available political alternatives. To use the jargon of the economists, there is a high search cost for alternative political organizations. Traditional occupational and class identification continues to play a major role in political outcomes.

The consequence of this political lag is often parliamentary incoherence. Any possible coalition, whether of the left or right, includes social groups with disparate interests. The left—whether in the 1924 Cartel des Gauches or the Democratic Party in the United States—includes strong unions and weaker white-collar workers as well as small businessmen. A conservative or Christian Democratic coalition includes entrepreneurs who enjoy relative inflation leverage and vulnerable petty bourgeois of the same social strata as those whom sentiment or anticlericalism or regional tradition places in the opposing camp.

The internal inconsistencies emerge most clearly during the politics of monetary stabilization, the fourth (negative) inflationary case to be considered here. Stabilization is not always welcomed, even by those groups hurt by inflation. The civil servant may find himself furloughed, as occurred in the German *Beamtenabbau* of the mid-1920s. The small proprietor may find himself deprived of credit and operating capital during the period of stringency; likewise the peasant may find that prices for his output have dropped drastically. If his mortgage has been lightened, new short-term operating credit has become costly. What is more, during hyperinflation or even Latin inflation, the aggrieved consumer/saver usually expects stabilization to bring about a recovery of the assets that inflation has eroded. Unless his society is willing to risk a grave depression and heavy tax burden, this expectation must be frustrated (as it was in both France and Germany during the mid-1920s). During the course of inflation it is the levies on real income that appear most preoccupying; the tax on savings is often concealed or believed less definitive. But after stabilization the levy on capital can be totted up. Moreover, any progressive income redistribution that might have taken place now ceases. Thus a direct government reduction or blocking of monetary assets, as carried out in Germany, Austria and Belgium after World War II, produces less resentment than the levy of inflation. Even if it is not a progressive tax, it is a more universal one.

Despite the difficulties, therefore, of accurately foreseeing gains and losses, there does seem to be a natural evolution to the political constellations that superintend inflation and stabilization: (i) workers concerned with high employment, (ii) that segment of entrepreneurs lured by export opportunities or speculative gains or able to exploit increased leverage, and (iii) middle-class constituents originally anxious to avoid heavier taxes, form a natural inflation-prone coalition. If the inflation originates in war finance, this coalition does not preclude conservative sponsorship. Since 1945, however, it has been more often characterized by the participation of the moderate left.

The third group above is especially volatile. When the levy of inflation itself becomes onerous and preoccupying, middle-class constituents revert to a more conservative coalition alongside less 'go-go' businessmen. Moderate and conservative leaders stress the protection of savings and the need for capital formation to compensate for the running down of assets that has characterized inflation. In 1974, as in the societies of the 1920s, business leaders could predict a necessary recession or crisis, what Caillaux termed the 'great penance' that must follow monetary debauch. The penance, however, has often been that of the working classes, which must suffer unemployment even if the real wages of those with jobs may actually increase.

While middle-class constituents may only slowly come to give priority to their stakes as savers and consumers (rather than producers), industry leaders previously acquiescent in inflation can join a stabilization coalition late but with more alacrity. They finally foresee a liquidity crisis being as likely to emerge on the inflationary path as on that of monetary contraction. Although it is difficult in an era of sticky wages, their costs can often be passed along to other sectors of the economy, sometimes by direct government credits. If real growth soon resumes, such a new coalition of (i) reunited business leaders and (ii) inflation-weary middle-class elements can successfully assemble around a programme of capital formation and the restraint of collective consumption.

But if prolonged recession results, or small proprietors get caught by a combination of credit stringency and tax increases, bewildered middle-class elements may turn again: now either to the left anew, or toward the radical right. Not inflation alone, but a harsh ending of inflation has provided the socio-economic ground for radical right-wing movements from the 1920s on. The first electoral success of the Nazis, and of other right-wingers, in 1924 drew in part upon the resentments of those who felt that their paper assets had been insufficiently revalued after the inflation. And the subsequent mass vote for the party depended a great deal upon farmers who had gained relatively in the inflation (by the wiping out of mortgages) but who were hurt by credit and price squeezes after stabilization (Maier, 1975, pp. 483–515). More recently the Poujade movement rose to prominence in the wake of the first major post World War II stabilization program carried out in France (Parodi, 1971, p. 77).

Inflation, Growth and Distribution. The emphasis on capital formation and the reduction of collective consumption has characterized conservative advocacy for a half-century or more. How many times have we heard the Delphic phrase that a country 'is living beyond its means'! What this lament amounts to is that a society is changing the ratio of capital formation to current consumption. The most noticeable way of proceeding is by refusing to curtail imports until compelled to by exchange-rate readjustment. Internally, this often signifies to conservatives that the wages and transfer bill of a modern society is growing faster than a normally glacial rate of change would warrant. Again, this is a question of perspective. From one point of view, labour in Western Europe and North America has shown remarkable restraint in view of the enormous differentials of income that persist despite taxes and transfers.

Recent conservative suggestions for indexation may have arisen in part, I believe, from a sense that older arguments on behalf of capital formation and stable money have lost their force (Friedman, 1974b; *The Economist*, June 15, 1974). Why should conservatives become more receptive to indexing? In Austria of the 1920s and Italy of the 1940s cost-of-living escalators reinforced the inflationary process. Supposed success in Brazil has been far from clear (Fishlow, 1974; Lemgruber, 1977; and for more general evaluations see Goldstein, 1975; Braun, 1976). Obviously, to index government bond returns or income tax calculations must be appealing. But wage indexation has also been proposed, perhaps because it seems to offer a way to restore the labour restraint that many feel has disappeared. Indexation appeals when 'guidelines' or social compacts fail. Indexation can work, however, only when labour (or corporations) accept their given share of the national income as satisfactory. It will sufficiently persuade workers to moderate claims only if they accept the productivity-linked concept of wages. The assumption is that labour may accept this concept if reassured that it need not constantly anticipate the next round of price increases. The matter is more complicated when national income is reduced by external forces, such as a deterioration in the terms of trade. The basis of indexation then becomes crucial, as discussed by Flemming (1976, pp. 124–5). This complication aside, indexation offers a chance once again to win a consensus on growth as a surrogate for redistribution.

The concept of growth as a surrogate for redistribution appears, in retrospect, as the great conservative idea of the last generation. By conservative I do not mean militantly right-wing, for indeed wide circles of social democracy and the left have implicitly embraced the covenant it implies. Nonetheless, in the confrontation with Marxism and socialism, conservatives had only three choices: an outworn insistence on the value of traditional élites and privileges, which had little prospect for success under conditions of universal suffrage; or a fascism requiring that all class rivalry must be submerged in the search to aggrandize national authority and territory (which emerged discredited by the war); or the non-zero-sum pursuit of economic growth in the hope that this might make the older doctrines of class conflict irrelevant. Inflation has played an important role in preserving a broad consensus around the third concept; for when growth could not keep up with expectations, inflation helped disguise the lag. But beyond a certain rate, inflation cannot play this role as social lubricant and instead aggravates the very distributional conflicts it helped assuage.

Thus inflation is integrally linked with the stability conditions of twentieth-century capitalism. Ultimately the society may have to resort to indexation; but at that point the left may well insist that income shares be not frozen, but made an issue of political determination. This will require explicit decisions on equality instead of *ad hoc* and covert ones. Will the result be a gain? Perhaps from the viewpoint of a rational social allocation of income and wealth. But whether it will assure political harmony or even civil peace is far from certain.

NOTES

1. Bresciani-Turroni (1937) also points out (p. 72) that employers might hold the withholding taxes from their workers up to two weeks, thus effectively appropriating much of the real value for their own uses.
2. The best sources for understanding the shifting balance of forces in Germany at the end of the inflation are the stenographic records of two joint employer-employee bodies—the Zentralarbeitsgemeinschaft and the Provisional Reich Economic Council—now held at the State Archives in Potsdam (GDR). They are utilized in Maier (1975), which is drawn upon here.
3. Another cost hits the humbler elements of society—that of constant shopping and queueing. Sensitive observers of the Austrian inflation pointed out the sacrifice of family time together because of frenetic shopping expeditions (Arlt, 1925)—a task that servants could be assigned in upper-class households. Twenty years later Kalecki would emphasize this aspect of inequality as an argument for rationing in wartime Britain. (Kalecki, 1947, p. 148)

72 Charles S. Maier

4. Data from *Bulletin de la Statistique Générale et du Service d'Observation des Prix*, XIX, f. 2 (Jan–Mar. 1930), pp. 206–7, and XX, f. 3 (April–June, 1931), 390–1 show the following:

Mean value of inheritance in France (pre-tax; per estate)

	1913	*1929*	*1929/1913*
Current value	15,342	40,900	2.67
Retail-price indexed francs	15,342	7,027	0.46

Mean value of inheritances over Fr.50,000

Current value	Fr. 243,634	Fr. 258,706	1.06
Retail-price indexed francs	243,634	44,451	0.18

(Dollar and price indices from Alfred Sauvy, *Histoire économique de la France entre les deux guerres*, vol. I, (Paris: Fayard, 1963), annèxes. Note the greater compression of the wealthier estates.)

For Germany we have comparisons only of the legacies cousins or more distant relatives inherited in 1928 v. those of 1908–13. The number of registered inheritances in 1928 was 16.4 per cent of 1908–13; the amount of bequeathed property involved was 22.9 per cent of the earlier period. The number of inheritances below RM 10,000 was only 15.5 per cent of the equivalent in the earlier period although the individual legacies were of almost 50 per cent higher value. The number of inheritances above RM 10,000 remained between 21 and 26 per cent of the earlier period (save for the inheritances to distant relatives of over RM 1,000,000—down to 17 per cent). Humbler legacies, however, may have escaped registration because they were concentrated in immediate family members, so the results are indeterminate. See *Statistik des deutschen Reichs*, Bd. 276 (Berlin, 1930): *Die deutsche Erbschaftsbesteuerung vor und nach dem Krieg*.

Remember, what these figures measure is the cost of war and reconstruction. Inflation represented a way of allocating that cost, not the cost *per se*.

CHAPTER 3

Inflation under Central Planning*

Richard Portes

I

'The political economy of . . .' is used nowadays to legitimize bringing 'non-economic' considerations to bear on an 'economic' problem. Finding it applied to a socialist centrally planned economy (CPE), a good Party member would see red. No important economic problem could be treated purely technocratically in such an economy, any more than Kantorovich could become President of Gosplan. Planning is a political process. But the contrast with capitalist mixed economies is not so great. It was only briefly fashionable to view economic science as a set of constrained maximization problems and markets as apolitical devices for solving them. Having been revived in order to stake out a position, the term 'political economy' is fast becoming redundant.

It is doubtless common ground among authors in this volume that even in the most perfect market economy, the problem of inflation has a political dimension, if only that deriving from the modern state's control of currency emission. Many might be inclined towards the other extreme for CPEs: there are no markets, allocation is entirely bureaucratic–administrative, so economic phenomena must be entirely political. This would be a quite misleading over-simplification. Markets do exist in actual CPEs, and it is precisely there that inflation matters.

*This paper is based on work done under Social Science Research Council (U.K.) grant HR3309, in which Stan Rudcenko and David Winter have collaborated with me throughout. I have also benefited from comments by Malcolm Anderson, Fred Hirsch and other participants in the Warwick conference.

73

Where central allocation does fully supersede the market, as
for commodities exchanged within the state productive sector,
there may be prices, but they are then merely accounting devices.
Most consumer goods and services are not however centrally
allocated (distributed 'in kind') among households, nor are labour
services so allocated among productive uses.

If inflation occurs in the consumer goods and labour markets
of a CPE, it does affect resource allocation and income distribution. At the interface of the household and state productive
sectors, these are not fully-fledged markets. For consumer goods,
the central planners determine the supplies to be offered at
the prices they have set, responding not to profitability calculations at those prices, but rather imposing their own priorities
on the allocation of available resources. For labour services,
the planners determine the structure of demand and the wage
rates offered. Households are, however, free to choose from
the goods offered what to buy with their incomes and, with
relatively minor exceptions, where to work. Thus there is market
allocation of labour on the supply side and of consumer goods
on the demand side (though there is a large share of collective
consumption, allocated administratively at zero prices).

In the CPEs I shall discuss, those of Eastern Europe (excluding
Yugoslavia) and the USSR, wage labour and material incentives
have been retained, and this in turn implies allowing households
to dispose freely in state shops of the money incomes they
earn from state enterprises. There are also sales of goods and
labour services within the household sector itself, in a wide
range of more or less open, more or less legal markets. Of
these, the most important are the *kolkhoz* (collective farm) market
for some foodstuffs, limited private artisan activities, and various
forms of moonlighting. Inflationary pressures generated in state–
household relations can spill over into these markets, where
the planners control neither supply, nor demand, nor price.
But these markets are limited in size and cannot themselves
be a significant autonomous source of inflation.

There is indeed a remarkable degree of consensus on the
cause of inflationary pressures in CPEs: a generalized excess
demand in real terms, created by the planners. This is manifested
in two distinct ways. First, there is the 'planners' tension' applied
within the state productive sector by setting 'taut plans' for
enterprises—output targets which cannot be met with the input

allocations provided. In the aggregate, the only recourse for the enterprises is to seek above-plan labour inputs, paying above-plan wages. The planners' tension is thereby communicated to the household sector through the demand side of the labour market, and the additional incomes then transmit inflationary pressure to the consumer goods market. Second, even if all output plans were met at the planned levels of employment and wage payments, there might be excess demand for consumer goods because of the planners' attempts to use more than 100 per cent of final output. Pressures in planning and plan-implementation for more investment, exports, defence expenditure, collective consumption and stockbuilding tend to draw output away from supplies for purchase by households.

This 'overfull employment planning' has of course been an essential part of the drive for rapid economic growth, and it has been most extreme in periods of fastest growth. But it has been characteristic of the socialist economies of Eastern Europe and the USSR from the installation of central planning to the present day. Yet after initial periods of severe inflation, these economies have over the past two decades maintained an enviable record of consumer price stability (rates of increase ranging from −0.4 per cent per annum for the German Democratic Republic to 1.6 per cent per annum for Poland 1955–75), with parallel growth of money incomes and real consumption. I have presented and discussed the data in a recent paper (Portes, 1977a), which also argues that 'hidden' and repressed inflation have not been as significant as is generally believed.

I shall therefore take as given the relative success of central planning in controlling inflation. Here I shall consider why and how the CPEs have avoided inflation since the mid-1950s, the weaknesses of and strains on their techniques of inflation control, and the recent experience of Poland and Hungary, where some open inflation has re-appeared.

II

It is obvious that the easiest way to abolish inflation is to set prices and wages centrally and to allow incomes to rise only in line with consumer goods supplies, taking into account household demands for financial assets. This is what the planners have always tried to do. But perfect administration is just as rare as perfect markets, and the early periods of CPE inflation show it is difficult to implement such a policy, however extensive the central bureaucracy and severe its sanctions. The authorities must give sufficient priority to this objective and develop the means to carry it out.

The planners and their political superiors have never wanted inflation, even in the USSR in the 1930s (Holzman, 1960). They do not need it and dislike its effects. Their recent success in controlling it has reflected more general improvements in planning and macroeconomic management, as well as some reduction in planners' tension and the priority given to output growth. It is often maintained that governments in capitalist mixed economies do need inflation and may like some of its effects, or at least phenomena they associate with it or are willing to trade off against it. I should therefore explain why the authorities in CPEs have no use for it.

First, central planners do not need inflation as a method of taxation, to finance state expenditure. Even without progressive income taxation, they have adequate instruments to enforce their desired allocation between consumption and non-consumption uses of output, or alternatively, to control real wages. Direct administrative control over the allocation of final output may not be fully effective, but households can only bid very small additional amounts of consumption goods away from the state when the planners also control the amounts of resources allocated to the production and importing of such goods. The major exception is agriculture, but here historical experience suggested that rising prices of industrial goods were not a very effective means of extracting surplus from the peasants, and other methods were used. Moreover, the planners do reinforce their control over the supply of consumer goods with direct controls over money wages. Within limits, they have even been able to *reduce* money wages occasionally, by raising piece-rate labour norms.

Nor do central planners need inflation as an 'impartial', 'anonymous' way of resolving real income distributional conflicts between workers or households. They have rather sought to enforce a conscious, centrally-determined distributional policy by operating on both money wages and the consumer price structure. Inflation only makes this more difficult.

It should not be surprising that the planners perceive no trade-off between inflation and unemployment, and hence no need to allow any inflation as a cost of reducing unemployment. There may in fact be such a trade-off, to a very limited extent, in the sense that 'overfull employment planning' makes enterprises willing to hire some workers who might otherwise be unemployable. But the planners believe they can ensure full employment through appropriate manpower planning and do not intend their 'taut' output plans to generate excess demand for labour.

Finally, neither the political authorities nor the economic planners in CPEs believe that they can make the population feel better off through money illusion. On the contrary, the longer consumer prices have been held constant, the more sensitive households appear to have become to any attempts to increase prices. This indeed has restricted the planners' room for manœuvre. Relative price changes calculated to keep the consumer price index constant have been perceived as increases in the price level; and price increases accompanied by money income increases, distributed fairly carefully over categories of households to 'compensate' them according to the composition of their consumption baskets, have been perceived as reductions in real incomes.

For these reasons, the planners have never seen any benefits they might derive from inflation, either in managing the economy or in political terms. Moreover, inflation makes their tasks more difficult in various ways, and they have a general aversion to rising prices and monetary disequilibrium.

There are of course pure administrative costs to changing prices. With several million consumer prices set and registered centrally, these are not inconsiderable, if one is contemplating a continuously or even sporadically rising consumer price level. A producer price 'reform', in which a co-ordinated revision of all enterprise wholesale prices is implemented simultaneously, normally takes several years for the price-setting bureaucracy to prepare. To enforce any planners' preferences on the consumer price structure with the price level inflating would require a very substantial additional administrative apparatus.

The planners abhor the 'spontaneous' phenomena associated

with inflation. They cannot control the redistributive effects of unplanned consumer price and wage changes, and they are especially sensitive to the spill-over of excess demand into the *kolkhoz* and other free markets. For the redistribution here is typically away from the urban proletariat to the peasants, private artisans and other less-favoured groups. After property rights have been openly and directly redistributed by a socialist revolution, inflation expropriates the wrong people.

Just as undesirable as price increases on free markets are the black markets and queues arising from repressed inflation. These are divisive, and create resentment and discontent with the system. Perhaps more seriously, the planners believe that repressed inflation on the consumer goods market will harm labour incentives. They assume there are limits to the willingness of the population to continue working so as to accumulate liquid assets which they cannot spend. And an 'overhang' of undesired money balances in the hands of the population always carries the danger of a sudden run on the shops in response to some real or imagined crisis. Excess demand for labour is just as bad as for goods. It is generally harmful to labour discipline, and in particular, it encourages labour-force turnover and migration, which housing shortages do not fully deter. The planners seem to regard all turnover as wasteful and disruptive.

Historical experience of severe inflation, including hyperinflation, in some East European countries, followed by 'currency reforms' which effectively confiscated liquid assets, have also left deep marks on the psychology of the political authorities, the planners, and the population itself. Moreover, there is a deep strain of conservatism, of monetary and fiscal orthodoxy, in the bankers and monetary planners of the CPEs. Marxist monetary theory reinforces this attitude. The planners invariably seek balance or surplus on the state budget; they tend to focus on stocks of cash and savings deposits held by the public as indicators of monetary equilibrium rather than attempting to match actual consumer expenditures to forecasts of aggregate demand; and they generally hold to a fairly unsophisticated, short-run version of the quantity theory. This may not be unreasonable in the CPE context (see the description of the monetary system below).

I shall now outline some structural features of CPEs which help the planners to contain in the productive sphere the excess demand they impose upon it. They also limit the effects on the household sector of shocks from abroad, from agriculture, from planning errors, or from impulses originating in the household sector itself.

The most striking characteristic of the monetary system is its extreme simplicity. There is a single, combined central and commercial bank (monobank) with many branches. Households may hold cash or savings deposits; there are no other financial assets. All enterprise assets and liabilities are entries in the monobank's books. Excess demand for productive inputs, no matter how strongly backed by enterprise liquidity, cannot affect the labour or consumer goods markets unless the bank allows enterprises to disburse additional cash in the form of wages.

One of the bank's most important functions is to monitor wage payments, checking them against the enterprise's plan. It can devote considerable attention to this, because its task in controlling money and credit is so straightforward. All that is necessary is to regulate advances to enterprises for working capital and to keep a check on the small amounts of consumer credit allowed for private housing and some purchases of durables.

An especially important aspect of the system is the way in which it separates domestic from foreign prices and domestic monetary variables from foreign exchange transactions (Pryor, 1963). Exports are sold by producers to the Ministry of Foreign Trade (through specialized foreign trade enterprises) at the same fixed domestic prices which they would receive from domestic buyers, and imports are bought by domestic users at their fixed domestic prices from the Ministry of Foreign Trade. The Ministry's domestic currency account with the bank is debited with these payments for exports and credited with the receipts from selling imports. On the other hand, it is credited by the bank with domestic currency in exchange for its foreign exchange receipts from exporting and debited with the domestic currency equivalent of its foreign exchange expenditure for imports, converted in both cases at the official exchange rate.

This exchange rate is purely an accounting device, with no relation at all to the ratios between domestic and foreign currency prices. At the end of the planning period, the Ministry's net domestic currency losses (or profits) are met by the 'price equalization subsidy (or tax)', paid directly from or to the state budget. The foreign currency account of course reflects the economy's actual foreign currency payments and receipts.

Under this system, no change in foreign currency prices has any effect whatsoever on domestic prices. If trade is initially balanced, a uniform change in all foreign prices does not even affect the price-equalization subsidy or tax. Inflation cannot be imported, except insofar as excess demand in the world economy might result in above-plan quantities exported or under-fulfilment of the import volume plan.

A deterioration of the terms of trade, while having no direct effect on domestic prices, will increase the price-equalization subsidy required from the budget, and this will be the monetary reflection of the real income loss. But the planners will determine and control what components of domestic final use must fall and how the reductions are to be implemented (cutting investment or defence, raising consumer prices, reducing money wages etc.).

Moreover, there are no foreign transactions on capital account except those initiated by the state bank. There are no domestic securities to purchase, and foreigners cannot buy the domestic currency, and so cannot hold it to sell subsequently. The bank (and only the bank) may of course borrow or lend abroad, but this has no effect on money balances held by domestic enterprises or households, nor on domestic asset prices and interest rates—there are none.

This insulation of the CPE economy from foreign inflationary impulses is accompanied by the breaking of various other macro-economic functional relationships. These relationships are often important channels for the propagation of inflationary shocks in capitalist mixed economies, and their absence again makes it easier for the planners to limit the effect of such shocks to once-for-all changes in prices or wages.

Thus a monetary error or production shortfall creating excess demand for consumer goods need not call forth any increase in domestic production, with a consequent increase in the demand for labour. The planners have alternatives, such as increasing imports or reallocating resources from investment to consumption, by which they can avoid transmitting the initial inflationary impulse to the labour market. Similarly, price increases do not generate factor incomes (disregarding small incentive funds related to profits). Wage increases raise production costs, but they normally have no effect on prices, at least until the next comprehensive producer price reform. The corresponding product-specific tax or subsidy is altered *ad interim*, or the cost change affects the overall budget subsidy or deduction from enterprise profits.

Finally, although trade unions do exist in CPEs, they have no role in money wage determination. The trade unions act as a 'transmission belt', mainly communicating central priorities and instructions downwards, as well as some worker attitudes back up to the leadership. They are used to promote labour discipline and socialist morality, especially among the non-Party members of the working class. They also act in settling labour disputes and grievances.

All this is helpful in supporting production-mindedness, and it leaves wage determination where the planners want it: entirely with themselves, except insofar as they decentralize to enterprise managers. They do this by establishing a national job evaluation system in which rates for job and skill categories are all set as multiples of a basic wage tariff, which they may then change from time to time. Each industry has a manual relating specific job types and skill qualifications to the national system, and the enterprise management are responsible for assigning each worker to a category. The planners also fix aggregate wage bill or average wage targets or both for each enterprise.

Thus there can be no 'relativities spiral', no 'leapfrogging', and consequently no pressure on the planners to allow the monetary expansion necessary to finance such 'autonomous' money wage increases. But the absence of any trade-union role in wage determination in CPEs is clearly not a sufficient condition for their success in controlling inflation. The counter-examples are the prolonged inflationary periods in the USSR, 1928–47, and in the smaller countries for several years following the installation of central planning. Trade-union behaviour during those periods followed the model sketched above. Moreover, there are both general pressures for real income increases and specific distributional tensions which do come from below, although they are not normally transmitted through the trade unions.

This is one point at which the planners' control has in fact weakened in recent years. Real income increases have been moderate but continuous in most of the CPEs since the mid-1950s, and the demonstration effects coming from the consumer societies of Western Europe have been especially strong in the more industrialized countries of Eastern Europe—the GDR, Czechoslovakia, Hungary and Poland. As expectations rise, the planners' room for manœuvre falls. In agriculture, incentives have generally replaced compulsion. This too has reduced the planners' autonomy, and the peasants' rising living standards have not escaped the notice of urban workers. Regional income differentials in some countries, inter-industry and inter-enterprise differentials in others, all contribute to distributional tensions. That income distribution is somewhat more egalitarian than in the West and wealth distribution considerably more so does not mitigate these conflicts—indeed, an egalitarian ideology and some progress towards equality make those differentials which do arise all the more noticeable.

The ability to take effective group action to assert real income demands is limited not only by the weakness of the trade unions, but also by the monolithic character of the Party. Nevertheless, groups like peasants, workers, and specific sectors and industries do have their political representatives, down to the enterprise Party secretaries. The workers themselves can exert diffused pressure through unwillingness to work harder or raise productivity, so that the planners are led to believe that further material incentives are required. All these forces increase the demands on the economy.

On the other hand, both planning and plan-implementation are much better now, and the planners no longer indulge in the excesses of the early years. Overfull employment planning continues, but on the whole it is less likely to affect the household sector. For example, it has long been conventional wisdom that consumer goods supply had the lowest priority among categories of final use, so that the planners would tend to use it as a buffer to absorb exogenous shocks during the plan period. But consumption goods supply-functions have been estimated for several East European countries since the mid-1950s, and they show little evidence of this effect. A shortfall in national income appears to have a *less* than proportionate effect on consumption, and there is hardly any sign that deviations of investment or defence expenditure from their trends 'crowd out' consumption (Portes and Winter, 1977). Moreover, the planners appear to raise the current year's consumption goods supply above its trend when the previous year has left households with real balances in excess of their trend value. This observation is corroborated by the literature on monetary planning from the CPEs themselves, which suggests an increasing willingness to adjust commodity supplies to meet monetary demands, rather than relying solely on restricting the latter (Rudcenko, 1977).

There have also been improvements in plan implementation at the enterprise level, especially in the banks' ability to enforce wage-plan discipline and the overall enterprise-budget constraint. An old controversy in the Western literature on CPEs revolves around whether the primary channel from excess real demand to monetary disequilibrium led directly through wage over-expenditure or indirectly through poor credit control and budgetary weakness (Hodgman, 1960; Holzman, 1960). Even in that literature, however, there was general agreement that the sophistication, authority and performance of the bank and the Ministry of Finance in the USSR had improved greatly from the prewar period. There would undoubtedly be a similar consensus in contrasting the early failures of the monetary authorities in the East European CPEs with their more recent record.

III

Although there has been virtually no open inflation in most CPEs since the mid-1950s, and allegations of repressed inflation have not yet been supported by the data (Portes, 1977a; Portes and Winter, 1978), there are two countries for which the picture is somewhat different. The consumer price index (CPI) in Poland rose at 1 per cent per annum from 1955 to 1972, but at rather more than 4 per cent per annum in 1972–5 (with some evidence of repressed inflation as well). In Hungary, the CPI rose at 0.5 per cent per annum from 1955 to 1968, then at 2.7 per cent per annum in 1968–76, with increases of 3.5 per cent in 1975 and 5 per cent in 1976. Some interesting lessons can be drawn from a brief discussion of the experience of

each country (see Fallenbuchl, 1977, for data and background—
but a somewhat different interpretation—on Poland; and Portes,
1977b, on Hungary).

Gierek came to power in Poland in December 1970 after
Gomulka's attempt to raise food prices brought open expressions
of discontent from urban workers. That was merely the final
provocation of a policy which had held average money wage
increases to less than 3 per cent per annum in 1968–70 while
the CPI was rising at about 1.5 per cent per annum. The
new government immediately rescinded the price increases and
allowed total money incomes to rise by slightly more than
10 per cent in 1971, with virtually no price increases, while
it worked out a new economic strategy. This was implemented
in 1972–6. It was a 'dash for growth', based on heavy investment
with Western equipment, together with rapid growth of real
wages, which were to give workers the necessary incentive to
increase productivity. In June 1976 the government tried to
raise the price of meat, again encountered open expressions
of discontent from urban workers, and backed down. The stalemate has continued, and the strategy is clearly compromised.

What does the story demonstrate, aside from the extraordinary
political insensitivity of the government and the fact that planners
always underestimate the income elasticity of demand for meat?
First, in their enthusiasm for monetary incentives (and partly
as a consequence of some limited decentralization), the planners
simply lost control over wages, and their commitment to keep
basic food prices down produced intolerable strains. Disposable
money incomes *per capita* rose by over 60 per cent in the
four years 1971–5, the average money wage in the state sector
by 50 per cent. This was evidently insupportable, and no price
control system could have held up against such pressure. Productivity did increase rapidly—output per man in socialist industry
rose at 7 per cent per annum in 1971–5 (though one cannot
separate the effects of the incentive policy from those of rapid
capital stock increases and of a simple recovery from below-trend
growth in the late 1960s). But the money income increases
were clearly excessive.

Second, although the planners lost their hold on monetary
variables, they appear *not* to have increased significantly the
overall excess real demand in the productive sector. In this
respect, the Polish experience in 1971–5 reverses the usual CPE

pattern, in which monetary disequilibrium is a consequence of overstrain rather than a cause of it. The investment boom was financed mainly by foreign borrowing, and the terms of trade improved. Investment *plus* the net export surplus (negative) as a share of domestically-produced output (a measure of the burden of non-consumption expenditure) rose only slightly, from 30.7 per cent in 1966–70 to 31.6 per cent in 1971–5, although investment was growing at 18 per cent per annum in the latter period.

Third, industrial workers in Poland are now fully conscious of their political strength, and they will resist any belt-tightening—any efforts to make them repeat the restraint of the late 1960s. The planners' freedom of action is severely constrained. If the population are still dissatisfied after five years of *per capita* real income increases at 9½ per cent per annum, as indeed they appear to be, it is hard to see what will or could satisfy them.

This suggests that Poland's inflation over the past several years is due not merely to the economic and political mistakes of the authorities, but also to their relative lack of authority itself. Throughout the postwar period, Poland has had overall the weakest monetary management among the CPEs (Montias, 1964; Portes, 1977a). This may be attributable in part to weaknesses in Party control over the society. These are evident in the Party's inability to eliminate the influence of the Church or to impose the collectivization of agriculture; and culturally and politically, many have continued to look to the West, regarding the Party as an unfortunate but perhaps indispensable buffer against direct Soviet rule. As in other countries, Eastern and Western, allowing money incomes to increase has been one response to such strains and tensions in the social and political system. It is therefore perhaps a tribute to the efficiency of central planning in containing inflationary pressures that Poland has managed to keep the rate of open consumer price inflation down to 1½ per cent per annum over the past two decades.

Whereas the Polish political context and Poland's recent growth strategy and monetary errors are distinctive, Hungary stands out because of the decentralizing economic reforms introduced in 1968. These brought significant elements of market allocation into the state productive sphere, while making prices more flexible and re-establishing some of the macroeconomic relationships which are absent in the standard CPE. The two features I would stress here are the remarkable ability of the remaining monetary, wage and price controls to withstand the pressures on the economy in the 1970s, and the importance of the distributional tensions created by decentralization and the Hungarian authorities' version of increasing material incentives.

The pressure was considerable. Real gross fixed investment rose 10 per cent in 1969, 17 per cent in 1970, and a further 11 per cent in 1971. Yet investment goods prices rose only 6 per cent over the three years. Hungary's terms of trade deteriorated by 14 per cent from 1973 to 1975, equivalent to about 6 per cent of national income. Yet the consumer price index rose only 6 per cent during that period. Although the enterprises no longer received money wage targets, and the bank ceased to regulate wage disbursements, the rate of growth of average money wages rose from 2.3 per cent per annum in 1961–7 to only 5.3 per cent per annum in 1968–75.

In my view, the continued control over wage levels through the fiscal system (the 'tax on wage increases') was a necessary condition for this impressive performance. But it was certainly not sufficient. A quite sophisticated set of price controls, which allowed some flexibility in relative prices while regulating the price level, was also important (until 1976, there was not a single year in which the rise in the price level exceeded the plan announced at the beginning of the year).

As in the Polish case, monetary incentives were a key element in the Hungarian policy change. But the focus was different, not on increasing real wages all round as a means of raising morale and stimulating a co-operative effort to raise productivity, but rather on income differentiation. A conscious decision was taken to reverse, to a limited extent, the highly egalitarian character of Hungarian incomes policy up to 1968. The planners perceived a conflict between efficiency and egalitarianism, and they tried to tilt the balance back somewhat towards the former, in line with the overall emphasis on markets in the reforms. Thus managers' incomes were to depend heavily on enterprise profits, workers' less so, but still significantly. Managers were exhorted to reward productivity and initiative within the enterprise with a more differentiated wage policy. An expansion of private sector activity was welcomed.

It was the effects of this policy which led the Party to halt further development of the reforms at the end of 1972. Just as in capitalist market economies, workers were unwilling to accept the legitimacy of an income distribution—in this case, a redistribution—deriving from market forces (cf. Hirsch, 1977a). They were not convinced by the argument that such a redistribution, by encouraging output increases, might ultimately bring higher real wages for all. They saw no reason why inter-enterprise differences in profitability, which might arise from differences in management ability, historically-given capital stock or the vagaries of price control, should result in differences in wages. Their sensibilities were offended by moonlighting, real estate speculation, country houses at Balaton, high earnings of private artisans, 'profiteering', 'money-grubbing' and 'materialism'.

Limited measures directed towards restricting the most visible of these phenomena were inadequate to calm the discontents of the urban, blue-collar working class, especially those in the largest state industrial enterprises, which were the least profitable. Thus in his speech to the Central Committee plenum of November 1972, Kadar, as First Party Secretary, stressed the relative drop in the position of industrial workers, argued that equality had to take precedence over efficiency and criticized petit-bourgeois excesses. The plenum decreed an 8 per cent all-round increase in money wages for manual workers in state industry and increased the powers of the central planning and price control bodies. There followed in early 1973 a new regulation on 'unjustified profits', which was in effect a tightening of the price control regulations, and subsequent revisions in the basic wage system were designed to restore more uniformity. There has been relatively little further recentralization since 1973, but any return to decentralization and extension of market relations have clearly been subordinated to maintaining a politically acceptable income distribution.

The Polish and Hungarian cases represent two distinct alternatives to conventional CPE policies and planning mechanisms. They demonstrate clearly the dangers of abandoning any of the key features of CPE monetary, price, and incomes policies in economies still emphasizing rapid growth. The weakness of the trade unions is clearly not a sufficient condition for the success of price and income control policies.

CHAPTER 4

Inflation and Income Distribution

David Piachaud

I

It is a rare economic or indeed social phenomenon that in recent years has been unaffected by inflation. Changes in earnings, profits, investment, unemployment and the rate of economic growth, in common with diverse other phenomena, ranging almost to England's batting performance, have all been connected in various ways with the rate of inflation, both as cause and as consequence. Since all these economic variables affect income distribution, the relationship between inflation and income distribution is necessarily complex. This chapter is concerned with inflation and the distribution of personal income. It concentrates on the British experience over the last twenty years, drawing heavily on the work of others recently surveyed by Laidler and Parkin (1975) and Foster (1976a).

It is a truism that those with fixed money incomes become worse off with inflation. But inflation cannot be considered in isolation from the response to it. The relevant question from the point of view of income distribution is to what extent incomes from different sources *are* fixed or have moved disproportionately. Nor is it only the response to past inflation that is relevant. The effects on income distribution also depend on how far inflation is foreseen, on how far adjustment is made to take it into account, and on how far the extent of foresight and adjustment differs between income groups.

To establish the effects of inflation on income distribution, we ideally need to know, first, what has happened to the distribution of incomes and, second, what would have happened to the distribution of incomes in the absence of, or with different rates of, inflation. The first of these questions we can, with difficulty and limitations, answer. The second in its nature can never be answered with certainty. Instead we must be content with lesser questions. Empirically and ex-post, we may consider what changes in income distribution have been associated with different levels of inflation, what connection can be made with inflation, and what, in consequence, is the scale of the effects that may be attributed to inflation. While the suitable analytical method varies according to the area under discussion and the availability of data, one generally appropriate approach used in this chapter is to analyse how far real changes after allowing for inflation—be it the real changes in incomes, in taxes or in asset values—have been related systematically to the rate of inflation.

In considering *income* and its distribution we must be concerned with income in an economic sense: we may appropriately adopt and adapt the widely used definition of Hicks (1946):

> a person's income is what he can consume during the week and still expect to be as well off at the end of the week as he was at the beginning.

Since data on personal incomes are not available in a form that fits this definition of income, we must break down the effects of inflation into a number of categories:

(i) the impact of inflation on original or market incomes, in real terms before government intervention;

(ii) the effects of inflation on the redistributive impact of government;

(iii) the changing relationship between income and command over real resources;

(iv) changes in wealth due to variation in the value of capital assets.

These four types of effects will be considered in turn in the four sections that follow. While this division is convenient, it must be said that, in so far as it isolates the effects of inflation on income distribution, it is, for two reasons, something of a snare and a delusion. First, this is because all four types may occur simultaneously and act on income distribution in several directions at once. Second, this is because most of what we can now know is based on 'snapshots' of the income distribution at a point in time, whereas in reality people do not occupy a fixed position in a static income distribution but change places through the stages of their life cycle; it is the impact of inflation on the distribution of incomes over the life cycle that is in many respects the most interesting question, but its answer is the most elusive. In the final section some of these wider, more intractable issues will be discussed and some limited conclusions will be drawn.

II

It is a sad fact that there are no British statistics of sufficient continuity and accuracy as to allow the impact of inflation to be measured against variations in the distribution of income as a whole. It is therefore necessary to adopt a disaggregated and rather disjointed approach, considering different types of original or market income in turn. Earnings, being the largest component of personal income, will be considered first, with the effects of unemployment; then incomes from investments, occupational pensions and imputed incomes from owner-occupation will be considered.

The traditional hypothesis on the effects of inflation on earnings has been the wage-lag hypothesis. The hypothesis is that with inflation, price rises tend to run ahead of increases in money wages, leading to lower real wages and increased profits (Keynes, 1923). A large part of the literature on inflation and income distribution has been devoted to this hypothesis, and will not be reviewed here. So much conflicting evidence has been produced that Laidler and Parkin resolved that: 'the only safe conclusion about the wage–lag hypothesis must be that it postulates a phenomenon which is certainly not universal, but which may from time to time have happened.'

The shape of the distribution of gross earnings of adult men has been remarkably consistent over a long period of time despite the substantial variations in labour market conditions that have occurred. For example the lowest and highest deciles (one tenth from the bottom and the top of the earnings distribution) as a proportion of median gross weekly earnings of full-time manual workers were 69 per cent and 143 per cent respectively in 1886 (Thatcher, 1968); in 1975 the corresponding figures were 69 per cent and 144 per cent (Department of Employment, 1976). This does not of course mean that there have not been shifts in the relative positions of different occupations and industries, or in the relative position of women, which indirectly were related to inflation. Such shifts were clearly influenced by the causes and nature of the inflation. (For further discussion of this point see the chapter by Maier, above) In the more distant past there were groups of workers who could for substantial periods find their pay eroded. Now that pay increases have become an annual event for almost all, compensation for inflation is more regular than in the past but there are still, of course, variations in the vulnerability of different occupations and groups to inflation. Yet how the ability of different groups to obtain compensation for inflation in their pay settlements varies with the rate of inflation and its nature is not at all clear. Similarly unclear is the long-run impact on income distribution of responses to high rates of inflation in the form of incomes policy. While in recent years there have clearly been substantial shifts in the earnings distribution due to incomes policy, principally to the detriment of higher earners, whether these are temporary rather than permanent remains to be seen. The casual evidence pointing to a squeezing of differentials takes inadequate account of fringe benefits, conditions of work and regrading. It is certainly hard to detect any lasting effect of previous incomes policies on the shape of the earnings distribution. How inflation has affected the shape of the earnings distribution must therefore unfortunately remain an open question.

Unemployment is inextricably entwined with inflation in a great deal of thinking on economic policy. The great question of the direction of the ultimate causal connection—whether the level of unemployment is the major determinant of inflation or inflation is the 'mother and father' of unemployment—is not at issue in this chapter; but that there is some relationship is not much in doubt. Therefore in analysing the relationship between inflation and income distribution the further relationship between unemployment and income distribution must be considered. While the differential between net incomes of those in work and out of work has narrowed over the last twenty years, net incomes out of work remain for the great majority of the unemployed substantially below net incomes when at work. The most recent and sophisticated estimate of the effect of unemployment on income has been made by Nickell (1977). He defined the 'replacement ratio' as the ratio of after-tax income of a household while the male is out of work (including all social security benefits and tax refunds) to the estimated potential income after tax while in work. For a sample of the unemployed in 1972, he found the average replacement ratio to be 0.72. Since 1972 there have, of course, been some changes. While benefit levels have not altered substantially relative to the net income of a man on average earnings—indeed they fell relatively from 1972 to 1975—it is likely that with rising unemployment the previous earnings of those unemployed will have been relatively higher, so that the replacement ratio will fall on this account and the number of unemployed for long periods will increase. The increased inequality in income distribution resulting from higher unemployment may still not have a clear-cut effect on the distribution of welfare where the additional unemployment is short-term, since there may be some positive benefit from not working; but the same is not true of long-term unemployment. There can be no doubt, therefore, that an increase in unemployment such as that in recent years must increase economic inequality in the wider sense. To the extent that inflation is connected with this rise in unemployment, this effect on income distribution is related to inflation.

Investment income comprising rents, dividends and interest payments is so diverse in content that nothing useful can be said of it in aggregate. The picture is further obscured by the interrelation of stocks and flows. The stock aspect will be considered in Section IV on wealth effects; in this section only the flows or yields are considered. The yields on three major sources of investment income are shown, together with the rate of inflation, in Chart I.

It is clear that there is no close relationship between yields and inflation but for two of the assets—government bonds and building society shares—the yields in recent high-inflation years are substantially higher than before. This is scarcely a comfort to those already holding fixed-interest government debt for whom,

CHART I   *Yields on Investments, 1956–76*

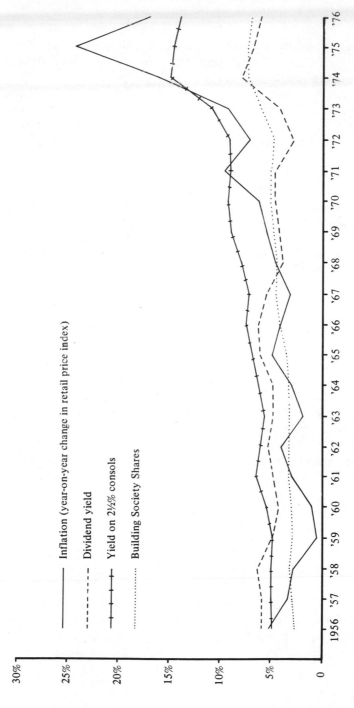

————— Inflation (year-on-year change in retail price index)
- - - - - Dividend yield
—†—†— Yield on 2½% consols
· · · · · · Building Society Shares

Source: Central Statistical Office, *Financial Statistics.*

in terms of flow of income, there is no compensation for inflation. Similarly, the dividend yield on industrial ordinary shares has shown no discernible upward trend. Of the three rates of return considered, only the income from a fixed money holding of building society shares would have increased along with inflation, and that by very much less than the rise in prices. Thus while all these comparisons are highly artificial in presenting changes in 'flows' separately from stock effects, they do serve to indicate that investment income as a whole has certainly not kept pace with inflation. (One corroborative indicator is the decline in real incomes of Church of England clergy whose stipends are largely financed from investment income). Insofar as it is the highest income group for whom investment income represents the largest proportion of income, this decline probably has, overall, an equalising effect. But the sad, and much cited, case of an indigent widow with her patriotism and War Loan is not mythical, and investment incomes are important to many low down in the income distribution—they too have lost when inflation has risen.

Next to the widow with War Loan, the most commonly cited victim of inflation is probably the pensioner whose occupational pension has been eroded. Unfortunately there is a dearth of up-to-date information on the performance of occupational pensions in payment. (The value of future pension rights is considered in Section IV). The survey of occupational pension schemes conducted in 1971 (Government Actuary, 1971) asked how much pensions in payment had been increased after ten years of retirement. It found that

> The evidence points to increases in the private sector averaging about 2½ per cent per annum over the whole ten years, in cases where augmentation was automatic. During the ten years the retail prices index rose by 4½ per cent per annum on average and so increases did not on the whole match price rises . . . In the more numerous cases where augmentation is *ad hoc*, the average rate of increase is much the same.

Thus, even in a period with inflation much lower than currently, occupational pensions in payment were on average falling in real value. Since occupational pensions have normally been fixed at retirement in money terms with no adequate mechanism for continued inflation-proofing, there seems little doubt that the fall in real value must have accelerated in recent years. This loss has most impact on the better-off pensioners who tend to be in the lower, though not the lowest, reaches of the overall income distribution at any point in time. However, they may be relatively well off in terms of life-time income and in relation to current needs. So the impact on income inequality in the broader sense is unclear.

Thus far we have been concerned with income that is actually paid (with deductions) to individuals. In order to arrive at economic income one item that must be included is the value of services, or imputed income, obtained from assets that are owned; and against these, interest payments must be deducted from income. Here only owner-occupied housing will be considered; in principle all services obtained from consumer durables should be included but these tend to be much less important and, where purchased on credit, the loans are usually for only one or two years. The imputed income from one's own house is a valuable service and is in its nature fully proof against inflation. What is influenced by inflation is the real interest payment. The real interest paid by borrowers depends on the real debt outstanding and on the rate of interest. With higher inflation, the rate of interest paid by borrowers has increased (in step with that paid to lenders and considered above), but this has been outweighed by the fall in the real value of the debt. Since, as will be seen, those borrowing from building societies tend to be in the higher income ranges, the fall in the flow of real interest payments increases the disparity of incomes.

At the same time, the rise in nominal interest rates involves a shifting forward in the real burden of debt servicing, with higher payments in the early years compensating for the payments in depreciated currency in the later years. The resulting cash squeeze for new house-buyers at the outset of the mortgage term discriminates against house-buyers who have little capital or access to supplementary resources, or borrowing guarantees from family or employer. This influence, therefore, also tends towards inequality within the sector of house-buyers. Once again, the overall effect is far from straightforward or certain.

III

We may now turn from original or market incomes to consider
the government's role in redistributing income. The gains to
the government from inflation have been summarised by Laidler
and Parkin (1975) as follows:

> First, inflation reduces the real value of government interest
> bearing debt . . . The second source of government gain from
> inflation is its influence on the real volume of tax payments
> . . . The third means whereby inflation redistributes income
> between the public and government arises from the 'tax' that
> *anticipated* inflation levies on holdings of that part of the
> non-interest bearing money stock which is the liability of
> government.

The second of these gains—'fiscal drag'—will be considered
in this section. But to identify fiscal drag as the only effect
on flows to the government would seem to be deficient and
politically selective. Where social security benefits are not inflation-proofed or where cash limits are applied to government
programmes, inflation reduces the real level or volume of benefits
or services the government 'gains'. It is ironic that some of
those who rail against fiscal drag at the same time question
whether we can afford inflation-proofed pensions, even though
both divert resources from private individuals to government.
The difference is that the former diversion is at the expense
of those best off, the latter at the expense of those worst
off. Thus any comprehensive analysis of how the government
gains from inflation needs to be extended beyond Laidler and
Parkin's limits to include the influence of inflation on the real
level of government expenditure programmes.

Social security benefits are the most important source of income
in all the lower income ranges. How has their real value varied
with the rate of inflation? Here the standard national insurance
retirement pension for a man or woman alone will be taken
as an example, being the largest benefit both in terms of numbers
involved and expenditure. In Chart II the rate of change in
the real value of the pension between upratings is plotted against
the rate of inflation. To indicate whether there has been any
sort of cycle of upratings, the points for each uprating are
connected together in sequence. It is clear that the changes
in the real value of the pension have not borne any systematic

CHART II *Pensions and Inflation, 1948–76*

Rate of change
in real value
of pension
 between upratings
(% p.a.)

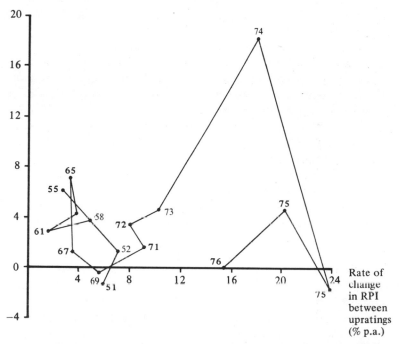

Source: Department of Health and Social Security, *Social Security Statistics*

relationship to the rate of inflation. The periodic upratings in pensions have involved large real increases both when inflation has been relatively low (1955 and 1965) and when inflation has been high (1974); equally, acceleration of inflation has been associated both with a more favourable real-value uprating (1969–71 and 1972–4) and with a less favourable uprating (1955–8, 1967–9 and 1974–5). The fact that the real value of pensions has been maintained and improved even in years of high inflation since 1951 is an indication of the gradual acceptance of the indexing principle which since 1975 has been made a statutory obligation. The effect of inflation on the real value of the pension has, therefore, been obscured by the government's response to inflation through both the size and frequency of upratings. Inflation has clearly had the political effect of focusing more attention on the circumstances of pensioners—it was in 1973 that a poster appeared: 'Warning to H.M. Government: Living on a pension can damage your health'. It is not impossible that inflation has led to pensions being higher in real terms than would otherwise have been the case.

Retirement pensions are, however, more favourably treated than most other social security benefits which still have no guarantee of inflation-proofing and have in the past signally failed to keep pace with inflation. In such instances—family allowances and death grants for example—one may reasonably assume that no government would have been likely to reduce their money value and it is then inescapable that their real value has been reduced because of inflation.

Finally in this section we must consider the relationship between gross and net incomes—in particular the income tax system and the effects on it of inflation. This relationship has been extensively investigated in studies of indexing in Britain (Liesner and King, 1975) and in the United States (Aaron, 1976). In the former case, Allen and Savage (1975) examined (a) the actual change in average rates of tax on constant real incomes that occurred from 1961/2 to 1974/5 and (b) what would have happened if the structure of rates and allowances had been held constant in nominal terms (the 'automatic change', representing inflationary fiscal drag); the difference they describe as (c) the 'discretionary change'. For a married couple with two children between 11 and 16, they obtained the results shown in Table 1. Thus if real income (in 1961/2 prices) remained at £1000 p.a. an extra 6.3 per cent of gross income would have been payable in income tax in 1974/5 above 1961/2; at the £2500 level an extra 4.5 per cent became payable, and at the £10,000 level an extra 14.1 per cent. Thus, the heaviest burden fell on taxpayers at the lower and upper ends of the scale, to the relative advantage of those in the middle. This arbitrary shift can be explained only by the interaction of the 'automatic change' and the government's incomplete response through the 'discretionary change'.

The question then is whether, in the absence of fiscal drag, the government would have been prepared to increase the nominal tax rates to the extent that effectively occurred. Judgements

TABLE 1   *Absolute Differences in Percentage Rates of Income Tax, Great Britain, (1961/2 to 1974/5)*

Gross Income (1961/2 prices)	(a) Actual change	(b) Automatic change	(c) Discretionary change
£700	+ 2.3	+12.7	−10.4
£1000	+ 6.3	+12.7	− 6.4
£1500	+ 5.6	+ 8.9	− 3.3
£2000	+ 4.9	+ 6.9	− 2.0
£2500	+ 4.5	+ 6.4	− 1.9
£3000	+ 4.6	+ 7.5	− 2.9
£4000	+ 7.5	+11.0	− 3.5
£5000	+10.3	+14.7	− 4.4
£10,000	+14.1	+23.1	− 9.0
£20,000	+ 8.2	+15.6	− 7.4

may differ, but it seems unlikely. Thus inflation probably resulted in a somewhat more progressive income tax system than would otherwise have operated. This is reflected in the changes from 1959 to 1973–4 in the distribution of personal incomes before and after tax. The Royal Commission on the Distribution of Income and Wealth (1976) calculated the following Gini coefficients indicating an increase in the equalizing impact of taxation:

	Income before tax (%)	*Income after tax* (%)
1959	39.8	36.0
1973–4	37.0	32.8

One result of fiscal drag has been that income tax has started to be paid lower and lower in the income distribution. As Trinder (1975) has shown, some of the largest increases in average tax rates have occurred at relatively low income levels. Thus, while the overall income tax system is probably more progressive, the change has not been straightforward or uniform. Once again, in analysing the effect of inflation, it is the discretionary response, in this case by government, that is crucial.

IV

In this section we shall be concerned with the effect of inflation on income distribution resulting from differences in the expenditure patterns of different income groups. In other words, to what extent has the degree of inflation differed between income groups?

Inflation is not a uniform phenomenon but conceals wide variations in price changes for different items—for example, public transport fares have increased much faster than costs of motoring and the price of books faster than that of television sets. Shifts in relative prices are not of course confined to periods of inflation. Inflation may exacerbate these shifts but as Bronfenbrenner and Holzman (1963) have written:

> It is often difficult, however, to separate the effects of general inflation on relative prices from those due to changes in other supply–demand relationships, including economic growth.

A number of empirical studies have been made of the effects of taking account of differences in expenditure patterns of different income groups or, essentially, of reweighting the general retail price index. The first major comparison of price changes for different consumers—or differential inflation—was that of Allen (1958). Using the 1953–4 survey of household expenditure, he derived sets of weights for pensioner families of one or two persons, for manual and clerical employees' families and for high-income families, distinguishing twenty-four sub-groups of expenditure. From 1949 to 1957 prices rose slightly faster for one-person pensioner families than for others but Allen concluded: 'The all-items index numbers for various consumer groups are found to be very little different.' Lynes (1962), using the same sources and methods as Allen, considered three groups of households with incomes at, or not very far above, the national assistance level over the period 1948–61. He concluded that: 'Price increases since 1948 have had a greater impact on those living on low incomes than the Ministry of Labour price index would suggest.' In 1968 the Department of Employment and Productivity introduced separate quarterly indices for one- and two-person pensioner households and published these indices from 1962. These official figures also showed an increase in prices somewhat faster for pensioner households than for all households included in the general index. Tipping (1970) estimated the average distribution of expenditure at various points on the income scale and from this calculated the following rises in prices for these income groups for the period 1956 to 1966:

Percentile of distribution of household incomes	*Retail Price Index for 1966 (monthly average: January 1956 = 100)*
5th (lowest income)	144.0
25th	139.0
50th	139.0
75th	138.3
95th (highest income)	138.0

The present author attempted to extend this work by using variable, rather than fixed, weights for the ten major groups of expenditure, by disaggregating the items within the groups of expenditure for each income level, and by taking a longer period—from 1956 to 1974 (Piachaud, 1976). The results are shown in Table 2. Over the whole period considered, prices

TABLE 2   *Percentage Increase in Retail Prices, 1956–1974*

	All items including housing					All items excluding housing
	1956 61	1961–66	1966–71	1971–74	1956–74	1956–74
5th percentile income level	17.7	21.4	30.2	35.2	158.3	135.1
25th percentile income level	14.0	20.4	29.6	32.5	141.8	124.2
50th percentile income level	12.9	19.8	29.4	31.2	133.1	118.8
75th percentile income level	12.0	19.1	29.4	30.6	128.5	115.1
95th percentile income level	11.3	18.6	29.5	31.1	127.4	115.0
Large low income families	13.4	20.0	29.1	32.9	134.0	123.1
All households	12.5	19.3	29.5	31.5	132.3	117.7

rose 26.0 percentage points more for the low fifth percentile income level—comprising almost exclusively pensioners—than for all households, and 30.9 percentage points more than for the high 95th percentile. Differences between other income levels were substantially smaller and prices for large, low-income families rose only slightly more than for all households together.

There was a broadly consistent pattern both over the intermediate
time periods and when housing was excluded from the index.

This suggests that those on lower incomes had experienced
a greater increase in their price level than those better off.
Muellbauer (1976) combining the estimates of Roberti (1975)
on the gross income distribution with my estimates of price
changes concluded:

> . . . thus, comparing the top of the distribution with the bottom
> the modest equalising trend in money incomes (of around
> 0.6 per cent per annum) over 1957 to 1974 is essentially
> wiped out by differential inflation.

In an earlier study Muellbauer (1974) calculated 'constant
utility' cost-of-living indices. This study, while differing in method
from the studies mentioned above, was consistent in its conclusion
that there had been an inegalitarian trend in prices. Muellbauer
(1976) has updated these computations to June 1976. He found
that from 1974 to 1975 the price level had risen around one-half
to one per cent more for the lower than for the higher income
groups, but that from 1975 to 1976 the gap increased to around
two and a half per cent over that one-year period. Muellbauer
writes of these two recent years:

> All the evidence points to the conclusion that these are the
> highest differences in rates of inflation over income brackets
> which have been experienced in the last twenty years. The
> tide which was stemmed in 1974–1975 through food and other
> subsidies was allowed to flow in 1975–1976.

One further aspect of Muellbauer's work bearing on inflation
and income distribution is relevant here. He has considered
the question of whom does the retail price index (RPI) represent?
Based as it is on expenditure weights, the index in effect gives
more 'votes' in determining the weighting pattern to those who
spend more. The RPI therefore most accurately represents an
expenditure pattern occurring in the upper range of income
distribution—estimated by Muellbauer to be around the 70th
percentile of household expenditure (corrected for household
size). The appropriateness of using the general RPI as a deflator
for incomes, as is common in most studies of income distribution
(including parts of this paper) is therefore open to question.

Differences in the impact of inflation may be indicated quantitatively by reweighting price indices, but there are more detailed and personal aspects which such procedures can never reveal.

In the studies described, the differences in price changes between income groups are entirely the result of differences in patterns of weighting. The price index used for each item is that prepared by the Department of Employment based on the average of prices in shops that are judged representative of where index households spend their money. These shops are not necessarily where low-income or high-income households do their shopping. While it seems likely that the prices paid by low-income groups for a given basket of goods have exceeded those paid by the better off (see Caplovitz, 1963 for U.S. evidence and Piachaud, 1974 for Britain), there is no evidence to indicate whether the prices in the shops used by different income strata are changing at different rates.

Relative price shifts, it is sometimes suggested, affect lower-income groups adversely because they are more conservative in their spending habits and slower in adjusting to changing prices. This untested assertion was not borne out in an examination of expenditure on one item which showed a substantial change in price relative to substitutes. From 1960 to 1973 the average price of all meats rose by 134 per cent while the price of chickens fell by 8 per cent. Over this period the National Food Survey (1961 *et seq.*) found that the poorer increased the proportion of all meat expenditure going on chickens by much more than did the better off (the lowest income group from 3.1 to 8.3 per cent of all meat expenditure and the highest income group from 9.1 to 11.7 per cent). This suggests that poorer consumers were less conservative but, due to inability to control for other factors that may be important, it is hardly conclusive proof.

It is convenient at this point to consider one other social effect of inflation. Most of this paper is concerned with income distribution between households. Inflation may also affect the distribution of income within households. Intra-household income distribution depends both on the extent of money transfers within the household and on the division of responsibilities for paying for different items. Information in this field is extremely limited but one investigation was recently made into the changes in money paid by husbands to wives for housekeeping (*Woman's*

Own, 1975). It was found that one in five mothers had received no increase in housekeeping money in the previous twelve months, and in the lowest-paid families the proportion was more than one in three. What was not investigated was the extent to which household responsibilities were re-allocated. But it is clear that in the absence of index-linked housekeeping payments, there is a real possibility that those who run the household and are supported by it, become worse off relative to the wage-earners as a result of inflation—which involves usually, but not invariably, a gain by men at the expense of women and children.

In this section we have been concerned with differences in the impact of inflation due to differences in price rises and in expenditure patterns. Yet, were all prices to rise uniformly or everyone to have the same distribution of expenditure and were the income distribution unchanged by inflation, it still might be that inflation imposed a differential toll. Inflation means a depreciating medium of exchange and standard of values. This is inconvenient for all, but the costs of adjusting to it, or the costs of failing to adjust to it, are likely to be most severe for those least intelligent, for those worst educated, and for the elderly with the longest experience of different and, relatively to present times, stable price levels. It is these people, who in general tend to be on the lowest incomes, who bear the heaviest psychological cost in trying to cope with the shifting terms of transactions that result from inflation.

V

Changes in wealth—in the real value of assets and liabilities—are an integral part of economic income. The one hypothesis about the effects of inflation that has been firmly established is that net debtors gain from unanticipated inflation and net creditors lose. In the economic literature at a theoretical level, great stress has rightly been placed on the distinction between inflation that is fully anticipated and inflation that is imperfectly antici-pated. The prevailing view is expressed succinctly by Laidler and Parkin (1975):

> If by anticipated inflation we mean not only a particular rate of inflation is expected by everybody but also that the

expectation in question has been acted upon by all concerned, then a fully anticipated inflation can, by definition, have no distributive consequences in the private sector. All bargains, be they about wages or about borrowing and lending, must, on these assumptions, be fully adjusted for inflation in such a way as to ensure that their outcome in real terms is just what it would have been at a fully anticipated zero rate of inflation.

But for this to be so, full flexibility will also be required by institutions in the money market and the capital market. In practice, full adjustment of the terms of borrowing and lending to anticipated inflation is impeded, perhaps most importantly by the influence of uncertainty over the reliability of the anticipation: we may guess at the inflation rate for 1990, but can do little more, so that we are not prepared to stake very much on even our best guesses (Flemming, 1976, and this volume). So even if all savers foresee the rate of inflation correctly (and accord with borrowers and everybody else in their foresight) they may still save with building societies and banks, knowing full well that they are getting negative real rates of interest, because no institutions are prepared to offer a better alternative. Thus, even with perfect and universal foresight, inflation would affect the distribution of income through the constraints and imperfections of existing financial markets.

To examine what has happened in practice poses certain problems. First, no precise definition of which capital assets and liabilities constitute wealth is possible. Here the practice of the Royal Commission on the Distribution of Income and Wealth will be followed in starting with physical and financial assets and liabilities and then extending the scope to include occupational and state pension rights. Second, it is necessary to look at the portfolio of assets and liabilities of different groups and assess how the real value of these portfolios has altered over periods with differing rates of inflation.

A number of such studies have been conducted in the United States, the most recent being that by Bach and Stevenson (1974). They concluded that it was doubtful if the redistributional effect of inflation as between debtors and creditors between 1946 and 1971 was less than $400–600 billion, or about one seventh of the 1971 total value of assets denominated in money terms.

They continued:

> Moreover, the total of monetary assets susceptible to erosion
> through inflation now is huge, so that each per cent of un-
> anticipated inflation in the future will transfer $35
> billion per year, and more as total monetary assets grow.
> The general direction of such transfers is clear—primarily
> from households to the government (taxpayers) and, to a
> lesser extent, to non-financial corporations ... Among house-
> holds, inflation transfers purchasing power from older to young
> people, and, contrary to the conventional wisdom, apparently
> from the very poor and the very rich to the middle and
> upper middle income groups. It is important to recognize,
> however, that the aggregate figures cover up a mass of differen-
> tial effects on individuals within and between groups.

The reason why the very poor and the very rich were more
vulnerable to inflation than middle-income groups was simple.

> The very poor have few debts (no-one will lend to them)
> and hold what few assets they have partly in monetary terms.
> The rich have also relatively few debts (though for quite
> different reasons) and hold a substantial part of their wealth
> in bonds.

For the United Kingdom the most recent and illuminating
study that deals with wealth effects is that of Foster (1976b).
This study concentrated on building society deposits and lending
to owner-occupiers which, as will be seen, created substantial
transfers between groups. Foster made ex-post estimates of the
redistributive effects of inflation on owner-occupier housing
finance. As he stated: 'The main problem in estimating redistribution is in assessing what the real interest rate would have
been in the absence of inflation'. He judged that 'building societies
would have had little difficulty in disposing of funds if they
had offered a constant real rate of 2 per cent throughout the
1961–1974 period'; thus, 'we can use 2 per cent (real) as a
base to make what seems to be a conservative estimate of
the inflationary redistribution that has been induced.' On this
basis he estimated the redistribution from lenders to building
societies to borrowers to have been over £3 billion (in 1963
prices) over the period 1961 to 1974, with the largest redistribution
in the later years. He then investigated who were the gainers
and losers and concluded that: 'elderly and low income groups
tend to lose and the younger and higher income groups tend

to gain.' In 1974, the year when the estimated redistribution was greatest, there was a redistribution of just over £1 billion of purchasing power at 1974 prices from the 55+ age group to those aged under 55; that was 1.35 per cent of total personal income in that year. As Foster stated, 'this represents a substantial loss for any group to suffer, but it is particularly so for the oldest age group who can least afford the rapid erosion of savings that such figures imply.'

At the same time, many of the losers will in earlier years have benefitted from the decline in the real cost of mortgage repayment. On a life-cycle basis, therefore, the effect of inflation here is likely to be less regressive and could indeed be expected to be progressive. But the data necessary to establish this do not exist.

For most households, investment income is a small proportion of total income; whether the yields on capital assets keep pace with inflation or not does not therefore have a profound effect on the overall income distribution, although it may be of the utmost importance to individual households. In periods of rapid inflation, changes in the real value of capital assets and liabilities, whether realized or not, are likely to have a much greater effect on the distribution of economic income. Of central importance, therefore, is the distribution and composition of wealth. In Table 3 Inland Revenue estimates of the distribution of personal wealth by range of net wealth are shown together with the asset composition at different levels of wealth; also included is an adjusted distribution using the Royal Commission's estimate of the number of persons excluded from the Inland Revenue's estimates, who are assumed to have no wealth. These wealth estimates are subject to numerous qualifications which have been extensively discussed (e.g. by Atkinson, 1972). Most relevantly here, consumer durables in 'household goods' are under-recorded and life insurance is valued as if everyone were dead. Nevertheless, these estimates are adequate for limited comparisons between wealth levels. It will be seen that the proportion of assets denominated in money terms is much higher for those with the lowest levels of wealth than for higher wealth levels and that, for the middle ranges of wealth, dwellings represent far and away the most important asset.

The fact that those with low wealth had a large proportion

TABLE 3 Asset Composition by Range of Personal Wealth, 1974

	Zero	£1–£1000	£1000–£3000	£3000–£5000	£5000–£10,000	£10,000–£15,000	£15,000–£20,000	£20,000–£50,000	£50,000–£100,000	£100,000 and over	Total
					percent by column						
Physical assets											
Household Goods	—	7.8	6.7	4.8	4.0	3.2	3.1	3.1	2.6	3.4	3.6
Dwellings	—	8.6	14.1	38.6	58.1	62.4	55.4	40.4	27.8	15.8	42.3
Other	—	5.4	1.2	2.8	2.1	1.9	3.2	10.1	17.0	22.7	8.0
Financial assets											
Cash & bank deposits	—	30.4	21.6	13.9	9.1	7.3	6.6	8.4	9.8	8.5	9.7
National savings	—	6.3	3.9	3.2	2.0	1.9	2.0	1.8	1.1	0.8	1.9
Building society deposits	—	8.9	13.2	12.2	8.7	8.7	12.0	13.0	11.1	5.4	10.1
Government securities	—	0.3	0.4	0.5	0.5	0.8	0.7	1.9	2.6	3.9	1.5
Debentures & preference shares	—	—	0.1	0.1	0.2	0.3	0.4	1.1	1.4	1.4	0.7
Other company shares	—	2.1	1.1	0.6	1.6	1.8	2.9	10.4	22.0	36.7	10.1
Life policies	—	31.7	25.1	21.3	19.0	17.4	18.0	13.4	7.9	2.9	14.9
Other	—	22.9	20.2	14.8	7.4	4.8	6.0	5.5	4.4	5.8	7.3
Financial liabilities											
Property debts	—	-5.1	-4.6	-9.3	-10.7	-8.3	-7.6	-4.4	-1.9	-1.1	-6.2
Personal debts	—	-19.2	-3.0	-3.8	-2.2	-2.1	-2.7	-4.7	-5.7	-6.2	-3.9
	—	100.0	100.0	100.0	100.0	100.0	100.0	100.0	100.0	100.0	100.0
					percent by row						
Proportion of wealth holders	n.a.	18.5	25.4	11.8	21.7	11.3	4.0	5.6	1.2	0.5	100.0
Proportion of wealth holders & other adults	52.0	8.9	12.2	5.7	10.4	5.4	1.9	2.7	0.6	0.2	100.0
Proportion of total wealth	—	1.3	5.6	5.6	19.3	16.7	8.5	20.0	9.9	13.2	100.0

Sources: *Inland Revenue Statistics 1976* and *Royal Commission on the Distribution of Income and Wealth Report No. 4, 1976.*

of their assets denominated in fixed money terms meant that they fared worse with inflation as long as the variable-price assets to some extent kept pace with inflation. However, in recent years the traditional pattern of asset prices under inflation has been broken at least for a substantial run of years. For the major types of assets in personal wealth in the United Kingdom, the year-to-year changes in real value have been calculated over the period 1956–76. The results are shown in Chart III. Although the points for each year are, for clarity, connected in the Chart, it should be stressed that what are shown are year-on-year changes, not cumulative changes compounded over time.

It will be seen that there is no consistent variation with the rate of inflation, so that there is no simple way to estimate the effect of inflation on real asset values. But it is apparent that a general change in relationships came about with the acceleration in inflation in the late 1960s. In the period 1956–68 inflation in the United Kingdom never reached 5 per cent per annum; since 1968 it has never been below this level. The average changes in the real value of the major capital assets in these periods of 'low inflation' and 'high inflation' were as shown in Table 4.

To illustrate the effect these changes have had at different wealth levels with their different asset compositions we may use the 1974 portfolios, as set out in Table 3. The assumption made in the illustration that asset composition is constant is of course highly unrealistic. Between 1960 and 1974 dwellings rose as a proportion of estimated total wealth from 20.7 per cent to 42.7 per cent. Since one of the advantages that comes with increased wealth is clearly increased opportunity to alter the composition of assets, the wealthier have greater ability to adjust their assets and protect their wealth. (This is supported by what appears to be the only relevant evidence on portfolio adjustment—that of Tait (1967)—but since it is based on the experience of 1931 it is hardly current confirmation). The results with all their limitations are set out in Table 5.

With high inflation it will be seen that there were losses at all levels of positive wealth. This suggests an equalising effect relative to those with zero or negative wealth who, according to the Royal Commission's estimate, comprised just over half

110

CHART III *Changes in Real Asset Values, 1956–76*

Year-to-
year change
(Per cent)

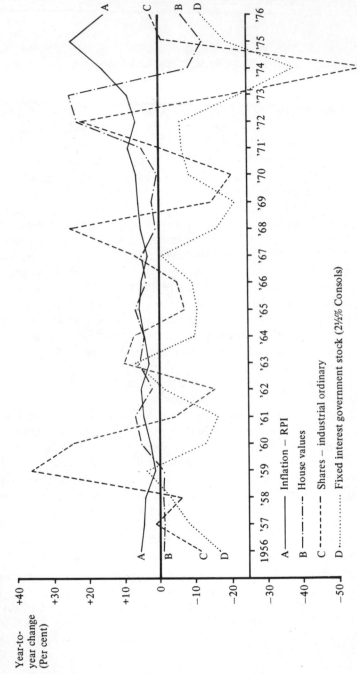

A ——— Inflation – RPI

B —·—·— House values

C --------- Shares – industrial ordinary

D ·········· Fixed interest government stock (2½% Consols)

Sources: Housing and Construction Statistics and Financial Statistics

TABLE 4   *Average Year-to-Year Change in Real Value of Assets (per cent)*

	Money	2½% Consols	Fixed interest preference stocks	Industrial ordinary shares	Houses
1956–68	− 3.1	− 7.1	− 4.9	+ 4.6	+2.4
1969–76	−10.6	−16.8	−14.4	−10.4	+3.4

Sources: *Housing and Construction Statistics* and *Financial Statistics*

TABLE 5   *Average Year-to-Year Change in Real Wealth by Level of Wealth Based on 1974 Asset Composition of Wealth*

Average change in real wealth (per cent)

Level of Wealth	Low Inflation 1956–68	High Inflation 1969–76	Difference (High-Low)
Nil–£1000	−2.0	−7.9	−5.9
£1000–£3000	−2.0	−7.8	−5.8
£3000–£5000	−0.7	−4.3	−3.7
£5000–£10,000	+0.4	−1.8	−2.2
£10,000–£15,000	+0.6	−1.3	−2.0
£15,000–£20,000	+0.3	−2.2	−2.6
£20,000–£50,000	+0.4	−3.4	−3.9
£50,000–£100,000	+0.9	−4.3	−5.3
£100,000 and over	+1.7	−5.0	−6.9

of all adults. Among those with some wealth, those with the least wealth suffered the largest proportionate real loss over the periods of both high and low inflation. The increased loss during high inflation is greatest for two groups: the many with little wealth and the few with great wealth. If the very wealthy can adjust their assets and, to some extent, protect their real wealth, then the wealth holders who lose most severely in proportionate terms are those with little wealth. On the other hand, a given proportionate decline in wealth will be more significant for the total economic position of those for whom wealth is more important within that total position, who are likely to be those with substantial wealth. For example, if a person derives half his income from assets yielding a ten per cent return, then a decline in asset values of one-fifth in a year would reduce economic income to zero.

Thus far we have been concerned with marketable wealth. Pension rights represent a form of non-marketable wealth. The extent to which occupational pensions already in payment were increased in line with inflation was considered in Section II. Here we are concerned with the value of the non-marketable wealth represented by the future pension rights. As the Royal Commission has shown, their inclusion in wealth statistics makes the distribution of wealth appear substantially less unequal. The effect of inflation on the value of an occupational pension scheme depends on the nature of the scheme. 'Money purchase' schemes will keep pace with inflation only in so far as the capital value and yield on the investments do so—which, on past experience they have markedly failed to do. At the other extreme, public service pensions fully indexed against inflation retain their full value. From the Government Actuary's survey of occupational pension schemes in 1971, it is possible to calculate what proportion of schemes retain the real value of pension rights up to the date of retirement. In 1971 four-fifths of members were in a scheme where the pension formula was based on 'salary service' or 'salary range' and most of the rest were subject to 'flat accrual per year of service'. For those where the formula was based on salary, the averaging period for salary was the last three years' pay for 62 per cent of members, the last one year's pay for 8 per cent and final pay for 12 per cent; for the rest it was pay over a longer period. Where the formula is based on a long period or where there is a flat rate of accrual, inflation will erode the value of the pension rights. For example, inflation at even 5 per cent a year will halve the real value of flat-rate pension rights in only 14 years. The majority of flat-rate accrual schemes cover manual workers only and in general have provided very low levels of pensions even before inflation has taken its toll. Thus it would seem that the better occupational schemes which tend to cover higher-paid workers retain their real value to a large extent up to the date of retirement, while the poorer flat rate of accrual schemes decline in real value.

The wealth represented by a pension right depends on the real value of the pension not just at the date of retirement but over the entire period of retirement. Prospective depreciation in the post-retirement period therefore makes pension rights less than inflation-proof, even when they are related to pay at retirement.

State pensions, as seen in Section II, have preserved their real value in the past and, for the future, inflation-proofing has been guaranteed. Thus accrued rights to state pensions are one form of wealth that is now immune to inflation (barring a real fiscal crisis of the state). Since state pension rights are far more equally distributed than other forms of wealth, the inflation-proofing of pensions acts as a counterbalance to the vulnerability of those whose assets are largely denominated in money terms. It acts as a general and possibly very important equalizing influence.

In this section we have been concerned with wealth effects on the personal distribution of incomes. Redistribution between the private sector and the government, to which much attention has been paid elsewhere, has not been considered specifically but incorporated by treating government bonds and money in the same way as other assets and liabilities. There has been no assessment of the effects of inflation on the taxation of wealth; this also has been generally in an equalizing direction, since the inflation of money values converts taxes on capital gains into effective taxes on real capital values, as well as increasing the progressivity of any given tax scale expressed in nominal values.

Finally, there are two important limitations in our assessment of the relationship of wealth to economic income. The first difficulty is that virtually no data on wealth and asset-composition are available in a form strictly comparable with income data. A second problem is that within Hicks' definition of economic income no distinction is made or is appropriate between realized and unrealized changes in asset values. For many purposes people do, however, make this distinction in their perception and practice: they may be obliged to do so by absolute limitations on their ability to borrow. Thus when considering the wealth effects of inflation there are as many, if not more, unresolved problems as in the other areas.

VI

Drawing together the threads from the four sections, we may start by considering the impact of inflation on certain broad groups within society.

First we may compare the old with the young. It was seen that the real value of state pensions has not varied in relation to inflation but that occupational pensions in payment have been eroded by inflation. The differential impact of inflation has resulted in a faster than average rise in the price level facing people in the lowest income levels, predominantly pensioners. In terms of wealth, the findings of studies in both Britain and the United States suggest that inflation has resulted in a substantial redistribution away from the old. Thus it seems clear that, while the government has maintained the real incomes of the poorest pensioners, rather better-off pensioners, as well as retired people living on investment income, have lost substantially with, and almost certainly because of, higher inflation. These are the main identifiable losers from inflation. In their current incomes they mostly are relatively low down in the distribution; on a life-time basis, they are typically in the upper ranges. Whether the inflation squeeze they suffer has involved a disequalizing or an equalizing influence on the income distribution therefore has no single answer: it depends on whether it is more appropriate to take a static or a dynamic view.

Owner-occupiers, who constitute the majority of all households and about three-quarters of households of working age, have wealth that has remained relatively uneroded by inflation. Interest rates of building societies have been adjusted much less than what would have been necessary for creditors to maintain their real capital intact and for borrowers to maintain the real value of their payments. This has given large real gains to those already in the process of purchase, although it has exacerbated problems for those seeking to enter or move up the owner-occupied housing market. Two conclusions suggest themselves here. First, government attempts to keep down mortgage interest rates probably served, in so far as they were successful, to increase the inequality of the distribution of income on a static view. Second, with interest rates falling in real terms and even becoming negative when inflation increased, all those with mortgages—now the majority of those of working age—gained in this respect from inflation. How widely this was realized is not known, but that it was so cannot have failed to influence attitudes to, and the acceptability of, inflation.

One other consequence of inflation for income distribution

will be mentioned. It is clear that net debtors gain from unanticipated inflation. Thus inflation is likely to shift income from those who save to those who borrow to consume immediately—there is no such clear-cut impact on those who borrow to invest, since inflation and the responses it provokes have tended to depress real rates of return. While this bias to immediate consumption may not, directly, have great quantitative importance it may, indirectly, have significant implications for people's attitudes. In the long run, the needs for investment in physical capital and human beings for the future may prove hard to reconcile with the personal attitudes of a society oriented towards credit and the present.

That inflation has different effects on particular groups to which an individual belongs at different times may mean that over the life cycle these effects even out. In the course of a lifetime, an individual may typically pass from work to retirement, from renting to owner-occupation, and into and out of debt. On the other hand, advantages may accumulate, for example from employment that provides the security to obtain a mortgage and incur debts and that also offers a more securely inflation-proofed pension. There is, however, a dearth of longitudinal data that would resolve such questions.

The limited conclusion that can be drawn from the evidence presented here is that there were no simple effects of inflation on income distribution. Inflation acts neither as Robin Hood nor as Robber Baron; neither the poor nor the rich are affected in a uniform way. The distributional effects of inflation have in the past depended both on the causes and nature of the inflation and on the responses to it of individuals, groups and government. For the future two considerations add further complications. First, nothing can be done directly about inflation, only about the economic policies that may affect inflation. Therefore, as Hollister and Palmer (1972) have written in their study of the impact of inflation on the poor in the United States:

> Instead of asking the question 'Does inflation hurt the poor?' we might ask the question 'Will a policy to stop inflation be helpful to the poor?'

Second, we have only the past to guide us in assessing how inflation may affect income distribution in the future; since so much depends on anticipations, adaptations, responses and remedies to inflation, the future may be very different. The marked change in the responses of financial markets to inflation in the most recent phase of high inflation is a telling reminder that expectations and anticipations are not static.

Finally, while we have been concerned with the effects of inflation on income distribution, the effects of income distribution on inflation should not be forgotten. To the extent that inflation is the outcome of people attempting, because of dissatisfaction with the existing income distribution, to improve their relative position, then inflation can only be overcome when there is a degree of consensus that the distribution of incomes is fair and just— which is a long way off.

CHAPTER 5

The Growth of the Public Sector and Inflation

Alan T. Peacock and Martin Ricketts*

Introduction

'What sex is to the novelist, inflation is to the economist. Discuss.'[1] This was set as an examination question a few years ago in one of the ancient universities and it reflects the obsessional interest of economists in inflation even during a period when the consumer price index normally rose at less than 5 per cent per annum and was accompanied by growth rates and employment rates which were historically abnormally high and prolonged. The treatment of policy objectives in isolation is now less of a feature of economic discussion than it used to be and, using the language of optimal control theory, economists have come to consider the problem of achieving price stability within the context of some government 'welfare function' in which objectives are traded off against one another. The acceleration in the rate of inflation experienced in many industrial countries has reactivated the obsession once again, but this is not simply because one important objective in the welfare function has been moving rapidly in the wrong direction. It is also because inflation has reached the proportions where its control is considered vital if the other important economic objec-

* At the time of writing, both authors were members of the Public Sector Study Group, University of York. They wish to acknowledge support to the Group from the Social Science Research Council. They are much indebted to the editors of this volume and John Flemming for useful comments.

tives are to be attained. A common example found in contemporary debate is that of a country, such as Britain, which relies heavily on international trade on both sides of the trading account and which has been experiencing a faster rate of inflation than its competitors. Such a country clearly faces the prospect of increasing unemployment if it is unable to retain its competitive position in overseas and domestic markets despite the range of policy instruments which it may have at its disposal.

A further feature of recent economic analysis of inflation is the attempt to identify culprits whose actions are mainly if not solely responsible for its acceleration. There are good analytical reasons, notably that the economy is a complicated interdependent system, which would lead one to be suspicious of this kind of witch-hunting. A prime suspect in the perpetration of the crime of causing inflation is the public sector. At a popular level the rate of inflation is seen as a function of 'excessive' growth in public spending, because of the difficulties associated with financing such spending and the fear that covering such spending by non-inflationary borrowing will raise interest rates and discourage private investment so as to lead governments to take the easy way out through recourse to note-printing (Confederation of British Industry, 1976). However this rather telescoped argument based on some version of monetarism can be refined in such a way as to provide a good *prima facie* case for associating the growth of the public sector with growing difficulty in controlling the rate of inflation.

This chapter considers the case in some detail. We begin in the next section with a critical examination of the conventional Keynesian analysis of the anti-inflationary control which the public sector is supposed to exercise through its power to tax and to borrow, to spend and to lend. This analysis is then confronted with an important policy constraint, namely the strong impetus given to the expansion of the public sector through popular support for welfare and environmental services. In the third section, therefore, we consider whether, given such a constraint, it is still possible to use fiscal policy as an anti-inflationary device. From this analysis an attempt is made to derive some testable hypotheses and, using cross-section data, we consider in our final section how far these hypotheses are consistent with the available evidence.

Keynesian Fiscal Policy and Control of Inflation

Several generations of students have been nurtured on a Keynesian macroeconomic model in which the role of government expenditure and taxation in combatting inflation is manifested in the control which the budget can exercise over aggregate demand. Recent examples are Branson (1972) and Blinder and Solow (1974). If producers are expected to raise prices they may be prevented from doing so by announcement of cuts in government expenditure or increases in direct tax rates. Both types of measure would lower aggregate demand and therefore put pressure on producers to hold prices down. Much of the textbook illustration develops the famous Keynesian multiplier analysis in order to demonstrate, often with considerable sophistication, the relative effectiveness, pound for pound, of using one method of fiscal control rather than another. It is generally recognized even at first approximation that the policy rules cannot be precisely formulated in order to be sure that inflation can be easily controlled, for there are the obvious difficulties encountered in foreseeing producers' behaviour and in measuring the lagged responses of producers to government expenditure and tax changes.

Even at the textbook level it is usually conceded that the relation between budgetary changes, aggregate demand and the price level can be rather more complicated than this. In the first place, while it is assumed that changes in aggregate demand influence the price level, account must be taken of any monetary consequences of budgetary action which would influence aggregate demand through changes in the terms of borrowing. Thus an increase in the budget surplus, the proceeds from which are used to reduce outstanding public debt, could exert downward pressure on interest rates and, other things being equal, this might encourage private spending on stockbuilding and on fixed investment which would offset the reduction in spending induced by raising taxes or cutting government purchases. In the second place, taxes on goods operate directly on costs so that ordinary profit-maximizing behaviour by entrepreneurs might lead them to increase prices if tax rates on goods are increased, even if these taxes lowered aggregate demand as well as affecting costs (Peacock and Shaw, 1976). Macroeconomic forecasting models, used by a number of influential policy makers, assume in fact that entrepreneurs simply mark up prices in response to tax increases and that the influence of aggregate demand (and therefore of the budget) is solely on the level of economic activity and not on prices at all. Finally, looking beyond the short run, the rate of inflation will depend on the interaction of aggregate supply and aggregate demand, and consequently budgetary changes designed to reduce aggregate demand or its rate of growth may have side-effects on aggregate supply. Hence the oft-heard advice that if the budget is to be used as an anti-inflationary device, its armoury should be directed at cutting private or public consumption and not private or public investment, the obvious point being that cutting the latter would adversely affect the growth in aggregate supply.

The trouble with this approach to the analysis of economic policy problems is that it fosters the belief, despite the usual caveats which its expositors insert with characteristic academic caution, that the budget is a mechanism at the disposal of some enlightened public officials not answerable to the electorate but committed to the public weal—in this case to the eradication of inflation. There is a corresponding tendency to regard consumers, wage-earners and entrepreneurs as passive adjusters to budgetary changes who have neither the wit to anticipate inflationary developments and government reactions to them nor the power to influence government in order to institute policies which they favour. A further problem with this approach is that it ignores the trade-off between meeting the price stability objective with other objectives which the budget is used to implement, objectives which might well be supported by enlightened bureaucrats as 'in the public interest' as well as by the electorate and their representatives who seek to control their actions. Thus a realistic model of the effect of the budget on price stability has to specify the 'opportunity cost of price stability', to hypothesize on public reaction to budget changes and how these might frustrate attempts to 'maximize' the policy objectives, and to measure the side-effects which budgetary measures designed to promote price stability may have on the pursuit of other objectives.

While it is not the purpose of this contribution to build such a model, an attempt is made to concentrate on one important aspect of the problem to which attention has been drawn. It is clear from the evidence available that democratically elected governments in industrial countries are under constant pressure to allocate a large proportion of resources to produce welfare and environmental services, as well as traditional services such as defence and law and order, owned and operated by the government itself. It is claimed that the larger the size of the public sector relative to the annual output of resources, the more likely it will be that the rate of inflation will be higher (Clark, 1977; Friedman, 1977a). The inference is drawn that countries favouring a large and growing public sector face a dilemma if they wish to combine price stability with pressure for bigger and better public services.

The Growth of the Public Sector and Inflation

Table 1 presents the main data on which our later statistical analysis is based. It gives some indication of the recent growth in the size of the public economy in OECD countries using various alternative measures. Taking taxes as a percentage of GNP (cf. Peacock and Wiseman, 1967), broadly speaking what has happened over the last twenty years is that, after a period in which the percentage remained fairly stable in most OECD countries, there was a marked increase in the percentage in the late 1960s in every country with the exception of France. The unweighted average increase in the OECD sample was 4.87 percentage points, ranging from −0.25 percentage points in France to +13.92 percentage points in Denmark. The rise in government current expenditure, on the other hand, is not so marked. The unweighted average increase was 1.7 percentage points, but it must be remembered that this indicator of public-sector growth excludes transfers (negative taxes) which (though not recorded in our data) grew at a faster rate.

More detailed evidence concerning the size and growth of the public sector in developed countries would confirm support for allocation and distributional policies which are to be conducted alongside stabilization and growth objectives. It suggests that in countries where welfare state imperatives are important,

TABLE 1   *Statistics on the Recent Growth*

	(1)	(2)	(3)	(4)	(5)
	Relative income/ head (1970)	*Average growth of GDP deflator (1965–72)*	*Growth/ head (1965–72)*	*Taxes % GNP (1965)*	*Taxes % GNP (1972)*
U.S.A.	1.65	3.9	2.7	24.88	28.06
Sweden	1.40	5.0	2.6	36.10	43.89
Canada	1.33	4.1	3.5	27.33	33.53
Switzerland	1.20	5.8	2.6	21.01	24.12
Denmark	1.10	6.4	3.6	30.90	44.82
Germany	1.10	4.4	3.5	32.65	35.97
Luxembourg	1.08	5.1	2.7	32.47	37.44
Norway	.99	5.3	3.8	33.80	45.71
France	.96	5.0	4.5	36.05	35.80
Australia	.95	4.6	3.0	22.79	24.28
Belgium	.92	4.2	4.4	30.03	35.20
Netherlands	.83	6.1	4.0	34.29	41.84
Finland	.77	6.0	4.8	30.74	35.75
New Zealand	.76	7.0	1.5	26.37	29.51
U.K.	.75	6.0	1.9	30.61	34.73
Austria	.66	4.1	4.8	34.30	37.04
Japan	.66	4.9	9.2	18.68	21.09
Italy	.59	4.4	4.2	28.95	31.07
Ireland	.46	7.6	3.8	24.98	31.09
Greece	.39	3.4	6.8	19.42	23.71
Spain	.33	5.9	5.4	16.01	21.30
Portugal	.25	4.9	7.3	19.00	23.38
Turkey	.12	9.3	4.3	16.49	20.45

Note: (a) Excluding transfers.
Sources: Columns 1, 2, 3, 10, 11: *OECD National Accounts Statistics 1972.*
    Columns 4, 5, 6, 7, 8, 9: *OECD Revenue Statistics of OECD Member Countries,*
    1965–72.

a higher rate of inflation and a lower rate of growth than might otherwise obtain will not be considered as too high a price to pay for achieving objectives which keep the electorate happy and promote social stability. However, to suggest that the opportunity cost of a growing public sector characterized by the growth of services which are perceived to confer important net benefits on a large proportion of the population is high *to those who represent them as voters and legislators* may be too much to concede at this stage of the argument.

of the Public Sector in OECD Countries

(6)	(7)	(8)	(9)	(10)	(11)
Personal income tax as % GNP (1965)	Personal income tax as % GNP (1972)	Social security % GNP (1965)	Social security % GNP (1972)	Government current expenditure[a] (1965) % GNP	Government current expenditure[a] (1972) % GNP
7.60	9.43	4.08	5.75	17.7	18.8
16.14	18.48	5.63	8.92	17.6	23.0
6.30	11.56	1.55	2.92	14.8	19.3
6.55	8.08	4.73	5.64	11.6	11.0
11.84	21.50	2.76	3.45	15.1	21.3
8.18	10.09	9.59	12.13	15.2	17.6
8.05	9.95	10.45	10.83	10.6	11.5
10.69	12.54	6.85	12.38	16.1	16.2
3.65	3.97	13.41	14.48	12.6	12.7
7.74	9.33	0.00	0.00	11.6	13.0
6.26	9.64	9.13	10.63	13.1	14.9
9.56	11.68	10.65	14.74	15.5	16.7
9.87	13.98	3.61	4.74	14.6	16.9
10.42	14.18	0.00	0.00	13.3	14.6
9.53	11.14	4.71	5.40	16.8	18.6
7.04	8.36	8.71	9.45	13.3	14.6
4.11	5.39	3.57	4.10	9.2	9.0
3.22	3.95	9.89	12.14	14.5	14.6
4.24	7.09	1.62	2.82	13.2	15.2
1.31	2.23	5.17	5.91	11.7	12.3
2.29	2.48	4.52	8.95	8.7	11.4
1.20	1.68	4.00	6.10	12.3	13.6
3.51	5.04	2.25	3.62	12.4	14.0

Let us explain this point in terms of the Keynesian conventional wisdom. The technical method of achieving the desired allocational and distributional objectives would be to devise methods of taxing which automatically increase revenue at a faster rate than the growth in money incomes of the working population and in which the tax system is progressive. This can be done by a combination of *ad valorem* taxes on profits and on goods (with appropriate exemptions) with a progressive system of income taxes. Such a tax package has the useful quality that the total yield of taxes will grow at a faster rate than money incomes without a change in tax *rates*, so that the announcement effects will be muted though the average rate of tax on all taxpayers will gradually rise.

But is this process of a growing public sector compatible with growth and stabilization objectives? So far as the latter is concerned, all that appears necessary is to vary taxes and other revenues *independently of public expenditure objectives.* If the rate of inflation is considered to be too high, then, if necessary, budget surpluses can be planned, or non-inflationary borrowing substituted for inflationary borrowing—this argument is highly simplified. So far as growth is concerned, any disincentive effects of growing and progressive taxation (and these effects have not even been established as operative) will be counterbalanced by the improvements in the quality of labour input resulting from growing government investment in human capital.

The analysis in our introduction, however, should warn us that this development of the Keynesian approach to match several objectives with a range of budgetary instruments rests again on assumptions about political behaviour which are suspect to say the least. Tax and expenditure decisions cannot be separated in the way just described and recent evidence collected for OECD countries suggests that in important industrial countries, growth in tax revenues, of which one major determinant is inflation itself, have simply led to a concomitant increase in government expenditure. Of course, preserving the nexus between government expenditure and tax growth may not necessarily be destabilizing, particularly if the combined tax-expenditure effect were expansionary (following the conventional 'balanced budget multiplier' analysis) and productive potential in the economy is growing. However, this ignores the possibility that the general level of wages and therefore prices can be influenced by cost-induced changes. Thus in the recent analyses of the causes of inflation in industrial countries, a great deal has been made, rightly in our opinion, of the emergence of wage bargaining based on real take-home pay. If the rate of increase in real take-home pay declines as progressive taxation takes an increasing proportion of incomes, then 'back-lash' effects are possible. Unions will in the first instance attempt to seek compensation through higher wages for the growing predations of the 'tax take' on disposable real income. Secondly, if the expected result of being successful in raising wage rates is that unions are faced with an increase in unemployment among their members as a result of the rise in wage costs per unit of output, then unions may seek to exert political pressure on government to expand aggregate demand in order to place firms in the position to be able to absorb the rise in wage costs without reducing output (cf. Auld and Southey, 1977).

The constraint on government action imposed by back-lash effects makes it very difficult to sustain the proposition that control of inflation by budgetary means can be exercised independently of the size and the rate of growth of the public sector. This is perhaps made clearer when one examines what the budgetary implications are of taking such effects into account. There seem to be three possible courses of action which may be used individually or in combination with one another:

(i) Try to exploit tax illusion. The Government might seek to substitute (at the margin at least) less 'visible' kinds of taxes for direct taxes, such as the income tax and social security taxes, in an endeavour to fool the taxpayers into believing that such a change will improve their real disposable incomes. Obvious examples are the raising of prices of nationalized industries or the rates of specific excise taxes. It has been claimed (Wilensky, 1976) that back-lash effects reflected in degrees of tax-resistance are positively correlated with the 'visibility' of the tax structure, that is the higher the proportion of direct to indirect taxes the greater the back-lash effect. We shall look at those aspects of this proposition which concern inflation at a later stage, but we cannot avoid expressing some initial scepticism at the prospect of relying on the techniques of the illusionist. Though it is possible to argue that taxes on expenditure and price increases in nationalized industry can be avoided, at least in part, by taxpayers, the social and income distributional effect of such changes (highlighted in Britain by the attention paid to the work of the Royal Commission on the Distribution of Income and Wealth) hardly fosters greater acceptance of reducing real disposable incomes through price rather than income changes.

(ii) Substitute non-inflationary borrowing for taxation. In the short run this could merely mean the substitution of one back-lash effect for another, for the costs of borrowing to the private sector would be raised, notably against the large number of home owners using mortgage facilities. In the longer run, of course, the interest costs of borrowing would in any case require extra taxation to finance them.

(iii) Substitute 'inflationary borrowing' for taxation, financing the public deficit by credit expansion. There is pronounced disagreement about the magnitude and timing of the effect of such borrowing methods on the rate of inflation, but no theorist claims that the effect would be other than positive in the circumstances envisaged in this contribution. That being so, this method of budgetary finance is clearly irrelevant in this context. Reliance would have to be placed on non-budgetary means to counter any such method of financing the public deficit for fiscal control of inflation would be abandoned. It does nevertheless suggest a possible line of empirical investigation, namely how far non-budgetary controls such as prices and incomes policies are to be found in countries in which the relative size or growth of the public sector is large.

The difficulties encountered in trying to reduce back-lash suggests a number of conclusions about both the economic theory and practice of fiscal policy. Firstly, the use of a policy model in which the public sector is delineated as a 'control system' with the 'government' in charge of efficient 'levers' which will produce the desired trade-off between price stability and other objectives is misleading. So long as governments are voted into office, then it seems more useful to accept that the correct analogy in these cybernetic terms is with a system in which the efficient operation of the levers is itself dependent on their effect on the actions of those whose actions the levers seek to control. Thus our methodological conclusion fits neatly with that of Brittan (this volume) in stressing the contribution of the economic theory of politics to an understanding of the political economy of inflation. Secondly, in employing this methodology one soon observes that the control of inflation by fiscal means is beset by the 'isolation paradox'. Individual taxpayers (voters) will recognize the dangers of inflation and support fiscal action to mitigate these, at least in principle. However, the political process encourages taxpayers to adopt strategies that enable them to seek to minimize the sacrifices that the fiscal action is expected to impose on the different taxpaying groups. However willing they may be to make some sacrifice, they will wish to protect their position because they cannot be certain that everyone will play the game. Their efforts will be all the more strenuous in situations where fiscal action to reduce the rate of inflation requires that the growth in average real disposable income of taxpayers must be zero or negative.

This second conclusion suggests a third. Though in principle individual taxpayers (voters) may prefer *at the margin* to have money in their pockets rather than extra welfare benefits provided by government, they will not risk supporting measures to reduce *both* taxes *and* expenditures because they will be uncertain whether the political process will produce results that leave them at least as well off as before or, alternatively, dissatisfied by being left no worse off while others are left substantially better off. Superimposing 'fine tuning' fiscal policy measures on this scenario, which would normally mean combatting inflation by reducing the rate of growth of government expenditure or increasing the rate of growth of tax yields relative to growth in aggregate demand, risks complete failure.

The above analysis implies that a political system that presents an individual voter with highly uncertain outcomes, and which gives him no assurance that he will not become the victim of the strategic behaviour of others, will be ill-equipped to provide a solution to the problem of inflation. It is evident however, that this essentially institutional hypothesis is not easily amenable to the usual processes of statistical verification, and in the next section we rely on some very imperfect proxy variables for what has been termed 'voter alienation'.

We now investigate two hypotheses in turn. The first relates inflation to the size of the public sector, and the second to its rate of growth. The second is perhaps the easier to justify in relation to the back-lash effects discussed earlier in this chapter. Whatever the size of the public sector the individual will always have an incentive to accept the benefits of public sector growth while attempting to avoid the costs. Size alone would appear to be more relevant to the problem of controlling or reducing inflation. The larger is the public sector, or more accurately, the more the individual perceives his own welfare to be dependent upon public sector activities, the more he will have to lose in the event of an unfavourable distribution of the costs of an anti-inflation policy (expenditure cuts, wage controls etc.). Given his assessment of the benefits to be derived from more stable prices, a larger public sector may tend to reduce the willingness of the citizen to bear the uncertain costs of achieving them.

The Empirical Evidence

The difficulties of deriving hypotheses about the relationship of inflation to the size and growth of the public sector from an underlying body of theory are clearly substantial. We have described above some of the mechanisms that may be involved if such relationships exist, and that would render obsolete the traditional textbook models of the economy based as they are on 'open' rather than 'closed' behavioural systems, i.e. systems in which collective choices and objectives are imposed exogenously rather than being the outcome of the system itself (Buchanan, 1972). No attempt is made here to test in detail a particular theory of inflation, but using cross-section data we investigate how far some of the simpler assertions about inflation are consistent with the available evidence.

Inflation and the 'Size' of the Public Sector. The simplest proposition mentioned in previous sections is that inflation will be associated with the size of the public sector relative to national income. This immediately raises the question of how the size of the public sector is to be measured. The use of total public expenditure, for example, raises such questions as whether to include the expenditure of the nationalized industries and how to treat expenditure on welfare benefits, debt interest and other transfer payments. Tax revenue, on the other hand, ignores the control that governments have over nationalized industry prices that can be used as substitutes for taxation, and the extent of government borrowing.

Ultimately, the appropriate measure to take will depend on the behavioural assumptions underlying the hypothesis. If public sector growth results in back-lash and hence inflation, is this

because individuals resent increasing state control over the allocation of resources (in which case welfare benefits and debt interest
should be excluded from any measure of size) or do individuals
simply oppose higher taxes *per se*, irrespective of the uses to
which this revenue is put (in which case all tax revenue and
nationalized industry net profits should be included)? Below
we investigate these possibilities.

CHART I

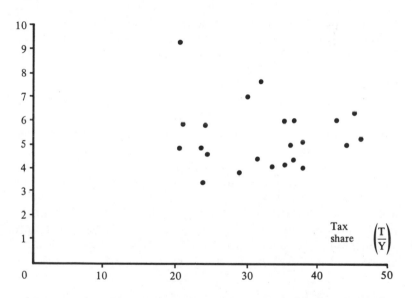

Taking total tax revenue[2] as a proportion of GNP and plotting
against the rate of increase in the GDP deflator between the
years 1965 and 1972 produces the scatter plot shown in Chart
I. It is immediately seen that for the twenty-three OECD countries
included, no support is derived for Clark's view (1977) that
a tax take in excess of 25 per cent of GNP will be inflationary.
All countries experienced inflation over the period 1965–72 whatever the share of taxes in GNP, and there is no evidence
that a larger tax take is associated with higher inflation rates.

The estimated regression equation is

$$I = 5.89 - 0.016 \left(\frac{T}{Y}\right).$$

(1.37) (0.037). \hspace{4cm} (1)

$$r = -0.095$$
$$R^2 = 0.009$$

(I = Rate of increase of GDP deflator 1965–72.

$\dfrac{T}{Y}$ = Total taxes as per cent of GNP in 1970.

Standard errors are given in parenthesis under the relevant coefficients).

A similar exercise using current government expenditure excluding transfers as a 'size' variable produced equally poor results, as demonstrated in Chart II. The correlation coefficient between the expenditure variable and inflation was calculated as -0.0001.

It may be argued however that these negative results are not sufficient to discredit the hypothesis entirely. Tests using cross-section data may be seriously misleading in that they imply a similar relationship between public sector size and inflation in each country. Since the basic hypothesis rests, as we have seen, upon the idea that individuals as wage bargainers and voters retaliate against increasing taxes, the extent and effectiveness of this retaliation may vary markedly between countries. Further, many other factors may be involved in the generation of 'pushfulness'—factors such as the level of income per head or the rate of growth in the countries concerned.

Inflation and Relative Income. One such view (Panić, 1976 and this volume) associates the rate of inflation in a country with the level of *per capita* income. It is argued that the lower *per capita* income is relative to that in other countries, the greater will be the inflationary pressures in the system. Here again the precise political mechanisms whereby rising aspirations and expectations are translated into inflation are not displayed in detail, but in this case there does appear to be more substantial evidence to support the hypothesis.

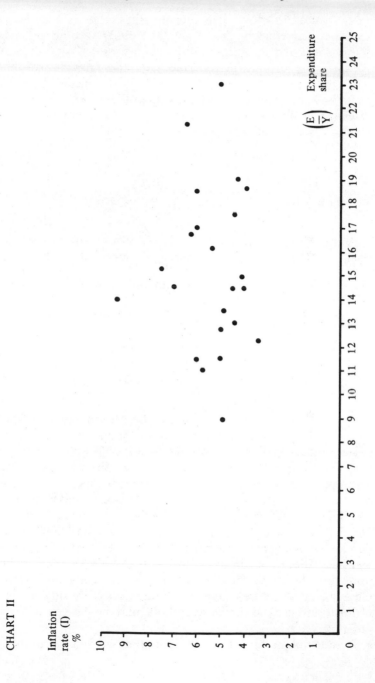

CHART II

Inflation rate (I) %

As a measure of relative income, the ratio of income per head in each country (Y_i^*) to total OECD income per head $(\overline{Y})$ was calculated using 1970 exchange rates. An additional measure of economic performance G^*, the rate of growth of GDP per head over the years 1965–72 was included, on the grounds that a higher rate of growth would be expected, *ceteris paribus*, to reduce inflationary pressure. The estimated regression equation is given as equation (2)

$$I = 9.46 - 2.60 \left(\frac{Y^*}{\overline{Y}}\right) - 0.46\, G^* \tag{2}$$

$$(1.06)\ (0.706) \qquad (0.152)$$

$$R^2 = 0.43$$

Both regression coefficients are significant at the 1 per cent level,[3] but the correlation is weak. Inclusion of the public sector 'size' variable $\left(\frac{T}{Y}\right)$ still fails to add to the explanatory power of the equation, however, as can be seen in equation (2b).

$$I = 9.33 - 2.63 \left(\frac{Y^*}{\overline{Y}}\right) - 0.46\, G^* + 0.004 \left(\frac{T}{Y}\right). \tag{2b}$$

$$(1.09)\ \ 0.775) \qquad (0.159) \qquad (0.034)$$

$$R^2 = 0.43$$

Inflation and Public Sector 'Growth'. The other major hypothesis discussed in previous sections relates inflation not to the size, but to the growth of the public sector. This argument may take two distinct forms. On the one hand, the political process is deemed to result in continuous government expenditure growth accompanied by an 'asymmetrical' reluctance to raise the necessary finance, thus resulting in a broadly 'demand pull' inflation. On the other hand, it may be argued (see the third section) that an increasing tax burden brought about by expanding government activities results in so-called 'tax back-lash' or 'wage retaliation', and hence to inflation of a broadly 'cost-push' variety. Once again, therefore, there is no question of testing a *theory* of inflation since the simple hypothesis may be derived in several different ways.

In attempting to verify this hypothesis, three measures of

public sector growth were employed:

(a) The change in the share of total taxes in GNP between 1965 and 1972 $\Delta\left(\frac{T}{Y}\right)$,

(b) The change in the share of current government expenditure (excluding transfer payments) in GNP during the same time interval $\Delta\left(\frac{E}{Y}\right)$, and

(c) The change in the share of direct taxes and social security contributions in GNP $\Delta\left(\frac{T_D}{Y}\right)$.

These measures are in percentage points and are clearly not independent of cyclical influences. (The period 1965–72 was chosen merely because comparable data from published sources were available spanning the period.) The estimated regression equations are as follows:

$$I = 8.98 - 2.74\left(\frac{Y^*}{\overline{Y}}\right) \quad 0.45\,G^* + 0.11\,\Delta\left(\frac{T}{Y}\right). \tag{3a}$$

$$\qquad (0.685) \qquad (0.147) \quad (0.070) \qquad R^2 = 0.50$$

$$I = 9.24 - 2.72\left(\frac{Y^*}{\overline{Y}}\right) - 0.45\,G^* + 0.14\,\Delta\left(\frac{E}{Y}\right). \tag{3b}$$

$$\qquad (0.717) \qquad (0.154) \quad (0.140) \qquad R^2 = 0.46$$

$$I = 8.93 - 2.91\left(\frac{Y^*}{\overline{Y}}\right) - 0.45\,G^* + 0.18\,\Delta\left(\frac{T_D}{Y}\right). \tag{3c}$$

$$\qquad (0.692) \qquad (0.145) \quad (0.103)$$

$$R^2 = 0.51$$

These results are very far from conclusive, but the public sector growth variables, at any rate on the tax side, perform better than the simple size variables included earlier. This would seem to be especially the case for the growth in *direct* taxes as a proportion of GNP (equation (3c)). The estimated coefficient is significantly greater than zero at the traditionally favoured 5 per cent level. On the whole it must be admitted, however, that the evidence in favour of the hypothesis is rather weak.

As an additional experiment, those countries with an income per head of less than half the OECD average were excluded from the data to see whether the more industrialized Western nations yielded similar results on their own. This required the exclusion of Turkey, Spain, Portugal, Greece and Ireland. The remaining eighteen observations then generated the following regression equation:

$$I = 7.23 - 1.82 \left(\frac{Y^*}{\overline{Y}}\right) - 0.24\, G^* + 0.14\Delta \left(\frac{T_D}{Y}\right) \qquad (3d)$$

$$(0.764) \qquad (0.125) \quad (0.082)$$

$$R^2 = 0.38$$

Although the same basic relationships appear to hold, the size and statistical significance of all the coefficients are reduced, as is the coefficient of determination. The coefficients of $\left(\frac{Y^*}{Y}\right)$ and G^* remain significant at the 5 per cent level while our public sector growth variable just fails to qualify.

The hypothesis that an increasing direct tax take is inflationary receives thus only a small amount of support from the above equations. This support is, moreover, reduced when the elementary point is considered that the causal relationship may well run in the opposite direction to that suggested. Fiscal drag might be sufficient to explain the positive association between inflation and the direct tax take, the latter in this case depending upon the former.

For a typical taxpayer in a given country we have:

$$\Delta \left(\frac{T}{Y}\right) \simeq \left(\frac{1}{Y}\right)\Delta T + T\Delta \left(\frac{1}{Y}\right)$$

$$\simeq \left(\frac{1}{T}\right)\Delta T - \frac{T}{Y^2}\Delta Y$$

$$\text{or} \quad \Delta\left(\frac{T}{Y}\right) \simeq \frac{1}{Y}\left(\Delta T - \left(\frac{T}{Y}\right)\Delta Y\right)$$

$$\text{Hence} \quad \Delta\left(\frac{T}{Y}\right) \simeq \frac{\Delta Y}{Y}\left(\frac{\Delta T}{\Delta Y} - \frac{T}{Y}\right).$$

Where tax allowances are not index-linked or adjusted to take account of inflation, it is therefore to be expected that a higher inflation rate $\left(\text{and hence a higher value of } \frac{\Delta Y}{Y}\right)$ will lead to an increase in the proportion of direct taxes to personal income, the size of the increase depending upon the difference between the marginal and average tax rate. It would require a detailed study of the tax systems prevailing in each country over the relevant period—the degree of progressivity exhibited by each, the amount of index-linking, the frequency of changes in tax rates and allowances—to determine how far equations (3c) and (3d) are merely registering some of the effects of fiscal drag.

Concluding Comments

The overall results from cross-section data would not appear to be very encouraging. However, this is not altogether surprising given that the simple hypotheses concerning the size and growth of the public sector are so tenuously related to public choice theory. This theory would not lead us to associate inflation with public sector size so much as with certain characteristics of the political system. To take an obvious, if extreme, example, a country in which decisions were taken on the basis of a unanimity rule would hardly be expected to suffer from tax back-lash since any undesired tax could always be prevented by the low-cost expedient of failing to vote for it. On the other hand, a representative democracy with a few major parties, lengthy election periods, a first-past-the-post electoral system, a majority decision rule within the legislature, and full-line supply of policies on the part of the political parties, would appear to give ample opportunity for the emergence of citizen 'coercion'

(Breton, 1974) and hence to such phenomena as pressure-group politics and tax back-lash. It might therefore be expected that small countries, with greater local power, more direct democracy and more 'earmarking' of taxes would give greater scope for individual marginal valuations to come into line with tax prices. Such hypotheses, however, are far removed from the simple tests conducted above.

In the light of these reflections it is perhaps understandable that our rather crude cross-section comparisons, including countries with vastly different political systems ranging from confederate Switzerland to Franco's Spain, should prove so inconclusive. If taxation has become inflationary it will require more detailed studies of individual countries as well as a closer inspection of the political mechanisms involved in order to show it.

NOTES

1. One candidate is said to have answered: 'I am not quite sure how I am supposed to answer this question but it may be said that both inflation and sex are characterized by a rising rate of interest'.
2. Unfortunately, available data did not permit the inclusion of public enterprise profits.
3. Pundits should know that throughout this chapter we test the hypothesis $H_0 : \beta = 0$ against the alternative hypothesis $H_1 : \beta > 0$ or $H_1 : \beta < 0$ depending on our *a priori* belief about the signs of the coefficients to be estimated.

CHAPTER 6

The Origin of Increasing Inflationary Tendencies in Contemporary Society*

M. Panić

Introduction

For almost twenty years now, prices have increased continuously in every part of the world. What is more, there has been a tendency for the rates of inflation to accelerate, culminating in the unprecedented increases of the mid-1970s which have still to be brought under control. (See, for instance, Maynard and van Ryckeghem, 1976; Panić, 1976.) The persistent accelerating price rises have affected countries irrespective of size, level of industrialization, dependence on external trade, social organization or political system, and have combined to produce the worst peacetime inflation in history.[1]

One of the major consequences of the worsening inflationary trends has been the virtual abandonment of the objectives of full employment and economic growth which dominated the economic policies of industrial nations after World War II, and which were pursued so successfully until the early 1970s. Instead, a new consensus seems to have developed according to which the two objectives cannot be attained until the problem of inflation has been 'solved'. This is implied strongly, for

* This chapter, which expresses the author's personal views only, was written before he joined the Bank of England. In preparing the final version the author benefited from comments made on an earlier draft by Samuel Brittan, Kenneth Dallas, John Goldthorpe, Fred Hirsch, Rafi Husain, Dudley Jackson, Michael Posner, David Stout and Keith Vernon. Keith Vernon also helped with the statistical work. None of the above is, of course, responsible for the views expressed, nor for any remaining errors and shortcomings.

instance, in a recent OECD review of the short-term economic
trends and prospects in member countries (OECD, 1976). Preoc-
cupation with the problem of rising prices has become, therefore,
the dominant factor in economic policies pursued by industrial
nations, together with great uncertainty about the means for
curing it.

The purpose of this chapter is to examine certain underlying
causes of contemporary inflationary tendencies which not only
appear to be consistent with observed worldwide developments
over the last two decades but also make it easier to understand
why the problem has turned out to be so difficult to solve.
In doing this, the chapter has little to say about the 'mechanics'
of inflation, not because it is unimportant but because its economic, social and political aspects are analysed elsewhere in this
book. Moreover, the 'mechanics' of the inflationary process—unlike its underlying causes—has received a good deal of attention
in economic literature (Bronfenbrenner and Holzman, 1963;
Laidler and Parkin, 1975).

Competitive Ethos and the Aspirations Gap

Human behaviour is influenced—even in the production and
distribution of material wealth—by many more factors than
a simple desire to acquire an increasing command over relatively
scarce goods and services. Nevertheless, it has been recognized
for thousands of years that this is an important means to
other ends.

> Material success was [the Egyptians'] first goal of good life
> ... A success visible to all men was the great good. These
> were the supreme values of the Old Kingdom [i.e. 2600–2500
> BC to 2100–2000 BC], and they continued in value throughout
> Egyptian history. [Frankfort *et al.*, 1949, pp. 106, 110]

Moreover, it was also recognized in the ancient world that,
unlike absolute wants, those which depend on relative wealth,
status and power, i.e. 'relative wants', were virtually limitless.
For instance, Aristotle makes the distinction when he points
out in Book I (ch. 8) of the *Politics* that 'the amount of property

which is needed for a good life is not unlimited, although Solon in one of his poems says that "No bound to riches has been fixed for man".' The desire for relative success and the inevitable competitive spirit to which it gives rise exist also in many primitive societies in our own time (Forde, 1934; Mead, 1937).

However, it was only with the advent of 'capitalism' that the competitive urge and the pressure of relative needs were combined into the dynamic force which not only made the Industrial Revolution of the eighteenth and early nineteenth centuries possible but has generated economic growth ever since. Indeed, reluctantly and despite protestations and claims to the contrary, 'socialist' countries have also found it difficult to achieve rapid and sustained economic progress otherwise (cf. Wiles, 1977).

In order for this competitive ethos not just to start economic growth but to maintain the momentum over a long period of time, there are two prerequisites, present in differing degree in all industrial and semi-industrial economies. One is the pursuit of self-interest in the achievement of both individual and collective objectives, i.e. the 'social good'. The other is the perpetuation of relative needs, which make a satisfactory pursuit of self-interest difficult unless the effort is either intensified or at least sustained, despite continuous increases in real income.

The rate of economic growth has been dependent, therefore, on the extent to which people seek out and seize opportunities for material gain. They may do this either because they desire wealth for its own sake or because it brings them social prestige, influence or power over other people. 'Socialist' economies, at least those in Europe, appear to be different, but the difference is largely one of degree rather than kind.

For the simple fact is, of course, that if wants are limited there is no reason for people to work longer than is necessary to meet these requirements. The environment in which this takes place is characteristically the one in which choice of goods and services is limited so that as their income rises people can buy only more of the same products. Once they have satisfied their basic needs and limited wants, there is obviously no reason for them to increase their income. Consequently, as income per hour rises, they will work fewer hours unless forced to do otherwise. For instance, given the very limited choice of goods and services open to them beyond a certain level of income, it is very likely that the Chinese (Donnithorne, 1974; Prybyla, 1976) could reach, within the foreseeable future, a standard of living beyond which it became meaningless for them to increase effort and income further.

Countries invariably 'take-off into self-sustained growth', as Rostow (1960) put it, thanks to a minority who 'blaze the trail' either individually or collectively. In both cases, the important thing is that this minority breaks with the existing traditions and expectations of a static society. Moreover, as it is they who rise, in dynamic economies, to positions of social pre-eminence and political power, it is their values and their ideology which soon become the dominant force in determining social patterns of behaviour. This is essential, because the minority cannot sustain economic progress on their own. It is in order to achieve this, for instance, that 'The ruling classes in any country are usually anxious that the people should be willing to work steadily and persistently . . .' (Lewis, 1955, p. 39). This is as true of governments as it is of private and state employers because by working hard people make it possible for them to achieve their objectives, whatever these may be.

In return, at least three conditions have to be satisfied. First, there has to be a reasonably high degree of social mobility which promises the industrious, the able and the inventive (and in 'capitalism' the thrifty) that they can rise to as high a rung on the social ladder as their ability and hard work can take them. Secondly, there has to be a system of differentiated rewards which encourages people to prefer to seek relatively scarce skills—or the jobs which are in relatively greater demand—as well as to work hard and conscientiously. To the extent that these incentives operate well, they will also make at least the relatively successful content with the existing social system. Thirdly, it is essential to provide a continuous stream of new goods and services in order to increase wants and encourage effort. In other words, technological progress is necessary not only to maintain a certain rate of growth of investment but also to secure a certain supply of labour. Otherwise, if wants became limited and the consumption expenditure of more and more people reached saturation level, the backward-sloping supply curve would make an inevitable impact on the rate of growth.[2]

With inequalities generating and sustaining growth and growth preserving inequality—even though it seems to decrease over time—it is hardly surprising that eventually a society is created

> in which one of the principal social goals is a higher standard of living ... When the attainment of any end becomes a generally recognised social goal, the importance of attainment of this goal is instilled in every individual mind by the socialisation process ... When this occurs the achievement of a certain degree of success in reaching the goal becomes essential to the maintenance of self-esteem. The maintenance of self-esteem is a basic drive in every individual. [Duesenberry, 1949, p. 29]

But it is not so much pre-occupation with absolute but rather with *relative* standards of living that provides the essential dynamic force in a modern industrial society. Moreover, relative income usually goes with *relative* status (Runciman, 1966); and the two together will also tend to be associated with *relative* power and influence. This appears to be as true of China (Prybyla, 1976) as it is of 'capitalist' countries (Miliband, 1969).

Consequently, modern economic growth creates an environment in which people may continue to feel worse off long after becoming able to satisfy their absolute needs. They will be influenced in this by those with whom they normally compare themselves. That is, whether they feel better or worse off will depend on the size of the aspirations gap:

> the gap between the standard of living and the status which people have and those that they would like to have ... The size of the gap will depend on changes experienced by individuals, groups and nations relative to those of their 'reference groups', i.e. those with whom they normally compare. [Panić, 1976, pp. 5–6]

If the competitive ethos inevitably creates the aspirations gap, it is the economic, social and political consequences of the aspirations gap that, as will be suggested later, tend to generate worldwide inflationary tendencies.

Normally, we will judge an improvement in our standard of living by the extent to which we can satisfy our needs in a more satisfactory manner. We may consume more of the same goods and services. More likely, we shall change the pattern of consumption to include higher quality items. But the change in consumption patterns is not purely a matter of the rise in real income. Our consumption behaviour is not independent of that of other individuals and families; and, besides, it has also a certain social function to perform. Consumption of goods and services of higher quality is also a way of signalling, by adopting their behavioural pattern, that one has joined a higher status group. More generally, because 'high-income families will spend more on consumption than low-income families, high standards of consumption become established as criteria for high status' (Duesenberry, 1949, p. 30).

At the same time, there is no absolute standard for judging what exactly is a high quality good or service, even less so a 'luxury'. It is in the very nature of the latter that it is relatively scarce; that, consequently, it commands a relatively high price and has a high income elasticity of demand. It is its very exclusiveness which gives special satisfaction to those who can afford it. By the time that it is mass-produced, assuming that it can be, so that many more people can afford it—it becomes a 'standard' good, compared with new 'luxuries' again available only to a relatively small number of people. The process of innovation, relative scarcity, inequality and the aspirations gap continues.

However, after a time frustration and discontent may appear and begin to grow. The reason for this is that during the early phases of rapid economic growth people may tolerate the existence or even an increase in inequality, but as Hirschman (1973, p. 545) has argued, 'this tolerance is like a credit that falls due at a certain date. It is extended in the expectation that eventually the disparities will narrow. If this does not occur, there is bound to be trouble and, perhaps, disaster.' The process which leads to this disillusionment has been analysed at length by Hirsch. Economic growth raises claims on resources which, simply, cannot be met from the world's existing productive capacity or indeed any productive capacity likely to be created in the foreseeable future. 'The locus of instability is the divergence between what is possible for the individual and what is possible for all individuals' (Hirsch, 1977a, p. 67). This process is reflected in various empirical studies which examine the link between relative income, people's satisfaction with life and their aspirations and which show that higher income groups are more satisfied, 'happier' than are lower income groups. (Easterlin, 1972; OECD, 1972; Abrams, 1973, 1974; SSRC Survey Unit, 1976).

It is feelings of disappointment and frustration generated in this way that ultimately lead to the tensions and conflicts which manifest themselves in, among other things, higher rates of inflation. Some writers (e.g. Mishan, 1967) attribute this to envy. But Hirsch (1977a, p. 11) is much nearer the truth when he says that 'Economic liberalism is ... a victim of its own propaganda: offered to all, it has evoked demands and pressures that cannot be contained.' Hirschman (1973, pp. 559–60) also concludes that it is not a simple question of envy. A society may well reach a point at which people become convinced that resources are 'limited' and that they are basically engaged in a zero-sum game. In the circumstances even the industrious, the able, the conscientious (and the thrifty) might begin to suspect that eventually only a few of them may be blessed for their efforts with riches, honours and power. By attempting a greater claim on resources, everybody hopes that he may enhance his chances of reaching El Dorado—or at least, that although his chances are extremely small they may become greater in this way than if he waits patiently for his 'turn'.

What makes the problem particularly serious now is the fact that the aspirations gap has become an international rather than a national problem. People in low income countries in different parts of the world, under different economic systems, demand and treasure goods normally consumed in higher income countries (cf. Rubin and Savalloni, 1966; Cukierman, 1973; Lloyd, 1974; Lockwood, 1975; Adams *et al.*, 1975).

There are many reasons for this apart from greater international specialization and exchange and the integration of more and more countries into the world economy. Developments of this kind are extremely complex and cannot be described adequately in a single paper let alone in a few paragraphs. Nevertheless, a number of them have taken place over the last fifty years—all highly inter-related—which have had a major influence on economic, social and political developments all over the world. It is these developments which also help explain the fact that the worldwide increases in prices have generally accelerated over the last twenty years.

First, one should not underestimate the impact—on people's expectations and behaviour—of man's demonstration of his capacity to control the economic environment. It was, of course, the great contribution of Adam Smith (1776) to show how nations, by their own effort and appropriate institutional changes, could increase wealth. But it is only over the last fifty years, and particularly since the early 1950s, that most people probably have realized the real potential of appropriate man-made policies. Thanks to unprecedented rates of growth achieved by many nations (even such relative 'laggards' as Great Britain), people could observe the real impact of certain institutional changes over a short period of time. There were, for instance, the enormous strides made by the Soviet Union to industrialize; and the success achieved by Germany in the 1930s to cope with the Great Depression, although both were accomplished at appalling social costs. Then, after the war, there were the impressive achievements of all advanced industrial nations, most of which adopted a more centralized, co-ordinated approach in their macroeconomic policies. Inevitably, success leads to expectations of further success.

Secondly, this was the period of decolonization, most of it completed by the early 1960s. Numerous 'new' countries emerged, all of them anxious to establish their own identity and play a more active, independent role on the world scene. They could not hope to do this so long as they remained economically weak. Besides, many of them had to cope with enormous problems of poverty, disease, illiteracy and general backwardness. Rapid economic growth provided the only way out. This, in turn, inevitably, led to the spread and strengthening of the competitive ethos and the emergence of the aspirations gap on a worldwide scale.

Thirdly, this has been the period of an intense and unusual ideological conflict. It is unusual in the sense that in the past it would have been resolved—or at least an attempt would have been made to do so—by military means. Now, nuclear weapons have made a solution of this kind impossible and the conflict has been transformed into an economic battle for the higher standard of living. The allegiance of individuals and nations would be won by the system which showed greater capacity to satisfy the ever growing demand for goods and services. But the war of compound growth rates had not only to be won but to be seen to be won—particularly by the new, 'uncommitted' nations. The incessant flow of information inevitably helped spread the aspirations gap internationally.

Fourthly, rapid economic progress and technological change require an educated labour force. It is no coincidence that the highest levels of literacy, as well as the proportions of people receiving the most advanced forms of education, are to be found in the most industrialized countries. Demand for a better-educated labour force comes from various sectors of the economy. For instance, the proportion of skilled manpower in industry has increased continuously over the last twenty-five years. At the same time, growing demand for better educational opportunities and facilities also comes from individuals as they realize the economic and social advantages of the more advanced forms of education and entry into certain occupations. The importance of education in the inflationary process is twofold. It reduces the relative scarcity of various skills and the quasi-rents earned by those possessing them and, in turn, inequalities in income distribution (Adelman and Morris, 1973; Ahluwalia, 1976). In this sense, it helps reduce also the aspirations gap and potential inflationary pressure. But this may be, at the same time, offset by the extent to which the established order in terms of the distribution of income, status and power—or rather the individuals and groups who represent it—is challenged by a growing number of those who feel sufficiently well-qualified and confident to perform high-reward tasks as well as, if not better than, those presently performing them. Education may therefore enlarge the aspirations gap, partly by increasing people's awareness of the importance of their skills in a complex economic process; and, partly, by widening their horizons to the extent that they can question the rationality and justice of existing social and economic relationships, including their own place in the established hierarchical order.

Fifthly, the scale of modern industrial operations, and the worldwide division of labour to which it has led, also contributes to the international aspirations gap. To begin with, a complex system of communications is required. But the immense improvements that have been made in worldwide communications also make people more conscious of what is happening everywhere on the globe. In particular, television and the cinema have made people aware of the standard of living enjoyed in industrial countries, including the life-styles of the more affluent sections of society within these countries. Moreover, rapid economic progress and the international division of labour are also dependent upon a highly-developed, low-cost transport system to extend the size of the market. The advances made in this area over the last thirty years have led to an unprecedented movement of people and ideas. Prominent among the mobile groups have been the educated élites of lower income countries, who play a major role in importing goods and life-styles from the more affluent nations and in this way exacerbate the aspirations gap in their own countries. Finally, one other influence in this direction is that of advertising which has expanded enormously since World War II. Thanks to transnational corporations it has been carried to virtually every corner of the globe. The usual defence of advertising in this context—that its failures prove that industry cannot create wants—misses completely the relevant point. Of course, even a mighty corporation like Ford may fail to persuade people to buy a reasonably well designed product like the Edsel car; or the fruit growers of America may fail to convince people that it is good for them to eat more prunes, despite great efforts from psychoanalysts to give them the right 'sex image' (Packard, 1957). But the important point is that the over-all effect of advertising is to promote a certain style of life and the standard of values which goes with it—not least by making those who cannot afford them feel inadequate, social failures.

None of the factors listed above explain *how* the inflationary process takes place. But the analysis of this section does indicate why there is an inherent danger in modern industrial societies of serious inflationary pressure and why the danger has increased over the last two decades.

*An International Comparison of Per Capita Incomes and
Inflation Rates*

If the central proposition of this paper is correct, the existence of a competitive ethos will inevitably create an aspirations gap between the more and less successful individuals and groups within a nation; and through them, for the reasons described in the previous section, also between nations. The importance of factors such as education, the spread of information and growing economic interdependence among nations is that the educated élites in lower income countries will tend increasingly to use as their reference groups those of comparable status in the more affluent parts of the world. Consequently, they will wish to enjoy similar standards of living. The more they are successful in imitating these standards, the more it is likely that they will widen the aspirations gap in their own countries—though the size of the gap and, therefore, of inflationary pressures will depend, among other factors, on the extent to which the élite are integrated into the community at large. In these circumstances, a strong inflationary pressure is unavoidable in the sense that there will always be a good deal of actual and/or potential 'excess demand' which the existing productive resources cannot satisfy in the short run. Indeed, as already pointed out, the continuing existence of the competitive ethos makes it extremely unlikely that this demand will be satisfied in the long run either.

If the distribution of income—national and, even more so, international—plays a major role in determining the aspirations gap, there should be a significant relationship between the relative level and distribution of income in a country and its rate of inflation. It would, of course, be naïve to expect that these two 'measurable' factors could account entirely for the observed difference. Countries will differ, often considerably, in their social and economic organization, system of government, cultural and historical traditions; and although all these factors will affect also the level and distribution of income in a country, important differences will remain, influencing not only the aspirations gap but also the means by which those trying to narrow the gap can do something about it. Nevertheless, the general proposition should be valid, at least in the case of those countries which are reasonably similar in terms of historical traditions and general economic philosophy.

This is one of the reasons why the simple, tentative empirical tests described in this section have been confined to a relatively small number of countries, predominantly members of the OECD. In the case of countries which are not members of the OECD, the sample was limited to semi-industrialized nations—judged, very roughly, to be those which have reached per capita income similar to, or higher than, that of Turkey, the poorest and least industrialized of OECD countries. The other important criterion was the availability, coverage and quality of the relevant statistical material. Several countries, were eliminated because data on income distribution were lacking or contained even more serious deficiencies than usual. Finally, four Latin American countries which would have qualified by the two foregoing criteria—Argentina, Brazil, Chile and Uruguay—were in fact excluded because their rates of inflation have, for some years now, been quite exceptional so that their inclusion would have seriously distorted the results.

However, despite the care taken in selecting the countries and statistical information, certain data weaknesses and limitations, described in the Statistical Appendix to this chapter, are unavoidable and should be borne in mind when examining the results. Caution is particularly required in regard to information on income distributions. Nevertheless, in spite of the data differences and deficiencies, the results presented in Tables 3 and 4 of the Appendix are consistent with the hypotheses put forward earlier in this chapter.

To begin with, there is a strong and statistically significant *inverse* relationship between the level of income and consumption reached in a country and its rate of inflation. (The conclusion is valid whether Yugoslavia is included in the sample or not.) In other words, judging by the experience of OECD countries, the prevalence of the competitive ethos leads to strong inflationary pressures—irrespective of whether the means of production are privately or socially owned; whether there are strong trade unions, weak trade unions or, virtually, no unions; whether countries are small or large; whether they depend more or less on external trade; and whether or not they have a 'democratic' form of government. Differences such as these may account for some of the observed variation in relative price increases. But one difference seems to count above the others: the lower the average level of income in a country, the higher will tend to be its rate of inflation. International inequality in income distribution appears, therefore, to play a significant role in the worldwide inflationary process.

Its impact is felt, as pointed out earlier, through differences in the distribution of income at the national level. Following the arguments in the preceding section, one would expect inequality in income distribution to be positively and significantly associated with the rates of inflation; and Tables 3 and 4 of the Appendix show that this indeed is the case. At the same time, there are a number of important and instructive differences. Taking the OECD countries only, the correlation coefficient has the correct sign but is not statistically significant if Yugoslavia is included. This is, partly, a reminder of the well-known fact that the Yugoslav economy is in a way unique—a 'socialist' market economy. Consequently, it does not fit easily into comparisons with either 'socialist' or 'capitalist' countries. At the same time, the results are also a useful reminder that a relatively high degree of equality is not, necessarily, sufficient on its own to protect a country from strong inflationary pressures. Equality, like wealth and poverty, is a relative concept and the degree of inequality acceptable in one type of society may lead to considerable friction and conflict in a different kind of society, i.e. one in which people expect monetary as well as non-monetary rewards to be distributed much more equitably (cf. Portes, this volume). Moreover, a relatively low income country will remain exposed to inflationary pressures caused by international inequalities in income distribution about which, of course, it can do nothing.

When Yugoslavia is excluded, the correlation coefficient becomes statistically significant. But so long as the analysis is restricted to OECD countries, this is due entirely to the inclusion of Turkey. This raises the question of whether the statistical relationship between inequality and inflation is really significant or whether the result can be obtained only by employing a biased sample of countries in order to obtain a 'freak' result. Table 4 of the Appendix, which relates to all countries included in the analysis shows that this is not the case. Indeed, the coefficient is now statistically significant at the 95 per cent level even when Yugoslavia is included. The problem with the OECD sample is that this particular organization comprises predominantly highly industrialized, high income nations. For a number of important reasons—some of which are mentioned below—differences in income distribution among industrial nations are much smaller than among semi-industrialized countries; and this will tend to affect the observed strength of statistical relationships if the analysis is confined mainly to one of these groups.

There is, however, an important distributional aspect in the inflationary process which summary measures of income distribution, such as the Gini coefficient, cannot capture:[3] namely, the extent to which individual countries take care of their low income groups by enabling them to enjoy a standard of consumption more in line with what is thought to be an 'acceptable level' in these countries. This can be measured, roughly, by the amount of social security expenditure per capita. The expenditure is, on the whole, progressive everywhere (Wilensky, 1975), so that it is lower income groups which benefit most from it. Hence, the level of social security expenditure can help reduce the aspirations gap and in this way also the inflationary pressure. Tables 3 and 4 of the Appendix show that, as one would expect, there is an inverse relationship between social security expenditure per head and annual rates of inflation. The correlation coefficients reported are statistically significant at the 95 per cent level in all the cases, though it is noticeable that the relationship is stronger for the OECD members than for all the countries covered together.

The relationships revealed, though important, are not exactly surprising. There is, for instance, the tendency first observed by Kuznets (1955, 1963) for incomes to become more equally distributed as the average level of income in a country rises.[4] This tendency is displayed both by data covering long periods of time in individual countries (Soltow, 1968; Williamson, 1976b) and by comparisons, on a cross-sectional basis, of the statistical evidence for a large number of countries (Paukert, 1973; Ahluwalia, 1976). Similarly, there is a tendency for countries to spend a higher proportion of their GDP on social security as their level of income rises (Wilensky, 1975). There are differences, influenced among other things, as Wilensky points out, by political factors. But, on the whole, the proposition seems to be generally true, as Tables 3 and 4 show. Not surprisingly, therefore, per capita levels of GDP, private consumers' expenditure and social security expenditure are all *positively* and significantly correlated with one another; and *inversely*, and in many cases also significantly, with inequality. (Similar results are, in fact, obtained also for shorter periods of time.) Given the high correlation coefficients between GDP per capita and rates of inflation, one would, of course, expect the other three variables also to show a fairly strong relationship with inflation.

But this is another way of saying that the dynamic forces behind contemporary inflationary pressures are, in fact, very similar to those which determine the degree of inequality both over time and between countries. Clearly, the leading industrial nations—say, the top half-dozen in Table 1 of the Appendix—enjoy an important advantage in the sense that they *set* consumption standards (both private and social) which the rest of the world tries, apparently with growing desperation, to follow. In doing this they also *set* production standards in terms of both the composition and quality of output *and* the efficiency with which it is produced. As Linder (1961) argued, new and improved products (and this is also true of services) will be developed first in high income markets and then exported elsewhere. Consequently, the capacity of leading industrial nations to satisfy the standard of living to which the rest of the world aspires will be greater than in the case of the long tail of countries trying to follow them. Moreover, the further down the income scale a country is; the bigger structural adjustments in terms of output, productivity and incomes that it has to make; the more limited the resources it has with which to make them; and, consequently, the greater the chances of growing disequilibria and inflationary spirals.

In many ways, it is this international aspect of long-term inflationary tendencies which makes the task of dealing with them so difficult. The strength of the relationship emerges clearly from the statistical analysis. When price rises are related in a multiple regression to the variables analysed in this section it is differences in levels of GDP and private consumption per capita which turn out to be the most significant statistically, as the following regression equations show. (In each case either inequality or social security expenditure per head was used, depending on which performed better. The period is 1959–76.)

P   = annual rate of increase in consumer prices
GDP = gross domestic product per capita
CE = private consumer expenditure per capita

SS   = social security expenditure per capita
I   = inequality (Gini coefficients)
(t-ratios are given in parentheses under the relevant coefficients)

(i) *All countries except Yugoslavia, Ireland and Portugal*

P = 4.5758 − 0.0004 GDP + 5.9952 I

       (1.92)   (1.36)

$$R^2 = 0.44$$

The GDP coefficient is statistically significant at the 95 per cent level.

(ii) *OECD countries, excluding Yugoslavia*

P = 8.7308 − 0.0008 GDP − 0.0023 SS

       (2.50)   (1.26)

$$R^2 = 0.62$$

The GDP coefficient is statistically significant at the 97.5 per cent level.

P = 8.8451 − 0.0013 CE − 0.0028 SS

       (2.64)   (1.64)

$$R^2 = 0.63$$

The CE coefficient is statistically significant at the 99 per cent level and the SS coefficient just fails to be significant at the 95 per cent level.

Actual price increases and those predicted by the last equation are shown in graphical form in Chart I.

Conclusion

What these results seem to indicate is that, as the global division of labour increases and the world economy becomes more integrated, inflationary and other pressures generated by international differences in levels of income and consumption are likely to become more intense. There is much more similarity in the four economic indicators shown in Table 5 among industrial

CHART I *Annual Price Increases in OECD Countries 1959–76: Actual and Predicted (Excluding Yugoslavia)*

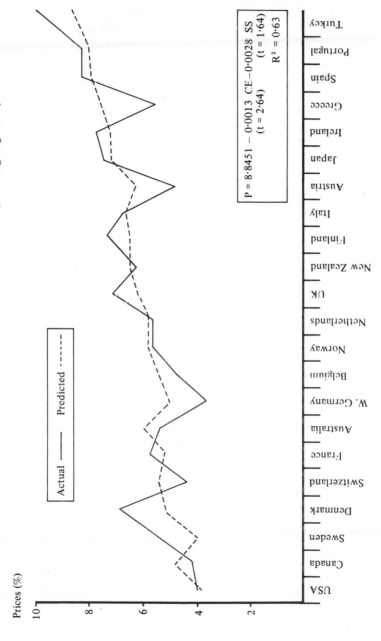

than among semi-industrial nations. The former also tend to be more homogeneous socially and politically.

Reductions of inequality within countries should help to lessen inflationary pressures, and higher levels of social expenditure per capita indeed appear to do so, at least in the case of the OECD countries. But they are obviously not adequate to offset the tensions and conflicts created by the international aspirations gap. What is more, if the gap between the leading industrial nations and the rest continues to widen,[5] long-term inflationary tendencies are bound to accelerate and the underlying socio-economic conflicts—of which inflation is only one symptom—could then easily be expressed in a much more disruptive and destructive form.

STATISTICAL APPENDIX

This Appendix presents the basic data and all the correlation coefficients referred to in the chapter, and also a brief description of some of the data problems.

To begin with, there are differences in the consumer price indices—i.e. in their coverage as well as in the sampling, compilation and weighting methods used—even among the OECD countries. (Vannereau, 1975). The coverage, for example, varies from the whole country (e.g. West Germany, Japan and Britain) to urban areas above a certain size (e.g. the United States and Canada), to the six state capitals in Australia (which account for most of the country's population), and to the capitals only in Portugal and Turkey. In the six non-OECD countries the indices reflect price changes in their capitals only.

The series for GDP and private consumer expenditure per capita were converted (by the OECD Secretariat) into US dollar at official exchange rates. The conversion suffers from a number of well-known weaknesses, including the tendency to exaggerate the difference between high and low income countries by understating, often seriously, the level of income and consumption in the latter (Kravis *et al.*, 1975; Usher, 1968).

But the most serious data problems, as one might expect,

appear in comparisons of income distribution in different countries. In his study of the distribution in OECD countries Sawyer (1976, p. 12) came to the conclusion that only the data for twelve of them were 'reasonably comparable'. The countries were: United States, Sweden, Canada, West Germany, Norway, France, Australia, the Netherlands, Britain, Japan, Italy and Spain. The available information about income distribution in

TABLE 1   *Selected Statistical Indicators: OECD Countries*

	GDP per capita in 1970 (US $)	Private consumers' expenditure per capita in 1970 (US $)	Social security expenditure per capita in 1970 (US $)	Inequality (Gini coefficients) c. 1970	Annual increases in consumers' prices 1959–76 (per cent, compound)
USA	4,879	3,029	385	0.40	4.0
Sweden	4,098	2,215	717	0.35	5.6
Canada	3,894	2,261	393	0.38	4.2
Switzerland	3,201	1,899	304	0.37	4.4
Denmark	3,192	1,914	444	0.37	6.8
West Germany	3,095	1,662	607	0.40	3.7
Norway	2,953	1,564	372	0.35	5.6
France	2,863	1,692	524	0.42	5.7
Australia	2,777	1,671	250	0.31	5.4
Belgium	2,658	1,596	492	0.41	4.8
Netherlands	2,474	1,420	453	0.38	5.6
Finland	2,253	1,184	295	0.47	7.4
New Zealand	2,193	1,307	259	0.39	6.2
UK	2,185	1,357	315	0.34	7.1
Austria	1,923	1,078	404	0.37	4.9
Japan	1,902	974	118	0.34	7.5
Italy	1,728	1,112	302	0.41	6.7
Ireland	1,335	935	148	–	7.7
Greece	1,091	762	131	0.46	5.6
Spain	961	646	41	0.39	8.2
Yugoslavia	714	375	82	0.35	14.3
Portugal	713	538	41	–	8.3
Turkey	360	251	7	0.57	9.7

Sources: GDP and private consumer expenditure: OECD, *National Accounts 1962–1973.*
Social security expenditure: OECD, *National Accounts 1962–1973*; H. L. Wilensky (1975); and ILO (1972).
Gini coefficients: M. Sawyer (1976); S. Jain (1975); and data supplied by the Centre for Studies in Social Policy, London.
Consumer prices: OECD, *Main Economic Indicators* and UN, *Monthly Bulletin of Statistics.*

the other member-countries was either not available or suffered
from such deficiencies that, in Sawyer's judgement, it could
not be compared with those of the countries listed above. Yet
even among the 'comparable' countries, in the few cases where
he could make a rough estimate of the under-reporting of incomes, Sawyer concluded that the extent of inequality was smaller
in West Germany and the Netherlands and greater in Australia
and France, relative to other countries, than indicated in the

TABLE 2   *Selected Statistical Indicators: Other Countries*

	GDP per capita in 1970 (US $)	Social security expenditure per capita in 1970 (US $)	Inequality (Gini coefficients) c. 1970	Annual increases in consumer prices 1959–76 (per cent, compound)
Mexico	649	19	0.58	6.4
Costa Rica	576	17	0.44	5.8
Peru	507	15	0.59	10.6
Jamaica	478	14	0.58	7.4
Colombia	361	5	0.56	14.4
Taiwan	342	5	0.47	5.8

Sources: GDP: UN, *Monthly Bulletin of Statistics* and IMF, *International Financial Statistics.*
Social security expenditure: Wilensky (1975) and as for GDP.
Inequality: Jain (1975).
Consumer prices: as for GDP.

figures in Table 1 (Sawyer, 1976, pp. 12–13). As for the remaining
eleven OECD countries, it was impossible to find data about
income distribution in Portugal; and the only data for Ireland
are, apparently, based on a household budget survey of very
limited coverage carried out in the mid-1960s (Sawyer, 1976,
p. 24). This is rather different from the information available
for the other countries, which is why in Table 1 no measure
of inequality is included for Ireland. The figures for the six
non-OECD countries were taken from Jain (1975).

Ideally, one would like to be able to use household distribution
of income—preferably per head, after tax but including transfer
payments, all adjusted for price changes appropriate to, say,
each decile. But, of course, no information of this kind is

available. Even the data for the household distribution of income have been collected in fewer countries than those for personal distribution before tax. It is for this reason that only the latter have been used, expressed in terms of Gini coefficients.[6] This particular measure of inequality has received a great deal of battering recently from Wiles (1974). However, all the existing measures of distribution of income suffer from various shortcomings (Sen, 1973) and, what is more, as Sawyer (1976) has shown, produce very similar rankings of countries. The Gini coefficient is still, despite its weaknesses, one of the most widely employed summary measures of inequality, and it is for this reason that it has been used in this paper. At the same time, it should

TABLE 3   *Correlation Coefficients*[a]
A.   *OECD Countries, 1959–76*

	GDP	Consumer expendi- ture	Social security	Inequality (excluding Portugal and Ireland)	Prices
GDP per capita	–	0.988	0.788	0.389	−0.715
Private consumer expenditure per capita	0.988	–	0.740	−0.357*	−0.725
Social security per capita	0.788	0.740	–	−0.279*	−0.649
Inequality	0.389	−0.357*	−0.279*	–	0.131*
Prices	−0.715	−0.725	−0.649	0.131*	–

B.   *OECD Countries, 1959–76*
(excluding Yugoslavia)

	GDP	Consumer expendi- ture	Social security	Inequality (excluding Portugal and Ireland)	Prices
GDP per capita	–	0.987	0.771	−0.487	−0.768
Private consumer expenditure per capita	0.987	–	0.718	−0.458	−0.762
Social security per capita	0.771	0.718	–	−0.354*	−0.705
Inequality	−0.487	−0.458	−0.354*	–	0.424
Prices	−0.768	−0.762	−0.705	0.424	–

Note: (a) All coefficients are statistically significant at the 95 per cent level except those marked with an asterisk.

TABLE 4   *Correlation Coefficients*[a]
A.   *All Countries, 1959– 76*

	GDP	Social security	Inequality (excluding Portugal and Ireland)	Prices
GDP per capita	–	0.862	−0.645	−0.633
Social security per capita	0.862	–	−0.595	−0.586
Inequality	−0.645	−0.595	–	0.390
Prices	−0.633	−0.586	0.390	–

B.   *All Countries, 1959– 76*
(excluding Yugoslavia)

	GDP	Social security	Inequality (excluding Portugal and Ireland)	Prices
GDP per capita	–	0.858	−0.706	−0.646
Social security per capita	0.858	–	−0.643	−0.607
Inequality	−0.706	−0.643	–	0.596
Prices	−0.646	−0.607	0.596	–

Note: (a) All coefficients are statistically significant at the 95 per cent level.

TABLE 5   *Variability of the Main Indicators*

	Mean	Standard deviation	Coefficient of variation (%)
Industrial countries[a]			
GDP per capita (US $)	2,839	823	29.0
Social security expenditure per capita (US $)	390	139	35.6
Inequality (Gini coefficients)	0.380	0.036	9.5
Prices (%, p.a.)	5.62	1.16	20.6
Other countries[b]			
GDP per capita (US $)	674	300	44.5
Social security expenditure per capita (US $)	44	50	113.6
Inequality (Gini coefficients)[c]	0.499	0.084	16.8
Prices (%, p.a.)	8.68	2.93	33.8

Notes: (a) USA, Sweden, Canada, Switzerland, Denmark, West Germany, Norway, France, Australia, Belgium, Netherlands, Finland, New Zealand, UK, Austria, Japan and Italy.
(b) Ireland, Greece, Spain, Yugoslavia, Portugal, Turkey, Mexico, Costa Rica, Peru, Jamaica, Colombia and Taiwan.
(c) Excluding Ireland and Portugal.
Sources: As for Tables 1 and 2.

be noted that the coefficients refer to those years for which income data were available. This means that from country to country they refer to a number of different years, mostly around 1970, which happen also to represent different points of the business cycle. As distribution of income varies over the cycle, mainly by affecting the share of low income groups (Beach, 1977), the figures may present a somewhat distorted picture of relative inequalities. Unfortunately, there is nothing that can be done about this.

Finally, the social security per capita series have been calculated from the data assembled by the International Labour Office (1972) and from those given by Wilensky (1975). The ILO figures include 'compulsory social insurance, certain voluntary social insurance schemes, family allowance schemes for public employees, public health services, public assistance and benefits granted to war victims.' (ILO, 1972, p. 2.) As they have been converted into US dollars at official exchange rates, they also suffer from the shortcomings mentioned earlier.

NOTES

1. Probably the most famous period of persistent and widespread inflation is the so-called 'Price Revolution' which took place in the sixteenth century. Yet, as Cipolla points out, the label is something of an exaggeration: 'It is generally held that between 1500 and 1620, the average level of prices in the various European countries increased by 300 to 400 per cent.' (1976, p. 211). But although extremely high by the standards of previous generations, these rates of inflation appear to be rather mild when compared with those experienced since the late 1950s. During the last twenty years prices have doubled in all the OECD countries included in Table 1 of the Appendix, going up by 300 per cent or more in ten of them. Increases in excess of these rates have, of course, been recorded in many parts of the world, particularly in Latin America and Asia.
2. Wiles (1977, p. 567) mentions the 'avoidance' of new goods in socialist economies as an attempt to beat economic scarcity and escape the awkward problem of inequality. It does not seem to be very successful, and for the reasons described later in this section is likely to be even less so in the longer term. (See, for example, Smith, 1976).
3. It needs hardly to be pointed out that Gini coefficients are quite inadequate for the purpose of representing many other aspects of inequality—e.g. social and political inequality—all of which may play an important role in the inflationary process.
4. The actual relationship described by Kuznets is of an inverted U-shape. Starting from very low levels of income, inequality first rises and then

160 *M. Panić*

falls with economic development. All the countries in the Statistical Appendix appear, however, to be on the right-hand side of the inverted U.

5. For example, taking the OECD countries only, there is no statistically significant relationship between level of GDP per capita (at constant prices) and annual rate of growth over the period analysed in this chapter. In other words, many of the countries with high levels of GDP and personal consumption per head were increasing their real incomes as fast as, or faster than, those with low real GDP per capita. Consequently, international disparities in income levels, far from falling, were in many cases widening.

In fact, given the size of the initial gap in incomes per head, even semi-industrialized countries would have to maintain exceptional rates of growth over a long period of time in order to catch up with leading industrial nations or even some of the 'laggards'. This can be illustrated by means of a simple example. Between 1959 and 1976 (i.e. the period covered in this chapter) GDP per capita increased (per annum, at constant prices) by 6.3 per cent in Spain, 3.2 per cent in Sweden and 2.4 per cent in Britain. Assuming now that the three countries are capable of sustaining these rates indefinitely, it would take the Spaniards until the end of this century to catch up with the British, and about fifty years to reach the Swedish standard of living. And Spain is, of course, reasonably well off compared with many countries in the world.

6. In a few cases the household distribution had to be used either because only data on this were available or because these were the only data based on a national rather than a sectional sample. To the extent that incomes tend to be distributed more equally among households than persons, the coefficients given in Tables 1 and 2 understate somewhat the degree of inequality in Yugoslavia, Turkey, Mexico, Costa Rica, Jamaica and Taiwan.

CHAPTER 7

Inflation and Democracy
Samuel Brittan

Inflation is a monetary disease. But this does not take us far without some further analysis of the forces which lie behind excessive injections of money into the economic system. It is doubtful if a completely general explanation, valid in all conditions, can be given. The aim of this chapter is to explore the links which may exist between the democratic form of government and inflationary policies. Some tentative reasons are given at the end for supposing that the present acute inflationary disorders may be transitional and could subside in time; but the underlying tensions of which they are symptoms will not necessarily subside and could express themselves in other, and even more unpleasant, forms. I have no illusions that I have been able to write in an entirely value-free manner, but the purpose of this chapter is diagnosis, not prescription. It should be obvious that the last thing I should favour is a preventive authoritarian regime. Quite apart from the cure being worse than the disease, a dictatorship can hardly be a remedy for contradictory policies which arise from the lack of checks on the aspirations of existing elected governments.

It will be helpful to set out first a few reasons why inflation may be tempting to a ruler pursuing his own interests without constitutional checks, before examining how the introduction of modern representative democracy affects the picture.

The Inflation Tax

Inflation has many aspects; but one thing which it is always and everywhere is a tax. At the very least it is a tax on holders of money. The revenue from the inflation tax is not

161

unlimited. In the simple case when all money is issued by the government, and there is no economic growth, the value of the tax revenue from a continuing rate of inflation, to which everyone has adjusted, is equal to the inflation rate multiplied by the real value of outstanding money balances. (The existence of a fractional reserve banking system dilutes the gain to the government.) As the rate of inflation increases, individuals and traders will hold a smaller and smaller fraction of their income in the form of cash balances. At the point where any further increase in the inflation rate is fully offset by a fall in the real value of cash balances, the revenue from inflation is at a maximum.

The revenue-maximizing rate of inflation clearly depends on how fast the demand for real cash balances falls off as inflation rises. This will vary according to the type of society, its state of development and its own monetary history. The range might vary, according to estimates collected by Friedman (1971), from 5 to 50 per cent. This might suggest a rationale for 'Latin American' rates of inflation; but it would also suggest that hyperinflation would not normally pay the rulers of a country, quite apart from the damage to trade and the risk of total destruction to the currency.

It is not, however, wise for the most selfish ruler to maximize the yield of the inflation tax in isolation from conventional taxes. For if there are limits to the share of its resources that a population will tolerate being taken for collective use, then the higher the inflation tax the greater will be the resistance to other forms of levy.

There is a further cost of inflationary finance that is rarely mentioned. Excess monetary expansion will yield inflationary revenue only to the extent that people can be induced to continue holding the currency in question despite the fact of its deterioration. There is no law of the universe saying that a particular currency must be used either for debt settlement or as a unit of account. People will withstand a surprising amount of debasement for the sake of dealing with the known and familiar. But, beyond some degree of debasement, citizens have to be forced to use their own currency by legal-tender laws and exchange control.

Temporary Gains

The discussion so far assumes a long-established and anticipated inflation to which all adjustments have long ago been made. Some of the largest 'gains' come, however, from the act of moving from one inflation rate to a higher one. One of the most important, as Laidler (1976) has pointed out, is the reduction in the real value, not merely of cash balances, but of fixed-interest government debt. This is a once-for-all, but permanent, effect. For even if nominal interest rates adjust to the new rate of inflation, holders of previously-issued government debt will never see their gains recouped. The trick can be tried a number of times, but not indefinitely. For if it is repeated too often the likelihood of a rising rate of inflation (i.e. an accelerating increase in the price level) will be reflected in the supply price of loanable funds.

Another governmental 'gain', known as fiscal drag, comes from taxes which are levied on nominal income. Realistically, there will always be some pressure to adjust thresholds and tax bands to inflation; and the revenue gain will depend on the adjustment lag. The latter is probably greatest when there is a sudden rise in the inflation rate above that to which government and citizens have already been accustomed. Revenue gains, however, fall off and become negative once the erosion in the real value of direct taxes during the interval for collection exceeds the gains from fiscal drag. This is estimated to occur in Britain at present at about a 30 per cent inflation rate.

But there are many taxes whose real yield falls off with the rate of inflation. These include specific duties on goods, poll taxes and land taxes. Such imposts have historically been more important than income tax or even *ad valorem* indirect taxes; and there has probably been more strife and bloodshed arising from attempts to adjust such specific levies to the changed value of money than on any other fiscal issue. Conflicts have ranged from the Peasants' Revolt of the fourteenth century to the 1977 British parliamentary skirmishes over petrol duty.

But perhaps the most tempting, although ephemeral, benefit from inflating at above the long term revenue-maximizing rate is simply the familiar time lag between the initial monetary

expansion and its ultimate effects. Again, the more frequently
rulers try to take advantage of time lags, the shorter the lags
become. The specific exploitation of time lags in modern full-employment policies will be discussed below when we come to
consider how democracy affects the temptation to inflate.

It will be noticed that many of the self-interested arguments
for governments *not* attempting to obtain the maximum theoretical inflationary revenue, such as the adverse effect on the willingness of people to pay other taxes or to hold the national
currency, are of a long-term nature. The arguments for inflating
at above the ruler's steady-state optimum, such as the exploitation
of time lags or the impoverishment of rentiers, are of a short-term
or once-for-all nature. It follows from this that highly inflationary
policies are characteristically a response to stress, when the
pressures on government are to finance a sudden increase in
expenditure at all costs. The characteristic stress that led sover-
eigns to debase in the past was that of expensive wars.

The Role of Democracy

The discussion so far has implicitly regarded the rulers as a
separate body from the mass of the population, with different
and perhaps conflicting interests. Democracy, however, is supposed to reduce or eliminate this conflict. There are at least
two different ways of looking at democracy. There is the classical
ideal of 'government of the people by the people for the people'.
There is the alternative interpretation, promulgated by Schumpeter (1942), of democracy as a system whereby rulers are chosen
by means of competitive bidding for people's votes. Politicians
attempt to maximize votes just as businessmen attempt to maximize profits. (Elements of the idea can be found as far back
as James Mill.) On this interpretation the machinery for bringing
about an identity of interest between rulers and ruled is akin
to that of the invisible hand in the commercial market place;
and, like the invisible hand, is subject to numerous imperfections
and distortions.

The Schumpeter vote-bidding approach is more realistic for
the purposes of this chapter. Just as the theory of business

competition can be adapted to deal with modified objectives, such as growth subject to a profit constraint, so voting theory can be modified to take in—for instance—ideological objectives subject to a vote constraint.

At first glance, a democratic system ought to be less inflationary than other systems. For it is no longer a question of attempting to extract the last ounce of revenue from an unwilling population by force or trickery. Public expenditure is now supposed to express popular wishes on the amount and composition of that part of their spending which citizens consider can best be carried out collectively; and the tax burden is distributed in a way that has at least majority consent.

Indeed there is no inflation bias in the simpler formal models of the operation of the 'vote motive'. These tend to follow the elementary competitive market models of the textbooks in assuming that information is freely available and that the only object of entrepreneurial activity is to satisfy known wants.[1]

The omission of information and search costs is much more serious in the political than in the commercial market place. Political entrepreneurs are under similar temptations to commercial ones to whip up expectations for their products—indeed more so to the extent that the issue is whether to be in or out of office rather than to affect marginal changes in sales. But, on the buyers' side of the market, the corrective force of direct and clear-cut personal experience is lacking. The route from a voting decision to a change in a citizen's own circumstance is complex and debatable. Indeed he does not have any personal incentive to acquire information about it because of the negligible probability of his own vote determining the outcome—a consideration which had led some American theorists to discover a paradox in why people vote at all. (The fact that they do shows that a narrowly self-interested view of political behaviour is over-simplified. But the smallness of the cost of voting and the way in which even minor inconveniences reduce turnout, suggest that the approach still embodies a useful simplification.) Above all the cost of a political decision is borne by people other than the voter. A customer buying a suit or a washing machine has to bear the cost himself. A vote for a candidate who offers to introduce or extend a particular public service, or to redistribute income in a certain way, or to favour a certain trade, usually assumes that others will bear the cost. This is realistic, as the gains of any particular policy are normally heavily concentrated among a minority while the tax and other costs are more widely spread among the electorate.

The bias of excessive expectation in democracy has a particular form. The benefits of specific programmes are heavily concentrated among minorities, who do have an incentive to keep informed and to organize. On the other hand, the costs are widely distributed among the bulk of the population for whom the loss is unlikely to be a decisive factor in casting their votes. The familiar example is that of a subsidy or tariff which benefits a few producers in large measure, but whose cost to each consumer or taxpayer is small. The minority can be quite a large one, ranging from home buyers to trade union activists; but their incentives to organize and inform themselves are still relatively greater than those of the population at large.

Does this mean that public expenditure will always be excessive because the tax cost of each item is spread thinly over most voters? Not quite. For general programmes which benefit the whole nation rather than specific interest groups will also suffer from the dispersion of interest. It thus seems that pure public goods, whether defence, environmental protection or public health regulation, are likely to be under-provided, whereas help for specific groups will be over-provided. But even this conclusion needs to be qualified. For if the providers of a public service are at all numerous or powerful, they will themselves form a group of concentrated beneficiaries with political power. Such arguments help to explain the military–industrial complex in the United States, and the allegedly excessive number of educational and municipal bureaucrats in Britain. The public is not necessarily over-provided with the final product, whether defence or education; but it is likely to be over-provided with personnel in these fields in the way elaborated by modern theories of bureaucracy such as those of Downs (1967) and Niskanen (1971).

Yet the taxpayer is not as powerless as a case-by-case examination of the political market would suggest. (As in other markets, a partial equilibrium approach can be misleading.) The taxpayer's gains from cutting down in any one item of expenditure may be very modest compared with the impact on the beneficiaries. But if one puts together a large number of programmes, the tax savings assume a large size. Thus attacks on public spending in general will always be more popular than attacks on any particular spending. The periodic economy drives, sometimes but not always associated with electoral change, can be regarded as counter-offensives by those who bear the cost of a combination of programmes. Such attacks will pay best politically, if their progenitors are as vague as possible about where the axe will fall beforehand; and *ex post* if they make across-the-board cuts, together with a few more severe attacks on very small and politically defenceless spending beneficiaries. It will not pay to attract opposition by a selective attack on major programmes such as council housing, even if they are not achieving their stated purposes. It is better to avoid threatening large groups more than necessary by adopting the approach: 'All these programmes are good, but we have to trim all back a little because we can't afford them.'

Inflation and the Vote Motive

It is because expenditure curbs and taxes are both unpopular that the temptation to inflationary finance arises in a democracy. But this temptation could hardly occur without the existence of lags in the inflationary process. If monetary expansion led to the immediate levying of the full inflation tax, it would be no more attractive than straightforward taxes of similar import. The existence of lags also provides scope for controversy about causal relationships, which in turn adds a crucial element of uncertainty.

The inflationary time lag occurs because monetary expansion can give output and employment a short-term boost of a Keynesian kind. If there were never such a boost, there would be an immediate cost to all government spending, whether financed by taxes, borrowing from the public, or monetary expansion; and in the latter case the inflation tax would have to be paid straight away.

If tax rates are difficult to vary in the short run, it might be rational to meet a sudden emergency or temporary bulge in spending through the inflation tax, even if there were no lags in its operation and no electoral myopia. The characteristic examples of such emergencies are major wars, which usually involve some inflation, even on the part of constitutional regimes normally committed to sound money—Britain in the Napoleonic Wars, the United States in the Civil War and most countries participating in World War I are examples.

Of course the short-term boost to output and employment is often the direct object of monetary and fiscal expansion, and not merely a way of financing particular spending projects; and an examination of full-employment policies is thus the best way to the root of the temptations and limitations of inflationary finance in contemporary democracies.

The Political Trade Cycle

A sizeable academic literature now exists on the political trade cycle; one particularly clear formulation is that of Nordhaus (1975). For the mechanism to work, three assumptions have to be made.

(i) It is possible to boost output and employment, at least for a while, by a monetary or fiscal stimulus, but at the cost of a higher eventual rate of inflation.

(ii) There is a lag between the effects of a monetary or fiscal boost on real activity and its inflationary consequences. Thus, in the run-up to an election, it is possible to have the benefits without all the costs of inflationary finance.

(iii) The electorate's memory is subject to fairly rapid decay, so that the incumbents lose less from high unemployment early on in their period of office than they gain from low unemployment nearer polling date. In addition voters have imperfect foresight so that they do not give full weight to the likely post-election consequences of policies.

The classic electoral cycle is then one in which employment and activity are at their peak around the election date. Then soon after the election there is a severe retrenchment with the object of getting the increase in unemployment over as quickly as possible. There would then be a fall in unemployment up to the next election. The exact pattern of the inflation rate (or of currency crises) would depend on the lags; the peak rate would be reached after or in between elections.

Nordhaus finds evidence of an electoral cycle in some, but not all, democratic countries. But the cases where the theory does not fit are as interesting as where it does. The classic examples of Presidents either not stimulating the US economy before elections, or doing so by controversially small amounts, were Eisenhower in 1960 and Ford in 1976. In Britain the main comparable example was Roy Jenkins in 1969–70, which was followed by Labour's surprise loss of the 1970 election.

Butler and Stokes (1974, ch. 18) find that there was a very close relation between unemployment and the government's perceived ability to handle the British economy between the end of World War II and the mid-1960s. In the United States, however, the economic variable that relates most closely to Administration popularity is the growth of real disposable income per capita in the year of the election (cf. Fair, cited in Gordon, 1975). It may be that in Britain in 1958–68, unemployment, which had a strong cyclical movement, happened to be a good index of economic conditions generally— better than any direct index of spending power. But once unemployment experienced a secular shift to a higher rate—it settled on a plateau in 1968–70—the old relationship disintegrated.

In the American case Fair has calculated that strict adherence to a vote-maximizing policy would require a temporary spurt in the growth rate to 20 per cent before each Presidential election—with an enormous recession afterwards. If this policy had been rigorously followed, the electorate would surely have been bound to see through it and it would have long ceased to work. It is only because manipulation is irregular and sparingly used, that the election cycle has lasted as long as it has.

Long-Run Stability

The political trade cycle can do only a limited amount of damage if it leads merely to oscillations in the inflation rate. The important question is whether there is any tendency to an upward drift, or even eventual explosion, over a run of such cycles. The crucial point is the tendency for the trade-off between unemployment and inflation to deteriorate and the Phillips curve to drift upwards. The simple Phillips curve PP′ shown in Chart I assumes that people are fooled by higher money rewards; that in conditions of excess demand they will be fobbed off with a higher rate of money payment. But this cannot last indefinitely. Once workers realize they are being paid in shrunken pounds or dollars in a labour market tight enough for them to obtain real increases, they will insist on still larger wage gains to offset inflation. Thus excess demand leads not merely to inflation but to accelerating inflation (strictly an accelerating price level and increasing inflation). Thus at any level of unemployment below some sustainable level wages and prices will increase indefinitely.

In the long run then there is no trade-off between unemployment and inflation. Demand management cannot reduce unemployment below a sustainable minimum determined by the real forces of the labour market. The only long-run choice is the rate of inflation that will accompany the sustainable unemployment rate. In other words the long-term Phillips curve is a vertical line.

There has been some debate on whether this is so, or whether the long-term Phillips curve is merely steeper than the short-term one. On the other hand there are those who argue that high inflation rates are eventually deleterious to employment. For convenience the long-run Phillips curve is shown on the diagram as a vertical line; but it would merely have to be steeper than the short-term one to give rise to an upward drift of both inflation and unemployment and a loss of political support.[2]

In the chart, the sloping straight line PP′ is a segment of a Phillips curve drawn for a period of zero inflationary expectations and a given mark-up on wage costs. The curved line running through E concave to the origin represents combinations of unemployment and inflation to which voters are indifferent. There is a whole series of such curves; and the ones nearest the origin give the government the greatest popularity, as they provide the most favourable combinations of unemployment and inflation.

At the start of the story the government is on the curve $V = 60$, signifying that it has 60 per cent of total votes (assuming

CHART I *Government Popularity and Deteriorating Inflation/Unemployment*
Trade-off

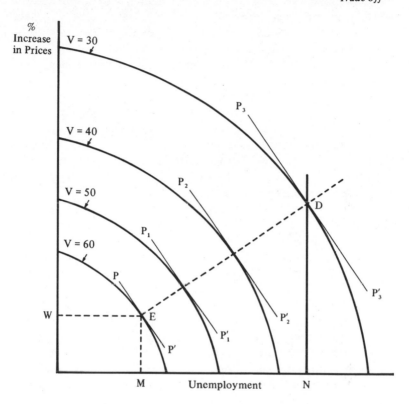

Key:

Curved lines represent combinations of unemployment and inflation to which voters are indifferent, and are labelled according to proportion of votes (V) gained by government.

Straight lines PP′, $P_1 P_1′$, etc. are segments of short-term Phillips curve giving trade-off between unemployment and inflation at successive intervals of time (assuming constant proportional mark-up on wages).

Vertical line from N represents long-run Phillips curve showing no trade-off.

ON represents sustainable rate of unemployment.

ED represents 'election path'.

for simplicity a two-party system). The government moves along the Phillips curve until it has reached the most favourable voters' indifference curve, here shown at E, where unemployment is OM, and inflation is OW. The Goodhart–Bhansali study (1970) suggested that voters' optimum position in the decade from 1958 was at 200–250,000 unemployed (about 1 per cent), then associated with a price inflation of 5 per cent.

But unfortunately this is not a stable long-term position. Over a run of political cycles the short-term Phillips curve will drift upwards. The government will still do its best to get on the most favourable indifference curve; but as it moves towards the right-hand corner along the electoral path ED, unemployment, inflation and its own support will all deteriorate. A long-term equilibrium is possible—if it is possible at all—only where the long-term Phillips curve (here shown by the vertical line up from N) is reached. Then unemployment will be at the sustainable level ON.

Although illustrative only, the chart does bring home that in the best of circumstances, democratic myopia and economic time lags will land the economy with an excessive rate of inflation. Unemployment will end up at ON in any case; but it will be approached along the path ED, which will take the economy to the higher rates of inflation in the top right of the diagram. It would have been possible to have combined the sustainable unemployment rate with low inflation, or even price stability and pleased more voters, if the government had settled for ON in the first place, and concentrated on long-run improvements in the working of the labour market to reduce unemployment, and forgone the temporary benefits of a short-term stimulus.

But this is by no means all. The point of long-run balance is one of much lower voter support for the government than at the beginning of the story—some 30 per cent in the illustration. If this merely leads to an alternation of governments, it may be tolerable. But governments may not be content to be voted out in this way and believe, not necessarily correctly, that they have found policies which will enable them to stimulate the economy without the usual inflationary consequences, i.e. to improve the short-term or long-term trade-off.

But the more serious point is that the combination of inflation rates and unemployment rate in the top right of the diagram may provoke more violent reaction than the mere change of party, and that there could be a breakdown in the whole political and economic system. The democratic doom thesis is that the sustainable rate of unemployment is beyond the limits of political tolerance and will lead to the abandonment of democracy and/or the present type of mixed economy.

If we combine the short-term political cycle with the long-term deterioration of the trade-off between unemployment and inflation, we reach the following account. Each stimulus takes the economy to a fresh inflationary height; and the subsequent check to demand raises the unemployment rate while administering only a limited and temporary check to the inflation rate, which resumes its upward drift once governments have become sufficiently worried about unemployment to restimulate demand. The model can be made more realistic by not insisting that *every* cycle reaches fresh inflationary heights, and instead looking for the upward trend over a succession of several cycles—even that could produce the explosion so vividly foreseen in Peter Jay's writings (e.g. Jay, 1976). All that one needs to generate this model is an employment target above the sustainable level and governmental determination to pursue it by fiscal and monetary expansion. The explosion will occur whether the gap between governmental aims and the sustainable rate is due to union monopoly, as in the Jay version, or to a governmental objective which is too ambitious in relation to other policies. The danger has been vividly described by Goodhart (1975):

If we cannot shift the natural rate of unemployment down to a more acceptable level by a prices-and-incomes policy [sic!] nor make the existing, possibly fixed natural rate of unemployment more acceptable, the economies of the West will remain faced with an internal contradiction which may well serve to destroy the democratic, capitalist structure of their existing system.

The Role of the Unions

There are many other issues to be considered, above all union influence. For all the pulp forests that have been consumed in discussing this question, no one knows how large a role union power has played in generating the dilemmas discussed in the last section. Even among those who accept that monetary expansion is a necessary and sufficient condition for a prolonged major inflation—and the evidence here is overwhelming—there is still every conceivable shade of opinion on the extent to which union behaviour has impelled the monetary authorities to inflationary action.

Flemming has mentioned (this volume) two ways in which unions may raise the sustainable unemployment level. First, changes in the pattern of union power—or in the use made of that power—must be added to changes in taste and technology as influences which bring about frictional unemployment. Secondly unions reduce wage flexibility and thereby throw more of the burden of adjustment to change onto output and employment. Against this must be offset the positive role of unions in reducing transaction costs by bargaining on behalf of their members and disseminating information.

These are all 'micro' effects. Much more controversial is the possibility of most or all unions acting together in a concerted wage push. Strict neo-classical economists are highly suspicious of its likelihood. This is because in their view unions (like all other economic agents) are already exerting their maximum degree of monopoly power ('everyone maximizes'). But there is a great deal to suggest that many unions normally operate with an unused margin of monopoly power. The electricity-generating workers—as we are constantly reminded in the press—are in a position to raise their relative wages by a combination of the strike threat and denial of entry to competitive workers willing to train. Let us assume that the power workers did try to maximize their monopoly wage bill and insisted on £500,000 per head per annum at the expense of somewhat smaller electricity consumption. If the power workers did secure such rises, then other groups would hardly let the position stand. The miners, sewer workers, dustmen and many others would all be able to take action to recover at least some of their relative position; professional groups might surprise people by showing the degree of monopoly power they possess if they chose to use it. There is thus a large conventional element in the balance of the labour market between different unions, which incorporates a mixture of historically determined and free market relativities, together with traditional ideas of status. It is a balance of forces, vulnerable to disturbance, rather than an equilibrium in a narrow market sense.

On this interpretation wage-push would arise if some or all unions, acting either in concert, or in response to common signals, tried to make more use of their monopoly power. This could be represented as an upward shift of the short-term Phillips curves shown on the chart. A great deal depends on whether the underlying aim is an increase in real or money wages. In the former case nothing will prevent workers being priced out of jobs and thus bringing about an increase in the sustainable unemployment rate, irrespective of whether monetary policy is very rigid or highly accommodating. If the union aim, on the other hand, is simply an increase in money wages, a monetary injection would maintain employment at the previously sustainable rate at the expense of a higher price level.

To admit the possibility of union wage-push does not mean that one should throw in the towel and abandon any economic explanation. A sudden shock to previously existing real income expectations, such as the fivefold oil price increase of 1973–4, can trigger off such wage-push. An increase in money wages is, as Flemming points out, a funny objective. But in the uncertainty which follows such events unions may put in large money wage claims to insure against adverse price movements without being too specific about their real wage objectives. Unrealistic real income aims on an economy-wide scale are likely to be transitional, as eventually some learning will occur. Moreover this learning is easier when a once-for-all contraction of real incomes is in the past and growth is once more possible, and it is simply a matter of not catching up with lost time. If the check to world growth since 1973 proves, however, more fundamental than the loss of a few years increased output— whether because of physical resource constraints or the increasing role of positional goods (cf. Hirsch, 1977a)—then the learning process could take a great deal longer, and both wage-push and electoral pressures on governments will be that much more intensive. My own suspicion is that the more fundamental limits to growth will make themselves felt gradually and that world output will continue to grow over the next few cycles even if at a reduced rate.

The increase in world inflation rates began in the late 1960s, well before the oil price explosion. The difficulty with a wage-push explanation is that no one has explained why there should have been an internationally synchronized increase in the use of union monopoly power during the period. An alternative explanation is available in terms of the inflationary turn taken in the US policies—partly due to deficit finance for the Vietnam war—and the currency link of other countries with the dollar.

The most important macro effect of union power may be one not so far mentioned explicitly. It may slow down the reaction of wages to a reduction in the growth of monetary demand. (In other words it will flatten the slope of the short-term Phillips curve to the right of the point of balance, the curve then becoming kinked.) This means that the transitional increase in unemployment involved in any attempt to reduce the inflation rate will be higher. Thus inflation will tend to be a one-way street. Any shock or policy error will tend to increase the rate, which will not fall back to its old level before the next shock.

Democracy comes in as an inhibition on methods which might otherwise be attempted for curbing the power of unions to force the authorities to finance inflation—on pain of pricing workers out of jobs. Just as democracy whips up expectations, it reduces the means available for fulfilling these expectations. There is first the difficulty of persuading the electorate that the normal processes of collective bargaining backed by the strike threat can be inimical both to the general standard of living and to the stability of the social system. An even greater inhibition is that of enforcing by tolerable methods legislation designed to curb coercive union practices which are used to prevent undercutting ('blacklegging'). One should not underrate changes in sentiment that come with time; but trade unionists' instincts of fraternity have up to now been too strong to be overcome by peaceful methods of law enforcement.

It is a delusion to suppose that incomes policy offers a way of coping with union market power by means of consent. This is a question which I have discussed at length elsewhere (Brittan and Lilley, 1977). Briefly, an incomes policy will always founder on the rock of relativities and differentials; and there is no such thing as a fair or scientific assessment of relativities. An *a priori* case can be made for a short-term emergency freeze or ceiling as a shock to expectations; but in practice such shock tactics have been accompanied by such other measures, and presented in such misleading ways, that they have done more harm than good to both inflation and employment.

The End of the Gold Standard

There is even now, however, a missing element. Democratic pressures for government spending and full employment policies, even combined with union factors, could not have brought the recent rise in inflation rates without a parallel erosion of institutional monetary constraints. With fixed rules of budget balancing, and gold-standard restrictions on the creation of money, an attempt to satisfy too many competing demands would lead to high government spending and correspondingly high taxation. The budget might balance at too high a level; but the size of the tax burden would provide a built-in constraint against indefinite expansion.

The necessary condition for the political overload on democracy to take inflationary form was, as Brunner (1975) has emphasized, the disappearance of the gold-standard rules. The disappearance was gradual. The first element to disappear was the convertibility of the privately-held domestic currency into gold in the 1920s. This loosened the link between the domestic money supply and the gold stock. The next stage, which also had its roots in the 1920s, but did not become *de jure* until Bretton Woods, was the transformation of the gold into a dollar standard. Most countries used dollars to settle imbalances in official transactions. Domestic monetary policies were limited by the need to maintain dollar convertibility; and only the United States was required to supply gold to other national monetary institutions. A further looseness was the adjustable peg mechanism, which enabled other countries to follow monetary policies partially independent of the United States. The constraints on the United States weakened once it became clear that gold convertibility was available only on the understanding that the option was not widely exercised; but the United States was not finally free to determine its own monetary policy until the formal end of gold convertibility in 1971; and it was not until early 1973 that most of the world went onto a floating system which removed even the temporary constraint of the adjustable peg and the link with the US inflation rate. Each of the successive steps appeared logical on its own merits; but the end result has placed the entire burden of checking inflation on the democratic self-restraint on which Schumpeter laid so much emphasis.

The sheer physical limitations of the gold supply in relation to world economic activity might in any case have made it difficult to maintain the pre-1914 form of the gold standard. The inverted pyramid of paper money, bank deposits and credit instruments standing on the base might have been extended further. The low physical cost of paper money and bank deposits, compared to mining gold, would have provided an incentive for such extension. But the paper and credit element could not be stretched excessively without making the gold base increasingly fictional and also making the system highly crisis-prone, as the interwar years showed. An alternative line of argument is that the system could have been made to work through periodic changes in the dollar price of gold. But quite apart from all the problems of whether other countries would have found the dollar link attractive in such circumstances, a politically set gold price has none of the automatic qualities of the orthodox gold standard: a system revised on these lines would have just been a series of discretionary dollar devaluations—a series of step debasements in place of the continuous ones which take place today.

The speculative reasoning of the age also contributed to the erosion of the role of gold. Whether the object of monetary policy is a stable price level or (as in the later writings of Keynes) to facilitate employment, it seemed absurd to tie the quantity of money in a loose and unpredictable way to the physical supply of a particular metal. It was surely more rational to have a paper money the quantity of which could be controlled by governments in the light of requirements; and differences between national objectives could be reconciled by floating exchange rates.

Such arguments were—and remain—valid in their own terms. The trouble was that they presupposed that governments were

Benthamite dictatorships rigorously devoted to some economist's conception of the public interest, rather than flesh-and-blood human beings subject to the push and pull of a highly imperfect political market place. But there is unlikely to be a solution through returning to some version of the gold standard. For myths have social value only when people do not realize they are myths. Once it is realized that the money does not depend on its gold backing for value, but only on its acceptability and quantity—and that the gold base is merely a device for limiting that quantity—then it is difficult to see governments again accepting gold convertibility at a fixed rate as an overriding aim for which real short-term sacrifices have to be made.

Unbalanced Budgets

The undermining of the gold standard went hand in hand with the overthrow of another moralistic constraint on monetary expansion—the balanced budget doctrine. Here again the traditional form of the doctrine had little logical basis. A Gladstonian budget covered mostly current government spending or non-revenue earning infrastructure investment, and it was a comparatively simple matter to say whether the budget was balanced or not. With the vast increase on the capital expenditure and lending side, the growth of expenditure by public bodies outside central government, and the complications of interest payments in an inflationary period, there are dozens of different balances which could now be used; and even if all agreed on a definition, it would still be far from obvious that the optimal size is zero. Again the balanced budget was but a myth or convention which provided a rough and ready built-in safeguard against monetary over-expansion.

The new philosophy which replaced the old restraints was that of demand management labelled (justifiably or not) 'Keynesian economics'. The doctrine, stated in its full rigour, holds that neither the money supply nor the budget balance is an independent objective of policy, but both are instruments for achieving a target pressure of real demand (measured by the ratio of actual output to assumed capacity output), itself geared to a specific employment objective. The demand management doctrine reigned for so long, partly because of the intellectual atrophy of the defenders of the old orthodoxy. So long as the main danger was seen as one of inflation (normally assumed to be within the 2 to 7 per cent 'creeping' range) rather than accelerating inflation, it was possible for the demand managers to say that some inflation was a price worth paying for full employment; and the argument was further confused by the poorness of fit in many countries of the old Phillips curve and its tendency to shift its position. There was also the vain hope that incomes policies would enable high demand targets to be set without inflationary consequences.

But it would be wrong to exaggerate doctrinal influences. Countries were not able to pursue full employment policies *à outrance* so long as there was some inhibition against large or frequent devaluation against the dollar. Paradoxically, monetary growth seems to have been more restricted in the 1950s and early 1960s by apparently irrational balance-of-payments fetishes than in the subsequent period when monetarism has been more fashionable. In the United States, the demand management philosophy never took full hold until the Kennedy–Johnson Administration of the 1960s; and no one knows what effect the ideological change would have had without the Vietnam War and the temptation to try to finance it without raising its full cost in taxes. Outside Britain and Northern Europe the Keynesian approach to deficits and monetary policy never really caught on; but Keynesian forecasting methods did; and these—together with the toleration of international bodies—enabled governments to live with their bad conscience when running deficits, France being a frequent case in point.

The Full Employment Era

The analysis so far still has important gaps. It does not explain why so many countries were able to maintain successful employment policies for up to twenty or thirty years after World War II, while also keeping the rate of inflation down to a creeping level. The tendency to explosive inflation began only with the late 1960s.

There is no shortage of explanations after the event, but we still do not know which are correct. There are any number of hypotheses about why the sustainable rate of unemployment should have risen. One of the most popular is the sharp increase in the ratio of unemployment benefit to average earnings in many countries, especially when tax, travel and benefits in kind are taken into account. Another explanation is in terms of structural changes, such as a decline in relative demand for unskilled labour at conventional wage ratios, or the disturbances to the pattern of industrial demand following the oil price explosion. Other hypotheses are in terms of government controls, which hold down the rate of return on capital; but such controls have in almost all cases been a response to an acceleration in inflation, which has already occurred for some other reason A different category of explanation is in terms of money illusion persisting for several decades at steady and moderate rates of inflation, which meant that trade unions and probably other groups settled for lower real rewards than they could have obtained in the prevailing state of demand; but once the increased inflation rates of the later 1960s had shattered the earlier expectations, money illusion was punctured very quickly and will not now be easy to recreate.

Changes in Prospect?

Does the above analysis, based on a combination of the imperfections of the political process and economic time lags, lead inexorably to ever higher inflation rates? Some caution is in order, if only because predictions based on extrapolations of the immediately previous decade have so often proved erroneous. The key to the doomsday machine is that Keynesian stimulation does increase output and employment in the short run, but only prices in the longer run. The process has been analysed by academic monetarists in their accounts of the 'expectations-augmented Phillips curve' (cf. Friedman, 1977a).

But it is a common experience in analysing economic change that no sooner has a particular relationship been established by analysis of past data and no sooner has it come into use among economists, then it breaks down—an example of the familiar interrelation between the observer and the observed. In short, once a monetarist diagnosis is publicly accepted in however crude and bowdlerized form, monetary expansion ceases to provide even a temporary stimulus to activity. This would be an inference from the theory of rational expectations; but it can be seen in all sorts of specific ways. An announcement of a series of high monthly monetary aggregates soon leads to a fall in government bond prices and thus to a rise in interest rates. This discourages investment both directly and via its effects on confidence; while any increase in inflationary expectations among wage bargainers soon leads to more inflation and less growth for any particular monetary stance.

While academic debate has been proceeding about whether there is no long-run trade-off between employment and price stability, or merely an uncomfortably steep one, actual events have overtaken the arguments; and high inflation has brought lower employment—either because of greater uncertainty, the difficulties of coping with high nominal interest rates and fluctuating asset values, or through government attempts to suppress the inflationary symptoms. Some of these perverse effects could prove as transitional as the employment-creating effects proved to be; but at least the route to high employment through taking risks with inflation can be seen to be well and truly closed.

Above all there is the fact that in any open economy the main immediate impact of monetary expansion is on the exchange rate. The effect has become much more rapid than it used to be, both because the temporary prop of the exchange rate peg has been removed and because monetary expansion itself leads to expectations of depreciation which defeat most efforts by the authorities to hold up the rate. An exchange depreciation is not only a force for inflation, but may also have a *contractionary* effect on real activity. A depreciation raises the domestic price level—directly and quickly for imports, through competitive forces for internationally-traded goods, and gradually through shifts in activity in the case of non-traded goods. As a result the real value of a given money supply falls, an effect which was obscured in the days of the (very occasionally) adjustable peg and accommodating monetary policy. The adverse effects are directly visible via real disposable income, interest rates, consumer confidence, asset values and many other channels. These may well outweigh any temporary boost from export profits, a stimulus which industrialists tend increasingly to write off in advance.

A similar process of disillusion with inflationary finance may be occurring on the union side. Much recent inflation can best be understood as an attempt to persuade powerful groups that they have won more than they really have, while disguising their real losses from others by means of a general depreciation of the monetary unit. Once this process is seen through, bargaining may be expected to be increasingly in real terms. This could aggravate inflation if there were large money wage settlements combined with the wrong sort of indexation clauses, such as the Italian *scala mobile*, and monetary policy financed the result. But there is at least a chance that unions will cease to demand or even welcome such monetary policies, and the struggle will become an open one about real shares and the distribution of unemployment resulting from given real claims. The relative mildness of British TUC calls for 'reflation' in the deepest of postwar recessions may be a pointer towards things to come.

It would be wrong to exaggerate. Western economic leaders have not so much lost their faith in monetary stimulation, as in its domestic variety. Demand expansion brought about via exports and world trade (or in some eyes through protection) is regarded as being much less dangerous—exactly why would make an interesting digression. The upshot is that governments are calling upon each other to expand demand, while being reluctant to do so themselves; but one must never rule out the perverse possibilities of international co-operation.

A look at the record may help. There has basically been one change of gear—from the prewar assumption of stable prices (with deviations in a deflationary direction) to the postwar expectations of upward creep. International evidence for inflationary acceleration is confined to two cycles, 1966–71 and 1971–5. This has been insufficient to establish a secure secular trend towards accelerating inflation. The Vietnam war and the magnification and concentration in a short time span by OPEC of the inevitable oil price increases, aggravated these two cycles.

There may not be comparable bad luck next time; and there is more caution about monetary policies on the world scene—despite the desire for mutual stimulation—than when President Nixon proclaimed he was a Keynesian and when there was a general consensus about a supposed shortage not merely of conditional liquidity but of international reserves.

A return to price stability or the postwar rate of creeping inflation is not being predicted. Nor is it being asserted that inflation will be below the 1965–75 average in future cycles. The rigidities of the established methods of wage and price determination may well remain; and there could still be a tendency for outside shocks to give upward boosts to the inflation rate, not easily reversed.

The residual effect of the full employment commitment may thus be to underwrite part at least of the levels of inflationary expectations brought about by such shocks. But this is not quite the same as the remorseless doomsday machine produced by the pursuit of unattainable full employment goals heedless of the monetary cost. It was on the basis of such a diagnosis that Professor Michael Parkin—almost the only writer in this area to contribute to knowledge by making a falsifiable prediction—asserted at the beginning of 1975 that world governments and central banks would react to the developing recession by pressing monetary and fiscal accelerators 'as hard as possible'. As a result 1976 was going to be a year 'of rapid real growth and falling unemployment', and 1977 'a year with inflation rates into the 20s and 30s rather than the mere teens' (Parkin, 1975).

Tensions Still Present

Although the threat of runaway inflation may recede, this does not mean that economic dangers to democracy would then be over. On the contrary, the tensions which gave rise to inflation could show themselves in other, and perhaps more dangerous forms. The disappearance of inflation as a temporary solvent would bring certain tensions into the open. The rivalry of coercive producer groups with incompatible real demands on the national product could appear more serious once they came out into the open and were no longer disguised as a mere wage–price spiral. Crouch (this volume) has stressed the role of inflation in enabling governments to postpone a resolution of interest group rivalries. The period when it was possible to drown relativity changes or the lack of them by a general rise in the price level might therefore come to appear the hallmark if not of a golden at least of a silver age. Similarly, the disappearance of 'reflation' and rapid 'growth' will make it more difficult for governments to appear to reconcile conflicting promises to different groups, and will thus bring to the surface the problem of excessive expectations.

The real problems of liberal democracy are not in the end about inflation. The spread of market relations itself tends, in ways explained by Goldthorpe (this volume) to undermine the status structure which provides capitalism with its legitimacy in the eyes of most people. One particularly serious problem arises from the contemporary belief that no constraints should stand in the way of an elected government, a belief sometimes given a traditionalist coat in Britain by expressions such as the 'sovereignty of Parliament' or 'the Queen in Parliament'. Another acute conflict, discussed by Dicey at the beginning of the twentieth century, is between the individual and the collective pursuit of self-interest. The two may not be compatible and the second may be explosive.

Whether these hypotheses are right or not, by disguising our problems as the semi-technical conundrum of inflation, we may be making them seem more tractable than they really are. Inflation may even have been a benign form of self-deception, a means of buying time. But we have come to the end of this period of grace.

NOTES

1. Introductions to the economic theory of democracy can be found in Barry (1970) and Tullock (1976). Most of the contributions to the subject are mentioned in Breton (1974).
2. There is now an immense literature on short- and long-term Phillips curves, the sustainable (or 'natural') rate of unemployment *et al*. The state of the debate is summarized in Friedman (1977a) which contains many key references. An approach by the present writer can be found in Brittan (1975a).

CHAPTER 8

The Current Inflation: Towards a Sociological Account[*]

John H. Goldthorpe

I

In seeking to contribute to the understanding of inflation the first problem that the sociologist must face is that of how exactly to effect his *entrée* into a field of enquiry which economists have taken as their own, and in which analyses in terms of the reigning paradigms of economic science are dominant. The approach to this problem which I shall follow derives from the argument that the limits of an analytical system are best indicated by the occurrence of 'residual categories': that is, categories which are introduced to deal with phenomena recognized as relevant to the enquiry in hand (the phenomena may indeed be more or less adequately described), but categories which are at the same time distinguished by their lack of theoretical fit with those that are central to the analytical system in use and 'positively defined' within it (Parsons, 1937). My strategy in this paper will therefore be to identify such residual categories in analyses of inflation currently offered by economists, and then to treat the phenomena which they comprise in a different perspective, reflecting certain analytical concerns of what I take to be the mainstream sociological tradition.

A further problem, arising from this strategy itself, might be that of how to decide on the particular economic analyses that are to serve as the point of departure—given that economists

[*] I am indebted for helpful comments on an earlier draft of this paper to most fellow contributors to the present volume, in particular to Fred Hirsch, Miča Panić and Alan Peacock; and also to Tony Courakis, Marcus Miller and Michael Posner.

are manifestly not at one in their views on the nature and causes of inflation. However, my sampling of the relevant literature encourages me to believe that this difficulty is more apparent than real. For while economists adhering to different theories of inflation tend to resort to residual categories at different places in their analyses—that is, they disagree (usually implicitly) about where in the explanation of inflation it is most needful to introduce such categories—they tend not to use residual categories to bring into the analysis *different sets of phenomena* in regard to the *same* substantive issue. Thus, I shall not have to face the complication of there being, so to speak, alternative ways of crossing the same analytical boundary. Moreover, at whatever juncture they are introduced, the phenomena covered by residual categories turn out to be of a basically similar kind: namely, modes of social action which cannot, in terms of the economist's analysis, be accounted for as rational, and which have therefore either to be seen as the results of error or ignorance, or to be labelled more substantively with one or other of the large array of emotionally-coloured terms which economists use in effect as synonyms for 'irrational' or at least 'non-rational'. It seems to me possible to cover the major instances of resort to residual categories—and to bring out their underlying similarities—by examining the views taken by economists of the part played in the inflationary process by (i) government; (ii) organized interests, in particular trade unions; and (iii) income receivers, in particular wage- and salary-earners.

(i) The agency of government in the inflationary process is most stressed by those economists who adhere to 'monetarist' theories: that is, who regard the fundamental cause of inflation as being excessive monetary expansion. Since the power to determine the money supply lies chiefly with government, then so too, it is argued, must the ultimate responsibility for the inflation that results when the money supply grows too rapidly (Friedman, 1956, 1960; Hayek, 1958, 1960; Johnson, 1972). Paradoxically, though, most monetarists would clearly prefer to regard governmental action (or inaction) as exogenous to their analyses: the intellectual tasks they take as central are those of tracing out the historical association between inflation and the expansion of the money supply, treated as a 'given', or of demolishing rival, 'cost-push' theories of inflation. However, having given government so crucial a role in their own account, they cannot in the end avoid the question—and their critics press it on them—of *why* governments act in the way they do. For even if excessive monetary expansion is accepted as being both necessary and sufficient to occasion a rise in the general price level, it can at the same time be regarded as no more than a (very) *proximate* cause of inflation: explanations are still required of why it is that such monetary expansion occurs.

The responses that monetarists offer here are of two main kinds. One, most favoured by 'hard-liners', is to preserve an essentially normative stance. From the monetarist theory of inflation, it is held, it is evident enough what, in general terms, a government must do in order to bring about greater price stability: that is, control the growth of the money supply more tightly, so as to keep it in a closer relationship with the growth of output. If, then, a government wishing to reduce inflation does not follow such a policy, it is, quite simply, either in error—its members, or those who advise them, are 'bad' economists; or it is acting irrationally (it is 'inconsistent', 'woolly-minded', 'ostrich-like', etc.) in not taking the effective—viz. scientifically accredited—means of achieving its end (cf. IEA, 1974; Laidler, 1975; Friedman, 1977a).

This response is intellectually safe, but at the same time intellectually feeble, in that it implies declining an explanatory challenge which would lead across the conventional boundaries of economic analysis. It is evidently seen as a danger that once a monetarist approach ceases to be normative *vis-à-vis* government, then—no less than a cost-push theory of inflation—it opens up issues which have not been the traditional concern of the economist but rather of the sociologist or political scientist. The second response, which has chiefly attracted 'soft-line' monetarists, also implies recognition of this point but is, in contrast, one of intellectual imperialism rather than autarky. In this case, the endeavour is to account for governmental action by extending the field of economic analysis: the problem of governmental policy in regard to inflation is defined in 'market' terms—i.e. in terms of the 'political market'—and a solution is sought in the analysis of political–market forces.

For example, in one of the most sophisticated essays in this direction, Gordon explicitly rejects the view that accelerations in money supply and prices are thrust upon society by the 'capricious folly' of governments; rather, they should be seen as 'the vote-maximizing response of government to the political pressures exerted by potential beneficiaries of inflation' (Gordon, 1975, p. 808). Gordon's main concern is in fact to investigate the determinants of the 'demand for' and 'supply of' inflation in terms of interest-group pressures for policies which imply raising the rate of money creation, and of the electoral considerations which may lead governments to accommodate these pressures.

This approach represents an undoubted advance on that of hard-line monetarists as regards both realism and intellectual interest. But it is important to note that it still cannot itself avoid terminating, explicitly or implicitly, either with the adoption of a normative position—governmental attempts to 'manage' myopic voters are themselves short-sighted and not in fact rational in the face of economic realities which will eventually confound all such political manipulation and compromise; or with the recognition that, when the determinants of the demand for and supply of inflation become themselves *explananda*, then the limits of even the extended version of economic analysis are reached, and recourse to residual categories of a 'sociological' character is required. For example, in seeking to account for cross-national variations in the rate of inflation, Gordon is led to invoke such factors as differences in the 'ideological orientations' of labour movements or in the time-horizons of the members of lower social classes.[1]

(ii) Just as the role of government is crucial in monetarist accounts of inflation, so is that of trade unions in cost-push theories. The key defining characteristic of such theories is the proposition that the state of the money supply is 'permissive or conducive, but not causal' in regard to rises in the general price level, and that causal primacy lies with recurrent and 'leapfrogging' demands for higher pay from organized labour (Phelps-Brown, 1975). However, as indicated in the previous section, some economists of a basically monetarist persuasion would also accord a measure of importance to trade unions in the inflationary process, that is, as sources of political pressure on governments to undertake excessive monetary expansion. In particular, monetarists of a Hayekian rather than a Friedmanite cast stress the ability of unions to force up the general level of wages faster than productivity increases, and then to induce governments (especially ones committed to 'full employment' policies) to expand the money supply in order to prevent the unemployment which the excessive wage increases would otherwise have caused (Hayek, 1958; Haberler, 1966).

Why, then, according to the economists, do trade unions act in the ways in question? Again, one finds that one form of explanation that is offered, and again chiefly by monetarists, is in terms of error and ignorance. Unions, it is held, simply fail to appreciate the adverse consequences—and ultimately for their own members as well as for the rest of the community—that their actions will have. In particular, it is argued by monetarists that union leaders, under the influence of 'bad' economics, have a quite mistaken understanding of the effect that monetary policy can exert on the level of employment: they do not see that there is in fact no lasting trade-off to be had between inflation and unemployment—that, in the long term, the 'natural' rate of unemployment in a given economy is bound to re-emerge, whatever the rate of monetary expansion, and hence that the only real choice for them is whether they will have this rate with inflation or without (Haberler, 1972; Brittan, 1975a; Brittan and Lilley, 1977, ch. 2).

While the monetarist tendency is thus always to imply that the solution to the problem of inflation lies essentially in the acceptance of 'good' economics by all concerned, cost-push theorists see matters as being considerably more difficult, and incline towards more complex, socio-political solutions or alternatively, it would seem, to despair. For, typically in their perspective, trade union action is not adequately accounted for through the categories of error and ignorance (though cf. Kahn, 1976) but must be seen rather as reflecting new forces at work within advanced nations—forces which can be accommodated neither socially, by existing institutional arrangements, nor intellectually, by the existing paradigms of economic enquiry. It is, then, in the case of these theorists that one has in its clearest form a resort to more substantive residual categories, in order to treat modes of action which economists' notions of rationality cannot apprehend.[2]

For example, Wiles (1973, p. 392) has argued that to seek a purely 'economic' model capable of predicting the general price level is now mistaken in principle, since this level will depend 'on what numbers the trade union leaders pick out of the air when they make wage claims.' The settlement of these claims—which are often economically 'absurd'—may have some relation to objective supply and demand, but only an extremely loose one; and a model could thus only be made determinate by including in it a 'non-economic' parameter relating to the subjective state of mind, or 'mood', of union leaders. Again, the 'leapfrogging' of wage claims and settlements, which is a process crucial to cost-push accounts of inflation, must be explained, according to Wiles, not on any rational basis but in terms of inter-union rivalry or 'jealousy'; or, according to Mishan (1974), in terms of a 'hypersensitivity' on the part of unions to pay differentials between occupational groups. Further still, cost-push theorists see it as part of the *Zeitgeist* that union leaders, rather than being in error in calculating the long-term consequences of their actions, are in fact little concerned with such calculations. Although union leaders may not actually belong to the New Left, Wiles contends, its influence still bears upon them:

> 'Do it', 'We Want It All Now', the cult of symbolic and temporary but forceful action etc., etc.—the New Left's antinomianism, irrationalism and total disregard for social consequences have been transferred from the academic/cultural sphere to collective bargaining. [1973, p. 378]

Similarly, Mishan argues that appeals for 'responsible' unionism have now lost all their force in an era which has seen a steady decline 'of patriotic sentiment, of civic pride, of *civitas*'. In his view, however, a more pernicious influence than the New Left is the youth and 'pop' culture,

> sporting a permissive 'own thing' ethic that is antithetic to traditional values and, more generally, to social order ... with passions reserved only for group or gang loyalties, for 'them' and 'us', for sporadic movements and ephemeral causes and cults. [1974, p. 24]

Finally, there is, of course, the category of 'ideology'—although it must be acknowledged that this is rather less used by academic exponents of cost-push theories than by their supporters in the media and politics. Union leaders, it is claimed, fail to act rationally because their actions are oriented to ideas of 'fairness' or 'justice' without serious regard for what their actual outcomes might be. And further, leaders and activists may in some cases embrace ideologies which they believe can only be realized once the existing economic and social order is destroyed; thus, for them, union policies which offer immediate gains, while threatening to lead in the long term to disruption and crisis, will not be unattractive.

(iii) In the main, monetarists do not regard the actions of rank-and-file wage- and salary-earners as contributing importantly to inflation: in pressing for pay increases or in seeking to preserve their security of employment, workers may help to maintain, or even step up, the impetus of the inflationary process; but, in so doing, they must be seen as essentially *reacting to* inflation rather than creating it. In contrast with their readiness to invoke error and ignorance in accounting for the actions of governments (and, in some cases, of union leaders), monetarists are indeed remarkably concerned to represent the population at large as behaving with great rationality in the face of inflation. Money bargains are in general made in terms which reflect the parties' expectations as to their real value; thus, under conditions of steady inflation, with the 'money illusion' dispelled, expectations (of prices, wages etc.) will be more or less accurately adjusted to the rate at which inflation is going on (cf. Laidler, 1975; Flemming, 1976).

Cost-push theorists are, however, obliged to take a different view. Although they tend to see union leaderships as having some degree of autonomy, they would typically wish to argue that in their militancy, their concern over differentials, and even their 'irresponsibility' (if not, perhaps, in their ideology), union leaders respond to the attitudes and demands—and sometimes to the 'direct actions'—of rank-and-file workers. For cost-push theorists, then, pay expectations are not simply being adjusted to inflation, so as to overcome the money illusion:

they are also being expanded in real terms, and further are becoming increasingly 'intransitive' as between different occupational groups. There is in train a 'revolution of rising expectations' which applies to pay increases, pay relativities and continuity of employment alike (Marris, 1972; Wiles, 1973; Mishan, 1974, 1976; Phelps-Brown, 1975; Panić, 1976, and this volume).

A partial explanation of this revolution which seems quite widely adhered to is that it represents the extension to the mass of the work-force of the 'spirit of discontent and acquisition' which formerly was the distinctive characteristic of the bourgeoisie and of the professional and managerial classes—and which, as such, was a key source of economic progress. However, as Mishan puts it, 'once this spirit takes possession of the masses, a socially beneficient outcome is no longer assured' (1974, p. 17). For the masses pursue material betterment through collective rather than individual means, and indeed seek to do so, encouraged by the experience of the postwar decades, on the basis of an effective guarantee of economic and social security provided by the state. Furthermore, the new acquisitiveness is expressed not only, or even primarily, in endeavours that serve to increase wealth overall, but is associated with a marked awareness of distributional issues, and a readiness to challenge the prevailing pattern of income inequalities.

At this point, consensus among cost-push theorists tends to break down, and they diverge, at least in the terminology of their accounts, according to their particular socio-political philosophies or prejudices. For example, distributional dissent is seen as the result of a pervasive envy and 'passion for equality' (Mishan, 1976, p. 7); or of discontent and resentment stemming from an 'aspirations gap' between actual and hoped-for living standards (Panić, 1976, pp. 3–6); or of 'frustration' and 'anger' created by a 'new consciousness' of the unacceptability of existing differences in incomes and life-chances generally (Marris, 1972, pp. 305–6). However, what is common to almost all these accounts, and for present purposes of main importance, is their resort to a residual 'psychologism'. That is, in the shift in analysis that is entailed from what have been termed 'in-order-to' motives to 'because' motives (Schütz, 1967); or, in other words, from the assumption of rational actors whose motives are capable of being discussed in terms of the conditions, means and ends of action to the assumption of actors whose motives can rather be understood only in terms of impelling emotions.[3]

II

Having identified what are, I believe, the major points in economists' theories of inflation at which residual categories are introduced, I wish now to reconsider various of the phenomena thus treated from a sociological standpoint. It would be tempting to say that in so doing my aim is to complement economists' accounts by making central to my concerns what is only peripheral to theirs. But in fact economists' and sociologists' approaches to the explanation of inflation seem almost inevitably to be as much competitive as complementary, and there is, I believe, a basic reason why this is so.

There are, and have been historically, clear differences between economists and sociologists in their evaluations of the capitalist market economy. Economists tend to see this as having an inherent propensity towards stability or, at least, as capable of being stabilized through skilled management on the basis of the expertise that they can themselves provide. Sociologists, on the other hand, tend to view the market economy as being inherently unstable or, rather, to be more precise, as exerting a constant destabilizing effect on the society within which it operates, so that it can itself continue to function satisfactorily only to the extent that this effect is offset by exogenous factors: most importantly, by the integrative influence of some basic value consensus in the society, deriving from sources unrelated to the economy; or by some measure of 'imperative co-ordination' imposed by government (or other agencies) with the ultimate backing of force.[4]

Thus, for monetarists, certainly, it makes no sense to regard inflation—or 'stagflation'—as being in any way the 'fault' of the market economy: it is, in their view, only external interference or distortion, such as may stem from unsound monetary policy or from the 'monopoly power' of the unions, that can bring about such disequilibrium. And while in the case of cost-push theorists, inflation may be seen as resulting to some extent from developments which are associated with the functioning of the economy, what is chiefly stressed is the connection between the 'revolution of rising expectations' and the experience over recent decades of continuous economic growth. In other words, inflation is linked with the actual achievement of the economy—with, indeed, its 'success'—rather than with its form.[5]

For the sociologist, however, the natural tendency is to look for quite specific connections between inflation, as experienced in capitalist societies, and the market economy; and in fact to regard inflation as being the particular manifestation, within a given historical context, of the social divisions and conflicts which such an economy tends always to generate. To be sure, a number of economists of varying stripe have at one time or another shown themselves willing to view inflation as a process which results when demands on the economy exceed its capacity, as different groups struggle to increase their share of the national income (cf. Aujac, 1950; Turvey, 1951; Zawadzki, 1965; Jackson, Turner and Wilkinson, 1972); and for cost-push theorists, the idea of distributional dissent must take on a particular importance. But the ambition of any sociological enquiry must be to go further here. It must be to investigate how inflation, understood as the monetary expression of distributional conflict, is ultimately grounded not in error, ignorance or unreason on the part of the actors involved, in the way that economic analyses are constrained to suggest, but rather in *on-going changes in social structures and processes*. And moreover, once such changes are established as analytically basic, the goal and potential of sociological analysis should then be to show how the actions of rank-and-file employees, union leaders, governments etc. are, if not rational in the economist's sense, still *intelligible*: that is to say, express a logic which is adequate from the actor's point of view, in the situation in which he finds himself, and which at the same time is apprehensible by the 'outside' observer.[6]

The argument that I would myself wish to develop, as a basis for sociological enquiry, is the following: that, so far as the advanced capitalist societies of the West are concerned, the current inflation is grounded in changes in the form of their stratification—in other words, in their structures of social advantage and power; and that these changes in turn stem from the changing interplay between the market economy as a stratifying force, that is, as a determinant of the distribution of advantage and of relations of super- and subordination, and *other* stratifying forces which are also at work in these societies. More specifically, I would maintain that over recent decades the generally rising rate of inflation reflects a situation in which conflict between social groups and strata has become *more intense* and also to some extent *more equally matched*, with these two tendencies interacting in a mutually reinforcing way. Less advantaged groups and strata have tended to become more free of various constraints on their actions in pursuit of what they see as their interests; hence, they have become more likely to 'punch their weight'—to press their claims closer to the limits of the power they actually possess; and in turn then, they have become more effective in their conflicts with other parties, gaining in this way not only immediate advantages but also a stronger position from which to fight for further claims. As a structure of relative advantage and power, the form of stratification which at any one time prevails in a society is likely to be highly resistant to change in the direction of greater equality; it will possess certain self-maintaining properties. But if, through external pressures or, perhaps, internal contradictions, such a change *is* brought about, then the nature of a stratification 'system' also gives rise to the likelihood of there being, so to speak, a burst of 'positive feedback', amplifying the change that has occurred—and, of course, threatening ultimately to disrupt the system, unless either its self-maintaining properties reassert themselves or external influences of a countervailing kind come into play.

In the case of present-day Britain, one can, I believe, identify three interrelated processes of change which together imply the emergence of a situation of the kind in question, and thus, concomitantly, a heightening of social conflict, of which inflation may be regarded as one expression. These I would label (i) the decay of the status order; (ii) the realization of citizenship; and (iii) the emergence of a 'mature' working class.

III

In what follows, my aim is to spell out as fully as space allows how I understand these changes, how I see the connection between them and the current inflation in Britain, and how the terms of my account differ from those characteristic of economists' accounts. I do not, it should be clear, make any claim to provide an adequate empirical test of my argument. Such a test could in fact be appropriately undertaken only on the basis of systematic *comparative* research. However, in an attempt at illustrating the possibilities of such research, the British case may be of more than merely parochial interest. The suggestion I would venture is that secular changes in the form of stratification evident in British society may be taken as the most developed manifestation of tendencies, or potentialities, which are in fact generally present in the societies of the advanced capitalist world—a speculation that I would then naturally wish to link with the position of some pre-eminence which Britain today also holds in inflationary 'league tables'.[7]

(i) *The decay of the status order.* Most sociologists would, following Max Weber (1925), accept the importance of a distinction between 'class' and 'status'. 'Class' pertains to differences in social advantage and power within the context of prevailing economic institutions. Thus, in the context of a capitalist market economy, class inequalities will reflect the pattern of property ownership and of the possession of economically valuable knowledge, expertise and skill, as distinct from the mere capacity to provide labour. The class situation of individuals holding similar positions within this structure of inequality may be decomposed into (a) their market situation—their chances of obtaining given levels of income, their degree of security of employment, their prospects of economic advancement; and (b) their work situation—their position in relation to systems of authority and control within the organization of production. In contrast, 'status' pertains to inequalities in social advantage and power which have ultimately not a material, but rather a symbolic and moral basis. Status inequalities are ones which arise out of the differing degree to which groups or collectivities within a society, by virtue of their descent, ethnicity, education, occupation, or other socio-cultural attributes, are able to benefit from—and actively exploit—prevalent beliefs and values concerning the criteria of social 'worth' or 'superiority'. The status situation of a group thus refers to its prestige relative to that of other groups, and hence to the location of its members in relational structures expressive of deference, social acceptance and derogation.

However, although analytically distinct, the concepts of class and status do of course relate to phenomena which are empirically closely connected. For one thing, different forms of social advantage and power tend in their nature to be convertible: economic advantage implies the possibility of acquiring 'prestige entitlements'; status advantages can often be translated into economic opportunities, etc. Moreover, and of chief interest for present purposes, status inequalities tend to stabilize class inequalities by providing them with a major source of legitimation. Class inequalities are essentially *de facto*, and, as more sophisticated defenders of the market economy have always been ready to recognize, are from any moral standpoint largely arbitrary (cf. Knight, 1947; Hayek, 1960; Brittan, 1973); hence, they are always likely to be socially divisive. Status inequalities, on the other hand, are an aspect of 'socially constructed reality': they imply some measure of cognitive and evaluative consensus on the attributes indicative of social worth and superiority. And, in turn, the existence of a status order implies that claims made by groups or collectivities to social superiority are, in the main, acknowledged by those thus deemed inferior, and in a transitive fashion. In so far, then, as class inequalities are correlated with a status order, they are able to derive from the consensual nature of this order a normative basis for the marked differences in both economic reward and authority which they entail, and which their actual source—the market economy—cannot itself provide.

However, while 'status' may in this way underwrite 'class', what I would wish further to argue is that, within modern capitalist societies, the status order is progressively weakened and disrupted by various forces that are in fact associated with the development and functioning of the economy. The status order—or, better, status orders—that have prevailed in such societies are not ones which reflect distinctive belief- and value-systems of capitalism; nor, moreover, are they ones which,

in the long term, are compatible with the wider social implications
of the capitalist mode of production. Their origins and the
high point of their development lie in the pre-capitalist past
of the societies in which they now exist in an increasingly
attenuated form. In other words, they may be taken as representing an important aspect of what Hirsch (1977a) has aptly referred
to as capitalism's 'depleting moral legacy'.[8]

To sustain this argument as fully as might be done would
require a monograph in itself.[9] But the following points are
salient. First, urbanization and the greater physical mobility
of the population, which are concomitants of industrialism *per
se*, largely eliminate the *local* status group structures in which
a status order tends to be manifested in its most concrete,
relational form. For such structures can rarely coalesce other
than as part of the multiplex relationships of relatively small-scale
communities. Thus, in modern society, a specific feature of
the attenuation of status is that it becomes less 'interactional'
and more narrowly 'attributional' in its basis (Plowman, Minchinton and Stacey, 1962). Secondly, within a growing market
economy, market relations and the principle of 'equal exchange'
tend to enter into an ever-enlarged area of social life, as the
dynamics of the 'commercialization effect' (Hirsch, 1977a) work
themselves out. This must then necessarily conflict with, and
undermine, the assumption implicit in a status order of a wide-
ranging structure of relationships that are formed not by the
'cash nexus' but rather by obligation—asymmetrical, but complementary and grounded in moral acceptance. Thirdly, in a context
in which segmented roles and market orientations prevail, not
only does status become attributional rather than interactional
but, further, growing dissent and uncertainty are created
over how in fact status is to be attributed. In part, this may
be a problem of increased social differentiation and mobility
resulting in greater 'status inconsistency' as, in particular, the
ascribed and the achieved characteristics of individuals diverge
in the prestige entitlements which they indicate. But, more seriously, the very notions of *generalized* social worth and superiority, which are crucial to a status order, are called into question
and tend to break down; and thus, as socially constructed
reality, the phenomenon of prestige itself decomposes.

Although, then, considerations of status may still remain of some consequence in shaping patterns of intimate association, in present-day society the existence of a status order of an integrated kind becomes highly problematic. There is little assurance that claims to social superiority that one group may wish to make will in fact be met by deference on the part of others, rather than by their indifference or dissent. Differential association or social segregation on what appear as status lines lose their legitimacy and are viewed simply as matters of fact or, indeed, pejoratively; and, most importantly for our present concerns, the legitimation of class inequalities is at the same time greatly weakened. As expressed both in the distribution of economic advantage and in authority in work relations, class inequalities come increasingly to be seen, and to be judged, for what they are—the products of the market economy—without the benefit of the normative camouflage which the status order previously created.

Once, therefore, this analytical context is established, it is possible for rank-and-file 'pushfulness', distributional dissent, union militancy and 'irresponsibility' etc. all to be viewed in a rather different way to that of the economists. To begin with, it no longer seems so necessary, in attempting to account for such phenomena, to invoke new cultural or ideological currents sweeping across the Western world, nor to give such prominence to rapidly rising expectations and to the psychological effects (however characterized) of the failure to realize them. It is not so much that *new* influences on wage- and salary-earners and their organizations need to be recognized, but rather the disappearance of old ones—that is, the weakening of the inhibitions formerly imposed by the status order. For once the normative ordering of status is removed, there is no obvious reason why the pay claims of different groups of workers should not expand and lead to the pursuit of relativities that are highly intransitive; nor, moreover, why in pursuing their claims such groups should not raise new challenges, both via their organizations and directly, to the authority of employers and managers—or, to be more accurate, to the *power* which the latter have in the past derived from the status order *over and above* their authority as functionally and legally grounded (Goldthorpe, 1974).[10]

Indeed, it may be held that what the mass of wage- and

salary-earners have learnt from capitalism is not acquisitiveness *per se*—which they probably never lacked—but, of far greater consequence, the practice of exploiting one's market position to the full. This includes, of course, maximizing the gains to be had from any 'strategic' advantage that may present itself; and, more importantly still, using the power of organization to improve a weak position or to reinforce and maintain a strong one. To claim, as Mishan does (1974, p. 17) that in their new aquisitiveness, the masses differ significantly from the bourgeoisie in their readiness to use collective action testifies only to the market economist's ability to disregard the history of capitalism over the last hundred years or more.

In sum, then, one may see the decay of the status order as having released, as it were, distributional dissent and conflict at a new level of intensity—reflecting not the emergence of new psychological 'impulses' which lie beyond the bounds of rational intelligibility, but on the contrary a clearer, more hard-headed, indeed *more* rational appreciation of the nature of class inequalities and of resultant balance-of-power situations.[11]

(ii) *The realization of citizenship.* Following Marshall's classic statement (1950), the idea of citizenship may be said to be realized to the extent that all members of a national society enjoy in common a body of civil, political and social rights. The achievement of citizenship is thus an inherently egalitarian undertaking. For example, to the extent that differences in civil and political rights are removed, the status order loses any legal basis which it may once have had (as in a system of 'estates') and becomes, to use Weber's term, purely 'conventional'. Moreover, the granting of social rights—to a minimum level of real income and to benefit from a range of social services—is, as Marshall puts it, a means of 'class abatement'. What is implied is that the welfare of individuals and groups will, up to a point, be determined independently of their market situation, and that class inequalities will thus be in some measure offset and their wider social implications reduced.

Those sociologists, mostly American, who have sought to elaborate on Marshall's analysis have concentrated on the way in which the development of citizenship may form a basis, within the capitalist order, for greater social harmony and co-operation: for example, by promoting the 're-integration' of the industrial work-force into the national community after the social traumata of the heroic phase of capital accumulation; and further, by replacing the status order as a source of legitimacy for class inequalities—which, where the basic equality of citizenship prevails, may be claimed as the outcome of meritocratic achievement (cf. Bendix, 1964; Parsons, 1971). However, this emphasis reflects a very one-sided reading of Marshall; and certainly in the British context at least, what would seem of greater relevance, as Lockwood (1974, p. 367) has pointed out, is Marshall's argument that 'in the twentieth century citizenship and the capitalist class system have been at war', and further that 'the basic conflict between social rights and market value has not been resolved'.

On the one hand, the implications of the growth of citizenship for the legitimation of class inequalities are, as Marshall recognized, double-edged. While the possibility is created of legitimation in terms of meritocracy, the threat also arises that with the realization of citizenship, the contrast between the principled equality of rights that it bestows and the unprincipled inequalities thrown up by the market will be highlighted, and that the latter will thus be increasingly called into question.

On the other hand, the growth of citizenship has undoubtedly made for a progressively greater 'equality of conditions of conflict' (cf. Durkheim, 1893), and would moreover itself appear to generate, as well as to give force to, new challenges to the *status quo*. Citizenship rights, in other words, possess their own dynamic. There are, as Lockwood has put it (1974, p. 365), always 'principles dormant in them . . . as yet unrealized in social relationships', and including ones which have 'the potential for exacerbating as well as diminishing the conflict of classes'. Thus, as Marshall's essay well shows, civil rights, which were 'indispensable to a competitive market economy' also provided the essential means for the achievement of full political citizenship; and, on the basis of civil and political rights together, there was further established the 'secondary system of industrial citizenship', whose key institutions were independent trade unions and collective bargaining. In turn, these developments were crucial to the success of the struggle for social rights, through which the role of the market in determining life-chances has been significantly qualified—and through which too the industrial power of rank-and-file employees, that is, ultimately their power to withhold their labour, has been considerably enhanced.

At the present time, it may then be held, the further working out of the logic of citizenship which is in train, on the basis of this new power of labour, is in the direction of reinforcing and extending citizenship rights specifically in the sphere of production. This is apparent, for example, in moves towards establishing employees' rights in jobs;[12] in rank-and-file pressure for a more general 'right to work'; and in the concern of unions to be involved as of right—whether through bargaining procedures or new institutions of industrial democracy—in all decision-making processes which affect their members' employment conditions and prospects (cf. Bullock, 1977). In short, one could say, the new thrust of citizenship, in its on-going war with class, is specifically aimed against the idea, coeval with capitalism, of labour as a commodity.

So far then as inflation is concerned, the main significance of this development lies in the constraints which it imposes on governments seeking to pursue standard deflationary policies. While there is little indication that the growth of citizenship has in fact served in any way to make class inequalities more acceptable,[13] it is, one may argue, in the context of a widening conception of citizenship that one must understand the present-day tendency of rank-and-file employees and their organizations to react strongly against any attempt by government to mitigate or control their 'pushfulness' in distributional conflict through measures which threaten their security of employment. In other words, it is not sufficient, in seeking to explain the force of resistance to such measures, simply to invoke changes in expectations created by two decades or more of virtually full employment following the Second World War. Workers' expectations that they will not be exposed to unemployment, or at least not of a widespread and long-term kind, have to be seen as ones which by now have a *normative* and not merely an *empirical* grounding—as ones relating to rights and not just to probabilities. Thus, such expectations will not be readily adjusted to what governments may wish to define as substantially changed economic circumstances. Rather, it must be regarded as an abiding feature of the political situation that governments (of whatever

party) whose policies are associated with high unemployment
will face not only severe electoral punishment, as opportunity
for this arises, but more immediately, perhaps, a loss of trade-
union co-operation in economic policy making and implementation, and direct industrial and political action in the form
of strikes, sit-ins, factory take-overs, mass demonstrations etc.
It is, of course, these more disruptive kinds of response which
economists (and others) have had in mind when they have
lamented union and rank-and-file 'irresponsibility' and the decline
of a sense of *civitas*. However, in the alternative perspective
offered here, it may be argued that a forceful reaction against
economic policies which are seen as leading to high unemployment
is, on the contrary, a result of the idea of citizenship being
taken more seriously than before. For it is undeniable that
unemployment operates with a strong class bias: its actual inci-
dence is greater among those whose class situation is that of
rank-and-file wage-workers than among those more advanta-
geously located in the class structure (Daniel, 1974); and further,
of course, it shifts the balance of power against the former
in their work relations with managers and employers. Thus,
the use of unemployment as an instrument of policy must serve
to accentuate, rather than to mitigate, the extent to which individuals' life-chances are determined by their class situation, and
hence must go directly counter to the principle of citizenship,
and, in particular, to the current tendency towards an expansion
of rights within the sphere of work. In these circumstances,
it is then scarcely surprising—indeed, entirely intelligible—that
workers should react to redundancy and unemployment, or to
the threat of these, with something more than the resigned
or fatalistic acceptance which they may have shown in earlier
periods, in which fluctuations in the level of economic activity
could plausibly take on the appearance of quasi-natural events.

(iii) *The emergence of a mature working class.* So far, I have
been concerned chiefly with changes in social stratification that,
in my view, help to account for—that is, to make rationally
intelligible—those actions of rank-and-file employees and their
organizations which in economists' analyses of inflation are typically treated via residual categories implying error, ignorance
or unreason. The significance I attach to the third development

that I shall consider is, however, somewhat different. In this case, my primary concern is not with the 'subjective' processes through which, as I have argued, workers and their leaders have come in recent years to fairly radical redefinitions of their social situation, but rather with more 'objective' ones, through which the potential of one major bloc of workers—industrial wage labour—to make its new definitions 'stick' is tending to increase. And following from this, my further aim is then to provide an alternative perspective, in particular to that of monetarists, on the actions of present-day governments when confronted with an inflationary situation.

The changes previously discussed have, of course, in themselves served to enhance the power of industrial labour. The decay of the status order has freed manual workers from inhibiting notions of their own social inferiority; and the growth of citizenship rights has in various ways widened and strengthened the forms of political and industrial action open to them. But it may be argued further that the full impact of these changes will be experienced only as a working class develops whose members have grown up entirely under the new conditions that have been created. And in this respect especially, I would suggest, present-day Britain may be regarded as showing within the Western world the leading edge, so to speak, of a generally emergent phenomenon.

In the course of the evolution of an industrial society, a general tendency operates—although more slowly and irregularly than is often realized—towards the creation of a working class that is 'mature' in what, to begin with, might be thought of as a demographic sense. First, a body of manual wage-workers develops whose members are detached from the rural economy and society, and permanently resident in large towns and cities. In Britain, where the general process of urbanization began earlier and went ahead more rapidly than elsewhere, the vast majority of the industrial work-force was in fact already located in large urban centres by the early twentieth century. In many other Western societies, however, this stage has but recently been attained or is still only approximated. Secondly, with the decline of the agricultural sector, and also of the traditional *petite bourgeoisie*, the recruitment of the industrial work-force from these sources steadily falls off, and so too thus does

the proportion of the industrial working class whose origins
lie in essentially pre-capitalist social contexts. While in a number
of advanced Western societies industrial workers who are of
such origins still today constitute a sizable—though diminishing—
minority, in Britain the proportion is very small and has indeed
been so for several decades.[14] Thirdly, the tendency towards
a working class which is in fact predominantly *self*-recruiting
is reinforced by the expansion, evident in all economically
advanced societies, of opportunities for professional, administrative, managerial and other white-collar, salaried employment.
For the effect of this is, of course, to produce a marked down-turn
in the probability that children born into more advantaged social
groups and strata will experience any *déclassement*, at least
of a permanent kind, into the ranks of manual labour. (Goldthorpe and Llewellyn, 1977; Goldthorpe, Payne and Llewellyn,
1978.)

In sum, then, a mature working class in the sense in question,
which has by now effectively emerged in the British case, is
one whose members possess a relatively high degree of homo-
geneity in their social backgrounds and patterns of life experience.
They are at least 'second-generation' urban—that is to say,
they have grown up in social milieux in which the influence
of traditional structures of status and authority is likely to
have been slight; and furthermore, they are for the most part
at least second-generation working-class—that is to say, they
have probably lived most of their lives within working-class
family and neighbourhood cultures.

As well as thinking of the maturity of a working class in
this demographic or socio-economic sense, one may, however,
also think in terms of socio-political maturity. In this case,
the chief requirement is that the successive generations of a
working class should have grown up alike within a stable national
community, in which citizenship rights have been upheld and
developed, and in which therefore workers have been able to
pursue their industrial and political interests by means of their
own organizations—in other words, by building up and acting
through the instrumentalities of a labour movement. In this
respect, the distinctiveness of the British case lies not so much
in Britain having been in the van historically in the extension
of citizenship rights to the working class, but rather in the

The Current Inflation: Towards a Sociological Account   207

continuity with which such rights have been maintained—this chiefly reflecting the freedom Britain has enjoyed from the disasters of dictatorship, internal war and enemy occupation. However, the British case, I would argue, points to the outcome that is most logically to be expected, so far as the socio-political character of the working class is concerned, from the prolonged association of a developing capitalist economy and a stable 'liberal–pluralist' or 'social' democracy. That is, the growth of a working class for whose members the existence of trade unions and of a labour movement is an established fact of life, and for whom, moreover, trade unionism—even if with little direct personal involvement on the part of the majority—is the normal mode of action by which conditions of work and standards of living are to be defended and as much as possible improved.[15]

Previous conceptions of a 'mature' working class have either implied, as in the Marxist case, a class ready to undertake the revolutionary overthrow of capitalism; or, as with American theorists of the labour movement, a class successfully re-integrated into the capitalist order (cf. Kerr *et al.*, 1960; Ross and Hartman, 1960). Both these views, I would suggest, reflect an undue optimism on the part of their adherents. More realistically, a mature working class, of the kind I would argue exists in Britain today, must be seen as one which is not revolutionary, or at least not in terms of the consciousness and ideology of either its leadership or rank and file; but, at the same time, as one which remains only very imperfectly accommodated by the capitalist system *per se*, in that its members lack any value commitment to the basic principle of this system—namely, that the life-chances and welfare of individuals are most appropriately determined by the 'free' working out of market forces. Rather, one could say, their major commitment—their major stake in the existing social order—lies precisely in those of its institutional and organizational features through which the influence on their lives of market forces and of their basic class situation has been most importantly qualified: that is, those features deriving from the growth of citizenship rights, and including of course those essential to the effective functioning of a labour movement.

Moreover, although a mature working class in the sense I have indicated is not revolutionary, its existence implies something more than the capacity of its constituent elements to engage forcefully, but severally, in distributional conflict along with other interest-groups. It has also the potential for action of a more concerted kind, both industrial and political, the ultimate threat of which is to create a major degree of economic dislocation and civil disturbance. Such action it may be expected to undertake essentially as a means of *defence*: that is, to resist any attempt to subvert those limitations on class advantage and power that have been successfully imposed or, hence, the greater 'equality of conditions of conflict' that has been established. This potential requires and reflects, on the one hand, the readiness, under certain conditions, of a working class with demographic and socio-political characteristics of the kind described to 'hold up the country to ransom'—or, in other words, the relative weakness of its moral and social integration into the existing order; and on the other hand, its reserves of grass-roots solidarity on which concerted organizational strategies can draw.[16]

If, therefore, one maintains the view that the current inflation is, generally, an expression of distributional conflict, and then adds the idea of a mature working class being a crucial element in the inflationary situation, a rather different approach is suggested to the assessment of governmental action from that usually taken by economists, and especially those of a monetarist persuasion. The problem facing government has now to be seen as that of coping not simply with inflation but also, and more fundamentally, with the conflict that lies behind it; and specifically, with the threat that the social divisions and antagonisms arising from an increasingly delegitimated structure of class inequality will prove no longer capable of institutional containment.

From this standpoint, of course, inflation will itself appear as having positive aspects for government: it allows the distributional struggle to proceed, and 'blindly, impartially, impersonally and *non-politically* scales down all its outcomes' (Tobin, 1972, p. 13, my italics). At the same time, inflation has the advantage of tending to diffuse the efforts of organized labour: a wages 'free-for-all' encourages sectionalism rather than solidarity. Moreover, in the perspective suggested, it also becomes more clear why, when government decides that inflation can no longer go unchecked, an approach to its control via some form of incomes policy is usually preferred. In this way, anti-inflation policy can be related, formally at least, to distributional issues, and thus some degree of accommodation can still be offered to the working class and its organizations as, for example, through a 'social contract' (cf. Crouch, this volume). And further, with an incomes policy in operation, it may be hoped to introduce greater monetary discipline with less risk of creating economic conditions in which a disruptive reaction from organized labour will be provoked.

On the other hand, however, it can also be seen that to the extent that a pure monetarist approach is adopted, the likelihood is increased of government being confronted with just such a reaction. A monetarist anti-inflation policy, like any other, must carry implications for the pattern of social inequality; and, in fact, its implications amount to an underwriting of market forces as the key determinant of inequality in its distributional and relational aspects alike—the major, but not the only, illustration of this being of course the requirement for an increase in unemployment, to an unknown level and for an indeterminate period.[17] In other words, a monetarist policy would appear designed to sharpen the social conflict stemming from the unpersuasive character of market criteria, once stripped of their normative camouflage; and, at the same time, to structure this conflict on broad class lines, bringing organized labour into direct confrontation with government in defence of its achieved bases of power and security. In turn, then, the serious danger, from government's point of view, would arise of the crisis of legitimacy now existing in the sphere of distribution being extended into that of political authority also.

When, therefore, hard-line monetarists characterize governments that refuse to embrace their policies as having fallen victim to error ('bad' economics) or unreason ('inconsistency', 'woolly-mindedness' etc.), the sociologist must have sympathy with the politicians who would for their part regard such judgement as simplistic or, at best, as symptomatic of an acute case of *déformation professionelle*. Furthermore, where it is acknowledged, as by more sophisticated monetarists, that the anti-inflationary policy they propose, although 'correct', has a problem of political marketability, it still will not do to see this as being simply the result of politicians lacking vision and responsibility, and pursuing short-term strategies that can be rational only if their authors' retirement from the political scene is imminent. It may reasonably be supposed that a basic, abiding, and eminently responsible concern of most politicians is that the legitimacy of government should be preserved; and hence, they will have a fully rational aversion to policies that risk leading government into situations in which its authority would face a head-on and powerful challenge. It could then be argued that it is ultimately on this account, rather than because of a pervasive political opportunism, that monetarist doctrines—and indeed those of economic liberalism generally—are, as Gellner has put it (1975, p. 146), 'ever destined for inevitable betrayal'.

IV

Given that my starting point was with economists' residual categories, it is evident that, in one sense, an explanatory approach to inflation of the kind I have suggested cannot stand alone, without economic analysis. Because such an account has nothing itself to say about the interaction in the inflationary process of specifically economic variables or quantities—such as the volume of money supply, the velocity of its circulation, the level of output or of wages, etc.—it obviously needs the addition of economic analysis to link it to the actual *explanandum* of generally rising prices. However, since economic theories of inflation employ residual categories—to deal with modes of action which they cannot treat as rational—in what appears to be a highly patterned way, it would seem possible to advance a sociological account which can, as it were, speak to all such instances, and which is not tied, so far as its validity is concerned, to any one particular economic theory. This is the case, I have tried to show, with my argument that the current inflation derives ultimately from changes in the form of social stratification, giving rise to more intense and more equally-matched social conflict than hitherto. This argument can be elaborated to suggest ways in which all the major forms of action handled by economists' residual categories—on the part of government, trade unions and rank-and-file employees—may be rendered rationally intelligible: that is, placed in social contexts so that what was previously treated as error, ignorance or unreason can be seen as a response by actors which is in accord with the logic of their situation.

At the same time, though, it becomes in this way evident that such a sociological account of inflation must enter into competition with economists' theories, at least in so far as these rest on the idea of an economic system that is inherently stable, or capable of being stabilized by essentially marginal adjustments of certain key variables—plus perhaps some *ad hoc* strengthening of its immediate institutional framework. For such theories must deny the need to extend analysis much beyond the interaction of economic variables, and, to the extent that they do go further, it is indeed entirely consistent that, in dealing with a *mal*functioning of the economy, they *should* then invoke some failure of reason. The approach to inflation inherent in these theories is an essentially technocratic one: inflation represents a problem in implying that something is going wrong in a system which is known in principle to be viable. Thus, determining the causes of inflation and finding a solution to the problem are *both* primarily intellectual exercises: the latter follows directly from the former. And given that a solution is available—in the form of 'good' economics—inflation can continue to exist only as a result of those with the power to act against it either not recognizing, or refusing to take, the appropriate, that is, the technically correct, course of action for bringing it to an end.

There is, then, little room here for any idea that difficulties for the economy may derive systematically from aspects of social structure and process, and most seriously from social conflicts that are closely associated with its own form and mode of operation. The possibility is not contemplated that the 'free-market' economy, even if self-regulating considered as a closed system, may none the less create for itself a social environment in which the conditions for its proper functioning are seriously undermined.

In contrast, for the sociologist, of whatever theoretical persuasion, the expectation must tend to be not only that free-market relations will in themselves be unable to provide a basis for their own stable continuance, but further that they will be a source of social divisions and antagonisms which may then lie at the root of what are experienced as economic problems. Hence comes the supposition that must be basic to sociological enquiry into any such problem, inflation of course included: namely, that the economic problem is to an important degree epiphenomenal. The claim necessarily made is that in order to understand the relationships between economic quantities in terms of which the problem is defined, one must understand the underlying, generative, relationships between social groupings—and that these will themselves present further 'problems' of a kind which are not open to merely technical resolution in the light of economic science.

NOTES

1. Cf. also the discussion in Brittan (1975b, pp. 138–40).
2. It is perhaps here worth repeating the point that such residual categories may well serve a valuable purpose in identifying phenomena which are of importance to the problem that concerns the investigator. The difficulty typically associated with them is that their application implies an undermining of, or at least an abrupt departure from, the conceptual schema which is central to the analysis.
3. For the classic critique of psychologistic explanations in the social sciences, see Popper (1945, vol. II, ch. 14 esp.) whose argument is, ironically, much informed by economists' analyses of the functioning of markets. The one 'cost-push' account of inflation among those cited which largely avoids residual psychologism is that of Phelps-Brown (1975)—who, significantly, writes as much in terms of economic and social history as of economic theory. Cf. n. 6 below.
4. Cf., for example, the accounts of the development of sociological thought, from the later eighteenth century onwards, provided in Nisbet (1966) and Giddens (1971). It should be recognized that sociological concern with the problems of a capitalist market economy has by no means always gone together with a political commitment to socialism. Rather, from Durkheim to Parsons and beyond, this concern has often stemmed from the fear of an irretrievable disruption of liberal–democratic institutions.
5. It is, one may note, sometimes claimed that through similar processes 'suppressed' inflation is being created in Eastern European countries with centrally-planned economies. But cf. Portes (1977a and this volume).
6. The particular style of sociological analysis here envisaged, which has ultimately a historical and a *verstehende* grounding, is of course one which effectively originates in the work of Max Weber, and in particular in his contributions (1903–6) to the *Methodenstreit* waged among German historians, economists and philosophers in the two decades preceding the First World War. For the idea of the analysis of social action in terms of the 'logic of the

situation', see Popper (1957, pp. 147–52; 1972, ch. 4) who explicitly follows Weber's lead, and the elaboration in Jarvie (1972). Those economists who inveigh most strongly against 'sociological' explanations, notably supporters of the 'Chicago school', seem most ignorant of the Weberian tradition—to which many of their strictures concerning sociologists' neglect of purposive, goal-oriented action do not in fact apply. For an egregious case of such ignorance, see Brunner (1975).

7. At the same time, I should make it clear that I do not regard such changes in stratification as the only possible source of inflationary pressures in modern capitalist societies. In other words, I am not claiming to advance a general theory of inflation. Indeed, I do not believe that such a theory is possible, unless perhaps, like some monetarists, one is willing to cut off one's analysis at a very early and intellectually unsatisfying stage.

8. It is of interest to note that the theme of capitalism's lack of a moral basis of its own, and its reliance on the—weakening—morality of an earlier era, have of late also been taken up, in a remarkably similar fashion, by both Marxists *and* economic liberals. Cf., for example, the discussion of 'the residue of tradition' in Habermas (1973) and of 'the vanishing heritage' in Brittan (1975b).

9. A review of relevant research is provided in Goldthorpe and Bevan (1977).

10. Note also that the position taken up here does not require any claim of 'expanding reference groups'—which would seem empirically dubious (cf. Daniel, 1975—though the crucial table on p. 20 is garbled): but that at the same time it makes quite intelligible a white-collar backlash, including increased unionization and militancy, against the erosion of pay differentials *vis-à-vis* manual workers.

11. Flemming (this volume, p. 31) writes that 'The reason that economists are so unsympathetic to appeals to trade union "militancy" [as a cause of inflation] is that it suggests that the *intensity* of feelings and the urgency of demands matter. This is not possible in the economist's world where everyone maximizes.' However, the implication of my argument is that it is in fact only of late that the actual behaviour of most groups of wage- and salary-earners has begun to approximate at all closely to the assumptions of 'the economist's world'—and that this *shift* is an important source of inflationary pressure.

12. Notably, via such legislation as the Contracts of Employment Act, 1963, the Redundancy Payments Act, 1965, the Health and Safety at Work Act, 1974, the Trade Union and Labour Relations Act, 1975, and the Employment Protection Act, 1975.

13. Meritocracy, as a legitimizing ideology, has fundamental weaknesses, by now thoroughly exposed by critiques—which again show a remarkable convergence (see n. 9 above)—from both economic liberals and Marxists. Cf., for example, Hayek (1960) and Offe (1970).

14. The foregoing arguments are based primarily on data made available to me by colleagues in the Social Stratification Research Committee of the International Sociological Association who are engaged on the 1970s 'generation' of national occupational mobility studies, the results of most of which are not as yet published. Cf. also, so far as the working classes of Western Europe are concerned, Kendall (1975, ch. 12 esp.).

15. I do not of course claim any historical inevitability for this process, and countervailing tendencies to both the demographic and the socio-political maturation of the working classes of the advanced societies of the West clearly exist—the most important, probably, being the absorption into their

labour forces of relatively large numbers of immigrant workers from the poorer countries of both the Western and the 'third' worlds. (Cf. Castles and Kosack, 1973, chs. ix–xi, esp.)

16. The importance of the growing complexity of the division of labour as in itself giving workers increased opportunities for exerting 'strategic' power seems to me easily exaggerated. Considerable power of this kind has for long been in their hands—witness, for example, the effects of the rail strikes of 1907 and 1911. What is significant is surely the increasing readiness, and organizational capacity of workers to use such power.

17. Also of major relevance, of course, are the likely implications for public expenditure.

ADDENDUM

On the Role of the Social Scientist
an exchange at the Warwick Conference 26 May 1976

PEACOCK: *What appears to me an implicit assumption in Goldthorpe's paper is that inflation is a problem which will never be solved within the market economy, or a social market economy, or even a mixed economy. Is this so? If so, then presumably there's no point in the present society recruiting sociologists, shall we say, into the government's service, unless as infiltrators to change the whole nature of the governmental process. What I want to know is: do sociologists feel that this is in fact their conclusion—that it's only a transformation of society, perhaps to the Hungarian or the Polish model where inflation is practically non-existent, that can overcome the problem? Is that really what is being said? It would be most interesting to know.*

GOLDTHORPE: *The difficulty with a lot of writing by economists is that they view inflation in an excessively technocratic fashion—as if inflation is something like a crossword puzzle or a chess problem that a clever economist can come along and tackle and solve. I think this unreflecting technocratic approach goes back a long way in the history of economics. I'm always fascinated by Keynes' comment that at some future point economics will be like dentistry—it will just be a technical matter. Now that seems to me absurd. My own position on this is that there may indeed be technical problems that one can treat in technical terms, but that, ultimately, the problem of inflation is a political problem: one's approach to it depends on what kind of society one wants to have. And in this respect, I have no more to say, as a sociologist, than the man who cleans my street. This is a matter, ultimately, for political action. As a sociologist, I will offer analyses. I might even say 'If you want to get from A to B, you might try doing it that way'—though I don't see this as being my major role. As a political actor, I will make my own political decisions and use what trifling amount of political weight I've got to push in the direction that I want to go. What I object to is economists thinking that inflation is just a technical matter and that they, in the light of economic science, can tell us what we ought to do.*

BRITTAN: *But it is a reasonable inference from your paper, isn't it, that, as a sociologist, you do not think anything can be done about inflation under the present system?*

GOLDTHORPE: *No—I don't discuss the matter of 'what can be done' at all. I object to this definition of the problem, as if it's like a leak in my pipes—so summon up lots of institutional plumbers.*

BRITTAN: *I don't have that approach. I don't think economics is ever going to be like dentistry. But it's still reasonable to ask whether you think that inflation is a problem which is incurable by political, technical, or any other means without a radical transformation of society.*

GOLDTHORPE: *I don't know. I don't think these are questions that one can answer as a social scientist. It's a historical situation, not an intellectual problem, that we are confronting here. I don't know how it will work out. I'm a good Popperian: I don't believe in historicist predictions about what's going to happen in the future, or in developmental laws of society—that's why I am not a Marxist. We have an open political situation. I don't know what will happen, and I can't see any point in pretending that I do.*

CHAPTER 9

Inflation and the Political Organization of Economic Interests

Colin Crouch

I

Although every account of inflation stresses the mutual entanglement of political and economic factors in the process, treatment of the political variables is rarely satisfactory. For neo-classical economists politics constitutes a messy interference with rationality, a combination of misplaced and doomed good intentions, woolly-mindedness and downright corruption. At best, political interference with market processes may be grudgingly accepted in order to come to terms with what are seen as 'psychological' factors—'psychology' being used, in a tradition that originates in Pareto by way of Elton Mayo, to refer to deviations from the rationality of market exchange. On the other hand, economists often have good cause to complain that political scientists are content to hint darkly that an interpretation which leaves out 'political factors' will fail to give an adequate account of events, without spelling out precisely what these factors are and what laws govern their operation. Indeed, they are often presented as being nothing other than the arbitrary muddle of personalities, patronage and public relations that economists always suspected them to be.

An example of the gulf in understanding between the disciplines, and of the damage it can do to an accurate understanding of the phenomenon, is a recent article by Parkin (1975). He here asserts that there are two opposed approaches to inflation—the economic and the socio-political. These are related to a model which immediately shows that the author has no interest in considering the 'socio-political' seriously; government actions are seen as directly influenced by the economy itself and by voters. All other social and institutional features of the society are dubbed 'other social and political factors', defined in primarily psychological terms, and have no direct effect on governments. The reference to 'voters' as the only political factor admitted to serious analysis is significant in that electoral behaviour, can, with some distorting assumptions, be assimilated to economic models. The two alternative approaches are then spelt out, whereupon it appears that the 'socio-political' extends to all economic schools other than the monetarist. The superiority of policy based on the 'economic' approach is then demonstrated by discussions of the superior success of the United States and West Germany in combatting inflation which concentrate solely on their willingness to accept regulation of the economy by unpoliticized central banks. No other institutional variables are considered: there is no historical context to the discussion; and no explanation is offered of why these countries have organized themselves in this way while others have not—apart, presumably, from strength of will and moral fibre.

Having established a model which permits no serious consideration of extra-economic factors and insisted on the incompatibility of economic and socio-political approaches, Parkin cuts short his inquiry into international variations in inflation experience at precisely the point where these factors become relevant. In the present article there will be no attempt to argue that a socio-political approach alone is relevant; but it will, I hope, be shown that such factors are both more substantial and more complex than Parkin allows, and that a satisfactory account of inflation has to combine them with the more purely economic variables.

Polity and economy may most usefully be distinguished as different ways of resolving the conflicts which would otherwise ensue from the unchecked pursuit of scarce goods by boundless private interests.[1] They differ in their orientation to the means–ends axis. If goals are pursued without restraint, they are secured by physical seizure, i.e. violence. The polity minimizes this challenge to social order by (i) monopolizing in a central institution (the state) the control of the means of violence; (ii) establishing a system of institutions which enable ends to be secured with the ultimate support of this violence but without constant recourse to it; and (iii) prescribing rules whereby social interests may have access to these institutions. This gives us the characteristic model of a political system, in which decisions to pursue chosen goals are made at a political centre, in response to the balance of effective interests, and are implemented through an institutional apparatus of bureaucracy, law and police services. Political decisions, though removed by institutions from constant recourse to violence, remain directly oriented to goals in that they seek to secure ends by command.

In contrast, economic action is oriented towards the means of securing goals. Through a system of exchanges, actors are able to pursue their private ends, but the system itself is silent about them. Regulation is secured, not through a central institution staffed by human agencies, but through competitive markets and an accepted unit of account. The former ensures that all actors are subject to the market and not able to dominate it—that is, not able to impose their goals on the system but only to pursue their goals through the system. The latter ensures that the private calculations can be made on a rational basis; and it is a formal, not a substantive rationality (Weber, 1922). Choices are made in terms of the indirect means-oriented unit of account (opportunity cost) and not in terms of a direct selection of goals, which would necessitate choice between ends in terms of their intrinsic qualities.

Models of both political and economic action assume that actors will try to pursue their interests to the utmost. However, internalized checks may prevent them from doing this. They may feel they ought not, in some ultimate moral sense, to maximize their interests, and this normative restraint constitutes a third, distinct form of regulation of social action.

Together these three modes of interest regulation are at the core of many models of society. Crudely they can also be used to differentiate the contributions of three central figures (and of their associated disciplines) who addressed themselves to the problem of what prevents the pursuit of private interest from destroying all society: Hobbes (politics), Adam Smith (economics) and Durkheim (sociology).[2] In reality, any system of social order will make use of all three of these sources of cohesion, but it was the extraordinary achievement of advocates of the *laissez-faire* political economy to outline a system that placed overwhelming stress on the economic. The achievement within capitalist societies of an unprecedented degree of political and moral freedom resulted from the liberation of these areas of action from detailed involvement in the task of social control. The achievement was always in part illusory. Capitalism depended on the survival of political institutions from an earlier (generally absolutist) period which made it possible to create the coercive legal framework it needed (Taylor, 1972), while the pursuit of amoral, individualized ends through the market system assumed reinforcement by a framework of moral restraint similarly inherited from the past (Durkheim, 1893; Hirsch, 1977a).

But the problem of the relationship between polity and economy under capitalism goes further than these familiar points. The market system can cope with interests only if they are constituted in a particular way; as soon as an economic interest reaches a position where it is able to affect the market, it is free from at least some aspects of regulation. This happens as soon as it is able to overcome the condition of individualization and atomization which is essential to perfect competition; in other words, as soon as the interest becomes organized. In Pizzorno's (1978) phrase, organization means a 'capacity for strategy', which might be defined as an ability to take action aimed at the direct achievement of goals. Such action has at least partly escaped the system of exchange and has entered the polity, where regulation can be secured only by engagement with the state. The phenomenon of organization will therefore require repeated political intervention, either to destroy the capacity to organize or to require the organized interest to operate through political rules. If the latter occurs, the segregation of economy and polity so crucial to classical capitalism is fundamentally threatened.

A further requirement of a capitalist economy is that only those interests that are capable of expression within the framework of privately appropriated market exchanges should be permitted any expression at all. If effective interests exist that are unable to realize their ends through the indirect processes of the market, they will automatically use direct means; that is, they will put pressure on the polity which will then become more active than the model of classical capitalism allows. Again, the process of either destroying such interests or forcing them into an economic mode will itself involve extra-economic action. The particular poise of a classical capitalist economy can thus be seen as very finely balanced—partly dependent on historical legacies for its initial establishment, and constantly facing the challenge of interests that cannot be assimilated to its mode and that either succeed in disrupting it or call forth extra-economic action to defend the system of exchange itself. It is possible to be more specific and indicate some of the forces that have created increasing problems of this kind for capitalism during the long period of its development. First, for a series of reasons, the organization of economic interests has intensified. Some of the reasons for this have been technical and derive from economic progress itself. As Galbraith (1967) and others have argued, much high-technology and large-scale industry requires conditions of stability incompatible with both the unpredictable nature of free competition and the multitude of producing units which is necessary for competition to take place. The quasi-political element inherent in the decision-making and allocative aspects of economic control becomes increasingly more important than subordination to market forces. The actions of such units necessarily engage the polity.

An increasingly important example is the organization of financial markets. It is possible for a small number of foreign governments or agencies like the International Monetary Fund to be so prominent in the supply of external credit to a particular country that their activities are not governed by a competitive market; their evaluations and expectations may then acquire the position of self-fulfilling prophecies, and might even be used to secure political changes. Such agencies have acquired capacity for strategy which may produce results different from the normal effects of a mass of creditors simply pursuing their own self-interest within an atomistic market.

More frequently commented on is the organization of workers. The latter present further problems of politicization, in that, unable to pursue their goals very effectively through market exchanges, they are particularly likely to seek to realize them directly through political action, whereupon the problem of regulating their action will pass to the polity. It needs to be remembered, however, that workers' capacity to organize is partly dependent on the level of employment. Thus, subject to certain limitations which will be discussed below, the economic mode is capable of solving certain aspects of this problem itself.

Finally, increasingly frequent interventions by the polity have been needed in order to maintain the capitalist economy itself. Society can be regulated by economic means only to the extent that social action takes a form amenable to incorporation in market transactions. There is no reason why actions should 'naturally' come in this form, and it is of course impossible for the market system itself to subsume activities that stand outside it. The polity has to intervene either to take care of the activity itself or to fashion it in a form that places it within the orbit of the market (Castells, 1975; Offe, 1975; Panić, 1976).

The state having once acquired an active role in the economy, for no matter what reasons, there are in-built tendencies for the process to intensify—which is why supporters of a pure market economy are justified, given their perspective, in opposing even innocuous degrees of intervention. To the extent that areas of social regulation are at least partly removed from the sphere of the market and located in the polity, social interests will have to take on a political role if they are to influence events. Thus, even if state intervention begins as a response to organization, it is itself likely to generate a further increase in organization. This partly explains why, although ostensibly it should be those groups who do least well out of the market economy who take to organization, in practice one finds at least as much organization among interests which do well from the market (Crouch, 1977a). Alternatively, once the state has become active on the issue, it may deliberately stimulate the organization of social interests, or at least encourage organizations of a certain kind. Organized social interests that remain unconstrained by political processes are as destructive of social order as profit-maximizing activity that is unregulated by the rules of free competition. The most clear example of this phenomenon is the well-known tendency of governments to encourage strong centralized trade union movements and to oppose fragmented, autonomous local movements. An example of a different kind would be the role played by the British government in urging the formation of the Confederation of British Industry in 1965.

This process of the centralized organization of interests accompanying state involvement has important implications for the political structure of classical capitalist society. Marx's aphorism about Parliament being the committee for regulating the joint interests of the bourgeoisie embodied an important truth. The limited suffrage of the bourgeois state restricted effective political participation to those who also occupied more or less dominant positions in the economy, ensuring no major strains in relations between polity and economy. The state's tasks were simply (i) to maintain the necessary extra-economic apparatus that guaranteed the functioning of the market economy; (ii) to conduct foreign and defence policy; (iii) to balance the government's own budget; and (iv) to institute a series of discrete interventions in order to remedy situations where, even on the basis of a limited and formal representation of interests, the unfettered operation of markets and their external diseconomies created 'problems'. An elected debating forum, from which was drawn a responsible administration supervising a small executive arm, fitted these conditions admirably. The polity, inheriting from the pre-capitalist period an aura of sovereign legitimacy, could occupy a position where there was no contradiction between this legitimacy and the notion of limited government.

The changes in the balance between polity and economy discussed above, together with the crucial factor of the extension of the franchise which extended participation to interests in clearly subordinate positions within the economy, threatened this balance in several ways. First, the bourgeois party gave way to the programmatic mass party, which replaced the concept of limited and discrete political interventions to resolve problems with the idea of using political power as a means for social transformation; the party would have 'policies' on nearly every aspect of social life (cf. Beer, 1965). Secondly, by the time of the Keynesian revolution in economic policy, the state's budgetary function had become that of regulating the economy as a whole, the balance of taxation and public spending being determined to that end with the overriding objective of maintaining full employment. Thirdly, concomitant with the rise in government activity has been the enormous expansion of professional, technical and bureaucratic staffs employed by the state in order to procure the means to the achievement of the politically-determined ends which cannot be left to the market economy. Finally,

the phenomenon of intensified organization of interests enjoying
a close relationship with the state (necessary if organization
is to be co-ordinated) plays an increasingly important part in
the goal-determining tasks of the polity.

All these processes challenge the place occupied by parliament
in the bourgeois state. The parliament made up of mass parties
provided a temporary rejuvenation of the institution: through
elections the size of the respective parties within parliament
is determined, and this in turn determines which party has
the right to seize the levers of the state in order to implement
its programme. But the change in the position of the state
within society wrought by the technical and bureaucratic complexity of its fiscal and regulating roles, together with the growth
of organized interests, renders the notion of parliamentary over-
eignty increasingly mythical. Instead of the state's relationship
to civil society being regulated carefully through the medium
of the bourgeois parliament, state and society stand in a complex,
interwoven relationship with the points of contact varied and
close.

So far the discussion has been concerned with the increasing
interconnectedness of the two spheres of polity and economy.
It is also necessary to consider the third mode of interest regulation: the normative. The remark of Harold Macmillan: 'If people
want morality, let them get it from their archbishops' (quoted
in Hirsch, 1977a, p. 134) was hopelessly out of date at the
time it was made. While expressing accurately the solution to
the problem of the source of normative constraints given in
classical economic theory, it failed to take account of the vast
process of secularization which had weakened the significance
of the church in industrial society. This is no place to spell
out in detail the history of the relationship between religion
and capitalism. But, in brief, just as absolutism produced a
separation of the state from society that proved crucial in the
development of capitalism, so the Reformation produced an
eventual separation of religion from any close involvement in
political and economic affairs that was no less important. While
this separation may have appeared to ensure the purity of
normative (i.e. religious) institutions, its long-term effect was
to press them into smaller and smaller corners of human life,
as science, art, economy and a whole range of human relationships

became freed from religious domination. In consequence, the state became the institution upon which falls the burden of maintaining some kind of consensus within the society, giving it an even more complicated and detailed involvement in social, particularly economic, affairs. The state is both the core political institution and the central normative institution of a modern society and many of the instances of state intervention that we label as politicization may represent, at least in part, normative rather than political action.

II

It is now necessary to see how these problems of institutional segregation in the capitalist economy become involved in the development and resolution of inflationary crises. The processes described in the previous section can all be seen as ways in which the basic social problem of competition for scarce resources has been exacerbated by the failure of certain kinds of regulation and by the overlapping of interests between the different modes of action. In particular, the processes of the organization of interests and their subsequent politicization impose demands for economic resources greater than those which can be satisfied. Unless there is a continuing high rate of economic growth or a major shift in the pattern of effective interests in the society, this can lead only to inflation. An important proximate cause of this will be the willingness of the state to sustain, through the money supply, a continuing high level of employment, but this 'willingness' itself needs to be explained.

Most obviously, the ability of subordinates to organize (both within employment relations and directly through the party apparatus of the democratic state) gives them a capacity to make political demands.[3] A fundamental demand for them is to reduce the level of unemployment, which brings instability to their lives and weakens them in employment relations. At the same time, subordinate interests also demand the high level of public spending associated with full employment policies, in order to compensate them for their disadvantages in market exchanges. However, important though these autonomous processes are, it would be erroneous to regard them as the sole pressures for the state policies concerned. Certain changes in the needs of the capitalist economy itself are also involved, both directly and in stimulating the political organization of subordinates. First, as Offe (1975) has argued, although capital as a whole needs certain continuing state interventions, including full employment itself, in order to maintain participation in the market economy, the cost of this state activity is experienced as a burden, a drain on resources, by capital. (This explains the paradox whereby, although capital can be seen as the beneficiary of much state action, capitalist interests themselves usually oppose intervention and regard it as purely wasteful 'welfare' which does not contribute to production.) This drive from within capital combines with the pure welfare demands of organized labour, and also with pressure from the groups of professionals whose career interests are associated with the continuing development of the public services, to form a powerful pressure for continuingly high public spending. Part of this expenditure eventually leads to an improvement in the efficiency of economic actors and thus contributes to economic wealth, but much of it remains as an economic 'burden' which removes resources from all interests competing for the market's already scarce goods.

A further process concerns the development of oligopoly and concentration of capital—which has massively intensified in the past decade. This calls forth state interventions of various kinds, and may have further consequences in that the organization of subordinates is likely to grow alongside the concentration of capital. The positive correlation between union membership and size of plant is well known, and it is also likely that oligopolies will be able to award wage increases less constrained by market forces. The processes may become cumulative; not only does oligopoly favour inflation, but as Maier argues elsewhere in this volume (p. 66), in an inflationary period it is large businesses that are more likely to have access to continuing credit.

The fact that industrial concentration and unionization were both increasing in most Western countries throughout the period of high inflation in the late 1960s and 1970s is evidence for the case that 'market power' was instrumental in causing inflation, even if one accepts Friedman's point (1966) that an existing state of monopoly power cannot account for inflation: the degree of 'monopoly power' of labour probably *was* increasing sharply. The contention has even more significance if one takes the broader view of what growing market power means in this context. The standard economic account assimilates union organization to ordinary monopoly theory. This overlooks the fact that in wielding organizational power, unions have to solve a series of problems that do not trouble business monopolies. These include the Olsonian problems of collective organization in the first place (Olson, 1965), as well as more psychological questions of workers' confidence in taking action. Some of these are discussed by Morton (1950). The more limited issue of the importance of changing ranges of comparisons has been recently discussed by D. A. Smith (1976). There is likely to be a lot of 'slack' to be taken up in the use of potential power by unionized groups, and at times when labour militancy is receiving prominent attention, workers in a variety of employments are likely to start taking up that slack. The tendency of economists to treat the fact of unionization as the single relevant variable ignores the evidence presented of increased pushfulness in the willingness of previously quiescent groups to strike, the use of new techniques of disruption, and other indicators (see Crouch and Pizzorno, 1978).

It is also likely that normative developments within modern capitalism have made their contribution to increased inflationary pressure, as several authors have claimed (Mishan, 1974; Panić, 1976; Hirsch, 1977a). While capitalism has produced no values of its own that foster restraint, a contribution to social order has been made during conditions of rapid economic growth by values that encourage people to satisfy all their goals through purchases of commercial goods and services. Once growth ceases, that same search becomes a major embarrassment and nineteenth-century fears of the unrestrained appetites of the masses, virtually unheard during the confident postwar years, again become prominent in conservative writing (Mishan, 1974; Brittan, 1975b).

This point may combine with other more structural factors to explain the predominantly economistic orientation of organized labour. The principal consequence of unionization is to improve the ability of workers to make advantageous wage bargains and improvements in working conditions. With the exception of gains made in job control at shop-floor level, it does not affect their position as subordinates alienated from a share in control over economic organization. Subordinates have secured an increase in bargaining power without any corresponding change in the system of economic organization. In the short run, only one thing prevents this situation from producing irreconcilable conflict within the economy: the fact that wages are fixed in money rather than real terms. In other words, inflation may result and, ironically, begin as a means whereby conflicts are contained. In this sense, inflation can be seen as spuriously providing the same solution to conflicts as an increase in economic growth: a relaxation of the zero-sum constraint on conflict (Crouch, 1977b, Part III).

Viewed in this way, the socio-political analysis of inflation follows the monetarist and demand-pull Keynesian accounts in seeing inflation as possible only because of the political manipulation of certain economic variables. It differs from them in regarding the polity as an arena of society which exists for more substantial reasons than human folly or corruption, and in treating its interventions in the economy as stemming in part from the needs of that economy itself; as a result, it is an analysis that does not lead to the same advocacy of apparently simple political solutions. For simplistic state action to be possible in order to reverse the state action that initially created the 'problem', the balance of power between interests within the polity which led to that initial action has to be changed. The removal of political power from a group can be achieved only by political action of a biased and coercive kind. It is for this reason that it is often argued that the monetarist solution, which constitutes the main thrust of attempts to return to a situation where economic issues are resolved solely within the economy, is in fact likely to lead to a considerable increase in state coercion in society.

These two objections to the monetarists' solution (bias and coercion) can be seen if one examines a central pillar of most of their proposals: the acceptance of a constraint on economic policy by putting it beyond the reach of political action, in the same way that the gold standard and the imperative of the balanced budget used to operate. As well as being non-political, such solutions have to be simple in the sense of being restricted to very few variables, for this alone makes non-intervention feasible. A level of unemployment of 2½ per cent was one such formula; restriction of the money supply is another. The fact that the need for simplicity is primarily political, whereas the technical issues involved frequently do not permit simplicity, is a major source of unreality in the proposals. More important, while the proposed devices may be non-political they are rarely socially neutral. Certain social interests gain both materially and in political power from the rigid pursuit of market rules, low public spending and high unemployment; that is, those who gain most from market transactions and who are not dependent on selling their labour for their livelihood. There may also be more subtle problems affecting the operation of ostensibly neutral agencies. For example, British financial institutions and by extension the Bank of England have been oriented to activities in world financial markets, entailing policies of an overvalued currency and stable exchange rates. West German banks have, in contrast, shared a national policy priority for the export of manufactured goods, leading to different exchange-rate policies. It is thus possible for these non-political institutions to have very different orientations, and these may well affect the willingness of various social groups to accept them as neutral and beyond debate. If organized interests do not trust an agency, then its dominance can only be secured through coercion, which is itself political. In sum, the pursuit of 'pure' economic regulation does not permit neglect of socio-political institutions, and in certain circumstances may give rise to considerable social conflict.

That an inadequately regulated amalgam of political and economic forces is at the heart of the problem of inflation is common ground among advocates of 'monetarist' and 'socio-political' measures alike. The solution considered so far is to try to shed the political altogether. If this is rejected the alternative is to seek more adequate regulation of interests at the political level. This is what is usually meant by those who call for political or institutional factors to be taken into account (Dahmén, 1973; Alexander, 1974). The argument is based on the assumption that *neither* the economy *nor* the polity functions as the models of liberal political economy require. Attention will here be focused on the inadequacies of the liberal bourgeois state.

Advocates of classical liberalism (e.g. Brittan, 1975b) describe
the problem as being an excess of democracy, in a model
of democracy which is limited to electoral participation. They
are easily able to show that electoral mechanisms make for
considerable irresponsibility in that nothing requires a generally
grossly-uninformed electorate to will the means to provide the
ends which it demands. But use of the idea of 'excess' conceals
the puny, limited nature of the participation afforded by the
electoral system, which virtually imposes ignorance and irresponsibility as means by which governors are protected from the
governed.

In practice democracy is not limited to elections but includes
a wide but, it will be argued, inadequate range of participant
institutions through which organized interests both express themselves and are controlled. The search for an improved regulation
of interests through political institutions therefore constitutes
a reform programme for the institutions of the bourgeois state—a
process already begun but not yet very advanced. Comparative
experience is of course highly relevant to this, and it is noteworthy
that three societies that have been particularly successful in
combining high growth, full employment and low rates of inflation
also evince advanced, though highly varied, forms of integration
of organized social interests: Sweden, West Germany and Japan.

Sweden is the most straightforward case, following the social-
democratic model of large concessions to working-class interests
in exchange for stability negotiated through elaborate national
institutions—though, it should be added, with the extra stimulus
of the extreme vulnerability of the Swedish economy to external
economic disciplines.

Germany, in contrast, is more often seen as a classic case
of market regulation. I do not wish to follow Parkin (see
above) into a partial, ahistorical analysis of countries, but it
is important simply to draw attention to the very precise role
allotted to organized interests in German society. The scope
and functions of trade unions, including their relations with
their members, are defined in legal traditions that predate by
many years the constitution of the Federal Republic; the involvement of unions in joint regulation with employers' associations
and sometimes with government agencies as well is important
in establishing economic targets; and in some industries a signifi-

cant part is played by co-determination. While in several respects modern Germany is a market economy with a lower level of government involvement than in several other European economies, it is by no means an individualistic economy, and the *state* in general (as distinct from government in particular) is a significant institution in regulating the behaviour of economic actors (Crouch, 1978).

Similarly, while Japan is noted for its compliant and obedient work-force, it would be highly misleading to regard it as having an individualistic market economy. The strong corporate loyalties of workers in the large oligopolistic Japanese concerns are very much the outcome of an exchange in which the interests of the work-force *as a collectivity* are recognized by employers; and while the role of unions is very different from what it is in Britain, it is by no means an irrelevant element in Japanese economic order. Many of the differences between the two countries have been well presented by Dore (1973), whose account is particularly valuable in showing the subtle differences in the balance of individualism and collectivism. Britain emerges as a society whose collectivism has evolved from the liberal individualism of a previous age. Managers and workers alike display a conception of their conflicting interests and of their mutual autonomy which is attractive in the sturdy independence and forthrightness which it fosters, but also dispiriting in that it reduces co-operation and the joint pursuit of efficiency to a minimum. This is the authentic legacy of British liberalism in industrial relations, and its correlate at the political level (unfortunately neglected by Dore) is unfettered collective bargaining with no state involvement. One lesson which British Conservatism may soon have to learn is that, now that the economy is dominated by highly concentrated bureaucratic corporations, private as well as public, and true entrepreneurship reduced to small and sometimes shady, non-productive corners, the only true heirs of nineteenth century English liberalism are militant shop stewards and work-groups in the more fragmented areas of collective bargaining.

The overwhelming impression left by Dore's study is the same as that left by a study of contemporary British politics: the great British compromise, for so long the most impressive example of class relations in the world, has become a tired stalemate. More precisely, the terms on which capitalist liberalism was amended in order to admit the interests of labour, while suiting most groups at a time of imperial strength and its temporary extension during the period of rapidly growing mass prosperity after the Second World War, seems increasingly to be a balance of interests which gives the worst of several worlds. Power has been conceded to workers at the level of fragmented job control (leaving industrial authority intact and free from any concerted attack at the higher levels); workers have had an illusory ability to wreak changes in the structure of rewards through free collective bargaining under full employment (but in reality their gains have been financed by growth or by inflation); unions have been able to generate a political wing which occasionally constitutes the governing party (but this has remained very separate from the industrial movement with a low capacity to secure its mobilization). The working class has long been exceptionally mature, in the sense described by Goldthorpe (this volume), but the maturity has remained rooted in a narrow particularism (Runciman, 1966; Goldthorpe *et al.*, 1968, 1969; Crouch, 1975). There is a powerful working-class collectivism, but paradoxically this remains, in its fragmentation, defensiveness and essential lack of politicization, more consistent with the classical liberal economy than with current state co-ordinated forms.

Now, in an economy with no constantly increasing resources to be shared out as part of the compromise, the low-level job controls are seen as merely restrictive, while the remoteness of workers from any real control leaves them suspicious of all actions by authority; free collective bargaining is felt to have its inevitable counterpart in either high unemployment or inflation; and no political force seems capable of securing long-term cohesion without a disturbance to the balance of interests that would be highly disruptive and coercive—there are certainly few normative bases for an appeal to order. The rejection by the Confederation of British Industry of the Report of the Bullock Committee on industrial democracy (1977) is the latest stage of this process. Industry wants trade unions to be more 'responsible' in the sense of exercising restraint and being willing to appreciate employers' problems; but there is resistance to any actual sharing of responsibility, in the sense of sharing the powers to make the decisions which set the framework within which moderation is supposed to be practised. The refusal of important sections of union opinion to accept such a share in responsibility anyway, preferring a role of uninhibited, if narrow and defensive opposition is of course just the other side of the same coin.

III

The requirements for a policy of increased acceptance and integration of organized interests may now be considered. Discussion will concentrate on the position of groups representing subordinates because this is where the problems are most severe. Three issues will be considered: (i) transcending the 'trust gap'; (ii) transcending particularism; (iii) tackling problems of relations between leaders and members of labour organizations.

The question of trust in industrial relations has been well analysed by Fox (1974), and the argument can easily be extended to relations among unions, employers and the state. The basis of trust may vary from being purely normative, amounting to virtual false consciousness on the workers' side that their employer will look after them, to a situation where decisions are made jointly on the basis of completely shared information and within a range of mutually agreed objectives. Where there is no trust there can be no co-operation and everything must be governed by either one-sided domination or very short-term bargaining. In such situations there will be extreme reluctance to forgo current consumption, and any attempt by one side to erect an ostensibly neutral constraint will be suspected of bias. The point has been well analysed by Lancaster (1973) in an article which uses games theory to show that where there is a division between those making investment decisions and those engaged in direct production (whether capital and labour or state bureaucrats and labour) there will be sub-optimal investment as neither side will be prepared to exchange current certainty for future possibility. To concentrate on the workers' side of the dilemma, there is no guarantee that a wage increase forgone will mean increased investment.

There are various ways in which this gap can be narrowed. It was suggested above (p. 229) that one reason for the greater willingness of German unions to accept bouts of exceptional restraint might be the export orientation of general finance policy, which means that a temporary down-turn leads rapidly to increased exports and a concomitant revival in manufacturing activity, real incomes and level of employment. The same expectation would not be justified in Britain. (An additional factor which makes the point about trust equally effectively, but less helpfully, is the fact that success breeds success. The German economy having once reached a position of strength, policy and predictions are more likely to be accurate, each occasion reinforcing the basis of trust in the future. The point is underlined by the observation that, since the great hiccups in the international economy from the late 1960s onwards, predictions have been less easy to validate and consensus in German economic policy and industrial relations has been less easily secured.)

More generally it might be argued that the more workers' representatives are involved in controlling economic variables, the more willing they will be to pursue restraint. This would include measures of co-determination, involvement in effective national planning instruments and participation in control of occupational pension funds and similar sources of investment— plans for which have recently been advanced, with varying degrees of success, in the Netherlands, Sweden, Britain and West Germany.

Finally, it must be remembered that external constraints may vary widely in their impact on different social interests. If a supposedly neutral and impersonal regulator in fact involves a distinct pattern of privileges and deprivations, there is unlikely to be agreement over its use.[4]

Securing the consent of union leaderships to schemes of this kind, in which they exchange a degree of autonomy for an increase in real power, does not present insuperable problems. As Pizzorno (1978) has argued, the chance of a seat at the table, the possibility of securing some control over future and not just current dispositions are strong pressures. Trade unions know that they can do most for their members in favourable economic circumstances, and if there is a basis for the expectation of success they will have an interest in co-operation. Indeed, the history of national union leaderships in Britain is more one of co-operating on an inadequate basis of trust (leading to the eventual disillusion of the membership) than of the opposite.

Turning to the transcendence of narrow perspectives, it is necessary to ask, without cynicism, what substantive jobs unions can be given to do. In strict economic terms all they can achieve are increases in income, which improved productivity was about to produce anyway, inflation or unemployment. In practice it is likely that they do more: requiring firms to improve productivity to pay for wage increases, squeezing oligopolistic profits, securing real improvements in working conditions. However, in periods of recession they can achieve little that is constructive if they remain rooted in economism.

The gap is that between the imperative to organize (which is logical in that labour's subordination to capital is partly dependent on individualization) and the constraints on what organization can achieve (given the pursuit of frequently self-defeating wage bargaining as unions' most readily available activity). Again, possible solutions appear in the extension of union activities to issues of the organization of production, corporate strategy and investment planning within industry, and to bargaining at the national political level over general economic policy and the advancement of workers' legal rights. At both levels a process of unions extending the range of their activities and powers, while at the same time acquiring increased responsibility in the full sense, is compatible with a strategy for the improved political regulation of organized interests.

In turning to the third issue—relations between union leaders and members—it has to be acknowledged that some of the measures relevant to the two previous issues are likely to worsen problems here. The general problem is of course a long-term one. It is easier to secure the integration of trade-union leaderships, not because of cupidity or corruption on their part, but because of differences between their position and that of their members. If organization brings capacity for strategy—that is, a capacity for long-term planning rather than mere immediate responsiveness to events—then that capacity belongs to the organization as such rather than to the members (Pizzorno, 1978). Further, many of the non-economic gains which governments can offer unions in exchange for restraint are gains for the organizations' own rights and powers—perhaps even powers over members. Further again, the interests of a union as an organization are advanced by the mere fact of participation in decision-making, because this affords the organization increased scope and useful, perhaps prestigious, activities; the members stand to gain only if some material benefit is secured from the participation, and this will be inherently long-term and uncertain. Finally, the Olsonian problems of an interest in participation in collective action, which make immediate and identifiable gains necessary for rank-and-file members, do not appear for the organizations, who are few in number and whose officials are often paid to participate.

It is these differences, rather than any tendency towards greater militancy among either leaderships or the rank and file which account for the greater likelihood of union leaderships transcending the narrowness of ordinary working-class perspectives. Similarly, the involvement of leaderships in planning and co-determination may partly resolve the trust problem for them, but at the expense of widening the trust gap between them and their members; the political system is then resolving some of the problems of cohesion by exporting them to intra-union relations. This may enjoy some 'success' in that unions have some compensatory resources of internal cohesion not available to the nation-state: small size, normative cohesion, extensive patronage and disciplinary sanctions, general 'wheeling and dealing'.

Such resources would require supplementation if the incorporation of organized interests were to be more strenuously pursued. Very different kinds of measures are available, ranging from legal obligations on leaderships to regulate the actions of members to more extensive participation by plant-level activists and others in union policy-making. At the same time, some of the extensions in union participation in industrial and national-political decision-making may actually facilitate solutions of this kind. To the extent that participatory organs extend throughout the structure, a wide range of actors will be able to transcend the trust problem and alternatives to mere economism in the pursuit of their interests will become possible.

IV

All the foregoing arguments have been consistent with the
central contention of section I: that the institutions of the
classic bourgeois state are incapable of providing an adequate
regulation of interests when so many of those interests are
organized and incapable of containment by economic regulation
alone. Inflation is one major outcome of such a situation. The
primary weakness of such a bold statement is that we have
had the development of institutions of this kind for a long
time now, and that even in the central homes of the liberal
political economy—Britain and the United States—the period
of predominance of the true bourgeois state was brief and
is long since past. On the other side, three important points
need to be made. First, it is doubtful whether, in most Western
societies but certainly in Britain, the process of the integration
of organized interests has yet proceeded far enough. The importance of organization has increased in the past decade or so,
as was discussed above. At the same time, certain barriers
which long protected the political economy from facing the
implications of the degree of organization which exists have
disappeared. The organization of the working class became a
major issue at the end of the nineteenth century, and that
was a period both of considerable discussion of the adequacy
of existing institutions of integration and of considerable social
disruption which lasted into the first decade of this century.
Since then there have been two world wars, a massive international depression that weakened organized labour considerably,
and a period of postwar prosperity that eased social tensions.
Now none of these factors is operative. A second reason for
drawing attention to the importance of the integration of
organized interests is that most accounts of comparative national
economies ignore national variations on this dimension, or
consider just arbitrarily chosen examples of institutions (such
as formal incomes policy). Finally, the most dominant voices
of the past few years have been those seeking a resolution
to the present impasse in a roll-back of political participation
rather than in its extension.

   The thrust of the argument of this chapter is in favour of

certain kinds of policy which would aid the more effective integration of interests, but these policies cannot be readily assimilated to conventional divisions between left and right. Opposed to such policies will be both monetarists and the advocates of unfettered collective bargaining; supporters might range from thoroughgoing corporatists to supporters of the worker-controlled economy. The political colour of particular versions of the kind of policy advocated will depend on the form and balance of interests involved in specific measures. How much disturbance is there to existing patterns of industrial ownership and control? How strong are concessions that are won in exchange for restraint? On what terms is the trust barrier transcended? By what precise mechanisms is intra-union cohesion secured?

The answers which would be given to such questions would be partly a matter of political will, but they would also be a response to the particular objective situation. Within Britain, with a mature, autonomously-organized working class and a strong legacy of liberalism which induces resistance to the corporate state, the kinds of policy most likely to succeed are those which give most concessions to subordinates' demands and maintain the highest degree of pluralism.

Political differences of this kind are crucially important. However, it is worth stressing that any pattern of political integration is likely to include both measures which enable organized groups to secure their ends through a particular set of institutions and other measures which restrain them. Accounts of existing instances of co-determination at various levels are always divided in their estimation of whether the system limits workers' autonomy or helps them secure their goals. The differences probably reflect a genuine heterogeneity within the institutions; at least, if the political integration of powerful interests is to be at all viable, such a heterogeneity needs to exist.

NOTES

1. The distinction between polity and economy adopted here has similarities to the distinction between adaptation and goal-attainment in Parsons' scheme of the functional dimensions of social order (Parsons and Smelser, 1956). The notion of normative restraint developed here also resembles Parsons'

concept of latency. There are, however, important differences from his approach, especially from his stress on value orientations rather than substantive interests.

2. The limitation of sociology to the study of the normative sphere may seem strange, but it is significant that most central schools of sociological thought, including those of Durkheim, Weber, Parsons and contemporary action theory, do take as their starting point the subjectively perceived nature of social reality.

3. It will normally be pressures from subordinates which create the excessive demands, because the economic system gives them least scope for pursuing their interests. However, in certain kinds of inflation dominant groups may be involved, as has often been the case in Latin America (Jackson, Turner and Wilkinson, 1972).

4. Jay's (1977) analysis of an economy in which the control of each company would be vested in all its employees (abolishing management, employers, unions and collective bargaining) falls at this point. Central to his model is (i) the maintenance in private hands of investment resources (banks, pension funds, private capital etc.) and (ii) a new political settlement under which governments would abide rigidly to monetarist orthodoxy. One can easily envisage such an economy becoming prone to crises of under-investment, similar to that of the 1920s, together with a fusion of the latent conflict in Britain between financial and industrial capital with current conflicts between employees and workers. While ostensibly a system of workers' cooperatives, it would really be one of labour-only sub-contracting by financial capital throughout the economy. Even if many of the beneficiaries of such capital are the members of occupational pension schemes, it is difficult to see such a framework of economic policy being accepted as neutral and depoliticized.

CHAPTER 10

Power and Inflation

Malcolm Anderson

I

In assessing policies to reduce the rate of inflation, two general questions may be asked. First, is the government trying to modify the right economic variables in the correct direction? Secondly, is the policy politically feasible—in other words has the government the power to carry it out? Economists have applied powerful analytical tools to the first question, but little progress has been made in answering the second question in a systematic way. As Crouch remarks (see above, pp. 217–8), the treatment of political variables in the inflationary process is rarely satisfactory. Giving precise meaning to the phrase 'not politically feasible' seems all the more difficult because it is often used by politicians as an obfuscatory justification for refraining from taking a course of action which they find distasteful.

There is common ground between Brittan, Crouch, Maier and other contributors to this volume in their view that the institutions of the contemporary state are weak in confronting the problems of controlling inflation. This weakness is all the more starkly exposed if we accept the conclusion that technical mismanagement, ignorance and real factors such as war are no longer crucial elements in an explanation of inflation (Hirsch and Oppenheimer, 1976). The origin of the weakness is assigned to various general causes—the effects of electoral competition (Brittan), the coalescence of groups into inflationary coalitions (Maier), the intermingling of the economic and political processes in a way which isolates political institutions from the mass of the population as well as bringing special interests directly into the making of policy (Crouch). Whatever the basic cause, the government and monetary authorities appear in certain circumstances not to have the power to impose policies. The way in which group conflicts are resolved has inflationary effects and the formidable persuasive, legislative and coercive powers of governments cannot, or can only partially, be used to bring the groups into a more orderly relationship with each other. The search for some method of systematically estimating a government's power to control at least some of the political variables is worth undertaking because a successful method would have important policy implications. It would help to solve the puzzle of why conflicts of objectives between governments and interest groups, or interest groups and other interest groups, may be resolved differently from what might have been expected, in view of the relative ostensible strength of the parties and their intentions at the outset of bargaining.

There are various ways of arriving at estimates of the power of governments in inflationary circumstances. The first, the comparative method, used by Maier, has the great advantage of bringing out the diversity and complexity of inflationary situations. By using this method, a typology of inflationary situations can be established, inferences drawn about the motives of policy makers, and assessments made of the outcome of their actions on the basis of a careful examination of the historical evidence. The second method is to develop general models of the political process which may be used to identify the main constraints on governments. These models may be of a sociological kind, such as the one proposed by Crouch; or economic models, such as that of the competitive party system used by Brittan. These are deliberate simplifications of reality in order to isolate key variables. The third method is the more piecemeal and partial modelling of particular sorts of power relationships, attempted in this paper.

None of these approaches can provide a definitive answer to the question of why governments fail to control inflation. Such an explanation would be dependent on a scientific theory of political life to which none but the most purblind ideologue would give credence. Each of the approaches can provide illuminating but partial assessments of the power of governments. Since the conclusions of political analysis are intimately related to its postulates, it is not surprising if the implications derived from the different perspectives outlined above tend to differ.

Clarifying the conceptual differences between them contributes, in the long run, to improved control over policy. As Connolly (1974, p. 180) has written:

> The concepts of politics do not simply provide a lens through which to observe a process which is independent of them ... they are themselves part of political life. It follows that changes in these concepts, once accepted by a significant number of participants contribute to changes in political life.

II

An essential preliminary to a political theory of inflation is a definition of inflation as an economic phenomenon and a clear view of the relationships between economic variables that result in inflation. I adopt the usual definition of inflation as an increase in the general price level. It is widely accepted that sustained inflation can only arise in association with a sustained monetary expansion. The view presented in Flemming's paper, a careful exposition of a neo-classical macroeconomic model, is taken as the starting point in this paper. If the monetary authorities are attempting and failing to hold back inflation, this can be explained by the action of powerful monopolies forcing a series of price rises to which the authorities respond by increasing the money supply. The monopolies initiate a process which leads to inflation, but the cause of inflation lies in the response of the authorities to these initiators. The authorities lack the power to oppose them.

There is a range of monopolies which could, in an economy like the British one, trigger the inflationary process. These monopolies can even exist within the apparatus of the state. In the past, central banks, firmly committed to fixed interest rates, could be the monopoly which triggered inflation. The operation of the dollar standard gave them additional freedom of action. As Meltzer (1977, p. 190) has written on the operation of the dollar standard: 'Most foreign central banks did not insist on the convertibility of dollars into gold and did not revalue. Instead, they purchased dollar securities and permitted prices to rise.' Producer groups which escape the rather weak controls of the Monopolies Commission or whose prices are fixed administratively can achieve substantial price rises. However, in Britain most publicity has been directed towards the real or supposed inflationary effects of labour-market monopolies. Although it is not possible to discount entirely the possibility of a conscious search for alibis, successive governments have appeared convinced that wage increases are the most important inflationary pressure.

Politicians and their advisors have asserted that wage settlements are the principal and perhaps the only cause of inflation. Brendon Sewill, a Cambridge economist who served as director of the Conservative Party's research department and subsequently as special advisor to Chancellor Anthony Barber, wrote (Harris and Sewill, 1975, p. 55):

> It is important to realize that it is the fear of a large-scale strike which renders governments impotent to stop inflation. If it were not for the strike threat, a pay and prices policy could be imposed, followed by a regime of strict monetary policy which, in a free competitive market, could be expected to produce price stability without excessive unemployment. Given price stability, interest rates would come down, exports would rise, sterling would strengthen, savings would revive, taxes could be cut, business confidence would return and fears of a slump would vanish like a bad dream.

The nub of Sewill's position is that the Conservative government would have no alternative but to comply with wage demands—it would be powerless to oppose the trigger which sets off inflation.

None the less, as Turner has remarked: 'The publicity which attaches to formal wage determination is not . . . a sufficient reason for regarding it as the main source of inflation.' (Jackson, Turner and Wilkinson, 1972, p. 1). Whether or not wage settlements have inflationary effects is a question for economic analysis and so too, in part, is the question of whether incomes policies are always or even usually the best indirect method of bringing down the rate of inflation. On the latter point, some of the best arguments such as those offered by Griffiths and Wood seem to belong to the other side.[1] Governments have, however, been convinced on both points and have acted accordingly: as a consequence, there has since the Second World War, with the exception of 1945–8, several years in the 1950s, 1964, 1970 and 1974, been an incomes policy of some sort. If governments had been convinced that the trigger of inflation was some other monopoly, it would have faced analogous problems of the exercise of power, although in some respects they may have been less intractable. The membership of trade unions forms a particularly large population, not susceptible to some forms of coercion. The use of the economic term 'monopoly' applied to trade unions can be misleading when used in a political context because it implies control of a market. Trade unions have complex internal political systems and are subject to external political and economic pressures, which form a network of constraints, limiting their control of labour markets. On the other hand they have unusual strengths. Negotiations with the trade-union leadership, in big set-piece confrontations, have to be conducted more or less in public so that the opportunities for exercising private pressure are severely restricted.

In a situation in which the government is trying to hold down the general level of wages through an incomes policy, any union in a strong market position has an incentive to breaking ranks and gaining a relative advantage. If some, but not all, other unions follow suit, this incentive remains. As Flemming points out, 'an effect of trade union monopolies is . . . to distort relative wages.' The government usually has very little by way of sanctions and rewards which it can apply to unions in a strong market position, other than those which it can apply or can offer to all trade unionists. There are, of course, exceptions when encouragement to various forms of strike-breaking may be given. When there is a danger to national security or public safety, it may be possible, as in the case of the strike at the Windscale nuclear installation in the spring of 1977, to threaten the use of force. In the British case (but not in other national contexts) the costs involved in threatening the use of force are too high; these arise partly out of the distaste for violent coercion and partly because of the probable reaction of the rest of the trade union movement. Similarly, constraint on the whole trade union movement, in the form of a legally enforced incomes policy with fines and imprisonment attached to infringements, is avoided. Thus, we get the curious fiction of a 'statutory' incomes policy which either has no sanctions attached to it or the sanctions are not enforced: the only difference from a voluntary policy is that the latter is passed by parliament in a legal form.

The central political question is what power relationships produce a government decision to retreat before trade-union demands. A satisfactory answer to this question would have important policy implications because governments would be dissuaded from using policy instruments that, predictably, they would be forced to abandon. Some may argue that the intuitions of politicians, based on the experience of exercising power, are the only possible guide in making major policy decisions. Notwithstanding that intuition and personal judgement will always be important in making these decisions, a rigorous theory of power would help to clarify the nature of the choices to be made, and to indicate that some choices involve predictably high costs. The recent literature on the concept of power contains some signposts towards the development of a theory with useful policy implications.

III

Power is a word frequently used in political debate but social scientists find it a particularly difficult and elusive concept. It has been used in such a broad and general sense that one political scientist, Allison (1974), has suggested that we dispense with the notion completely, but this is an eccentric view. The attention paid to the concept in recent years supports Elster's contention (1976, pp. 249–50) that: 'The notion of power would seem the most important idea in political theory, comparable to utility in economics.' Elster goes on to point out that the theory of power is in a poorly developed state in some ways similar to the theory of utility fifty years ago: at that time there was no clear understanding of the relation between the notion of utility and the notion of preferences, just as today there is no agreement on which comes first 'the absolute notion of power *tout court* and the relational notion of power over *someone* (or something).' But there the analogy breaks down: 'There are no substantial similarities or structural analogies between power and utility, no reason to think that we shall witness a clarification of the theory of power comparable to our advances in our understanding of utility.'

There are two ways forward. First, we may accept that power

is a very broad concept and that any analysis of power is inextricably involved with evaluative judgements and with moral and ideological positions. This is the position of Lukes (1974, p. 26):

> ... its very definition and any given use of it, once defined, are inextricably tied to a given set of (probably unacknowledged) value assumptions which predetermine the range of its empirical application ... The concept of power is, in consequence, what has been called 'an essentially contested concept'—one of those concepts which 'inevitably involves endless disputes about their proper uses on the part of their users.' Indeed to engage in such disputes is to engage in politics.

One can hypothesize that a certain distribution of power in communities (such as that underlying Maier's inflationary coalitions) makes inflation inevitable, but such a hypothesis would require a broad definition of power as a phenomenon with many social and political manifestations. Such broad definitions can usually be quickly identified as committing their exponents to certain practical political positions.

A major recent debate on power was provoked by Dahl in his celebrated study of New Haven. He argued that the assertion that someone has power is a statement about an actual, observable exercise of that power (Dahl, 1961). Since in almost any community several groups can be observed exercising power, in the sense of making others do things which they do not wish to, the Dahl view is associated with a liberal–pluralist political position. His best known critics, Bachrach and Baratz (1962, 1970), argued that there is a form of power that takes the form of placing issues on, or excluding them from, the agenda of political discussion. This, it could be argued, is a much more important kind of power than the exercises of power that Dahl observed, which could safely be left to subalterns. Lukes took the debate further, arguing that the powerful could manipulate the views of the less powerful so that the latter saw certain actions which would be in their interests as either impossible or undesirable; no overt exercise of power is therefore required to prevent them taking these actions. The Bachrach and Baratz position and, even more, the Lukes view of power are identified with the radical left because of the association of the concept of power with the manipulation, and possibly exploitation, of the powerless by an élite. These, however, are the kind of stated or implied conceptions of power that must be used if we are to make any generally applicable statement about the relationship of the power of particular groups and inflation. Differing general accounts of the distribution of power seem, as a consequence, plausible and intuitively correct depending on the nature of the audience receiving them.

This does not make such accounts worthless or absurd, but those who advance them must recognize that they are directly engaged in practical political debate as well as theoretical argument. Others will identify them as belonging to different sides of a political conflict and draw policy inferences from their analyses. Three examples of explanations of inflation which depend on an implied general theory of the distribution of power can be mentioned.

The first is the argument that with increased specialization of labour, modern economies have become increasingly interdependent in the sense that if one function is not performed this can have the effect of preventing the performance of many other functions. Withdrawal of the labour of certain groups of workers can have extremely damaging and expensive effects. This gives a number of groups of workers a blackmail power which has to be bought off if employment in other sectors is to be maintained. Another scenario (cf. Maynard and Van Ryckeghem, 1976, p. 256) is that inflation is

a symptom of an internal contradiction of capitalism which puts the system under threat. Labour movements are everywhere seeking a larger share of the national income and are conducting wage bargaining accordingly: profits are being squeezed. The capitalist is seeking to maintain the share of profits which are indeed necessary if investment is to be financed: inflation results.

A third perspective is based on the symbiotic relationship between the state and the 'monopoly sector'. (O'Connor, 1973). The state has to support certain monopolies in order to keep key industries in being and maintain levels of employment. This involves intolerable levels of taxation on other sectors and therefore the necessity of taxing through inflation. The first view is a conservative or *status quo* one in that the policy inference is that some sort of orderly control of strategically placed groups of workers has to be imposed if prices are to be stabilized. The second is, in effect, a 'class war' view, in that capitalists are seen as promoting inflation in order to maintain their share of the national income and are thus thwarting the drive of underprivileged classes for equality. The third is a neo-Marxist view, in that the internal contradictions of capitalism are leading to an unresolvable 'fiscal crisis of the state'. There are not testable theories in that they contain broad evaluative judgements about the nature and distribution of power. Most events can be interpreted in the light of them, and the failure of particular policies would not constitute a refutation of any of them. However, consistent anti-inflationary policies are usually based on theories such as these: they are important theories to the extent that participants in politics believe in them.

The second way forward is to seek a more limited and testable theory. Most of the running in recent years in this field has been made by the exponents of 'rational choice' or economic models. Following the lead of Schumpeter (1942), Downs (1957) and Olson (1965) there has been an attempt to postulate a *'Homo politicus'* similar to (and in some cases identical with) the benefit-maximizing, cost-minimizing *'Homo œconomicus'*. This has not had much useful application in general analyses of political processes and behaviour. There are no fixed and knowable gains to be derived from many political processes, no stable unit of exchange such as money—what political actors regard as a gain and a loss tends to change over time. General assumptions about the motives of political actors are difficult and perhaps even impossible to formulate. For example, Nozick's (1974) attempt to give an account of what motivates political man, on the basis of a survey of views of human nature to be found in the writings of political theorists, and his choice, for his own purposes, of a mid-point between the conceptions of Hobbes and Godwin—the 'justice loving egoist'—is singularly unconvincing. Assumptions about motives must relate to a particular group at a given period.

When considering the motives of political actors, in relation to inflation, it is necessary to consider group interests and what we mean by the term 'interests'. Group interests can, at least in principle, be the subject of empirical investigation if we take as a definition of group interest self-regarding wants over a specific period of time. There are, of course, many who have argued that the notion of interests involves normative elements and have held, like Plamenatz (1954) that interests are wants which, given the resources of a particular society, particular people have a strong claim to have satisfied. Debates about interests have often been, to quote Connolly (1974, p. 48), part of 'a larger debate about the structure and style of the good society.' But there is no reason why, in defining interests as wants, we should consider the wants as good or legitimate before accepting them as interests. There is, however, a distinction developed by Lively (1977) between immediate and long-term interests. Long-term interests involve an evaluation of what people might want in, say, ten years time: notions of what they ought to want are bound to enter. The problems associated with the notion of 'long-term', 'real', or 'higher' interests can be ignored for the sort of analysis of power with which this paper is mainly concerned.

As well as a specification of the interests of the groups that might trigger an inflationary process, there are a number of other elements which have to be included in any empirical political theory of inflation. One of them is a framework for analysing several rounds of the same conflict between one of the groups and the government or the monetary authorities, because it is unlikely that a conflict between them will be a once-for-all matter. Tactical concessions in one round may be a means of strengthening one's hand for the next. What happens in any given round will affect the starting position for the next: particular outcomes may affect the power resources of the parties involved in the conflict. We also need an expression for feedback from other issues: for example, one can argue that the trade union leadership was more powerful, in the sense of 'activation of commitments', in the early 1970s in the pursuance of wage claims because of the industrial relations legislation of the Conservative government. Our theory must also take account of the phenomenon, labelled by the now famous phrase of Bachrach and Baratz—the 'mobilization of bias', whereby the arrangements for resolving conflicts systematically favour one group rather than another. Also institutional 'gatekeepers', such as courts or professional economists or the quality press, may limit the range of possible outcomes. An excellent account of the role of the quality press as a gatekeeper is given by Hirsch and Gordon (1975, p. 37), in which they describe the press in Britain as 'an influence which sets the boundaries and to a large extent the agenda of political action, which in turn helps to determine the content of party programmes.'

IV

An ambitious and potentially useful model for analysing the relations of governments with groups which act as triggers for inflation is contained in Barry's economic analysis of power (1974, 1976). Barry's theory is similar in style to the theories found in Downs, Olson and others but he is much more careful in defining the application of his theory and in working out its implications. Barry's account can be drastically summarized without, I hope, seriously distorting his thinking. His starting point is a deliberate avoidance of the quest for a general theory of power. This is based on the belief that there is no hope of operationalizing a general theory of power, no way of measuring the power shares of all the political actors in the community, because for this we would require a theory of what causes things to happen. Power is normally used as a descriptive term like illness: we know when a person is ill but there are many different forms which illness can take. According to Barry, if we know what sort of power we are talking about, this will avoid the confusions which general theories of power inevitably create. Forms of power can be classified according to ways of getting people to do things. If we follow Barry in adapting Talcott Parsons' categories—'activation of commitments', 'persuasion', 'inducement/coercion' and 'physical constraint'—we can engage in more rigorous modelling of, at least, some of these categories. Theorizing, at least for the last two categories, can quickly become technical, employing graphical and mathematical techniques. Value assumptions are present but, as in 'positive' economics, there is an attempt to reduce these to a minimum.

Technical complexity should, however, be avoided as far as possible if the intention is to explain or predict observable relationships.

The model proposed by Barry for one form of power, the 'inducement/coercion' form, is appropriate to the examination of government relations with labour market monopolies. There are a number of plausible assumptions in the model, such as that costless threats and promises are unusual cases. In many situations, carrying out a threat or promise would result in a net loss to the issuer even though he acquired the compliance of the person to whom they were addressed. In such cases, trying to exercise power by inducement/coercion would be irrational unless the intention was to retain credibility for the next round of the conflict. In considering the exercise of power of actor A over actor B by the manipulation of rewards, there are two factors to be taken into account: the size of the rewards in B's values which are necessary to gain his compliance—and the more distasteful the demand, the larger the reward will have to be; and the cost to A of any given reward for B—we have to assume a transformation function of A's costs into B's rewards. If we assume that it costs nothing in net terms to A to reward B, there would be an optimal point (x) on compliance line (0) for A to offer rewards to B (see Chart I). If A's costs of rewarding B increase with the size of the demand made on B, then the net cost of rewarding B will always and increasingly be less than A's gross gain from securing compliance. A will always attempt to maximize his net gain and the highest net gain available (nw) will always be to the left on compliance line 0 of the highest gross gain (px) (see Chart II). We can also assume that the efficiency of rewards will be 'lumpy': in other words there may be nothing effective available between a given level of reward and a much bigger reward for securing A's compliance. If we assume that rewards are lumpy rather than finely graded, then Barry argues that we will have graphs such as that of Chart III. There are segments on the compliance line 0 (tu, vw) where increases in gross gains are unavailable and even larger segments (t'u', v'–) where net gains are unavailable.

A somewhat different analysis must be applied to threats. What is involved in threatening effectively is different from

CHART I

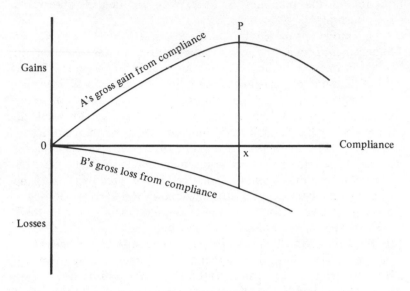

rewarding successfully: one of the points to emerge from the discussion of deterrence theory is the questionable rationality of A actually carrying out a threat to B, if B refuses to comply. However, for our purposes we may assume that A's net gain from B's compliance to threats is the expected value of A threatening B. Expected value means that each of the possible outcomes is discounted by the probability of its occurring; for example, the cost of carrying out a threat is discounted by

CHART II

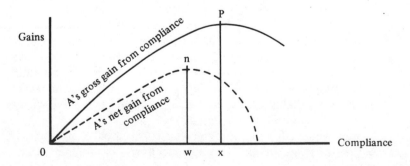

CHART III

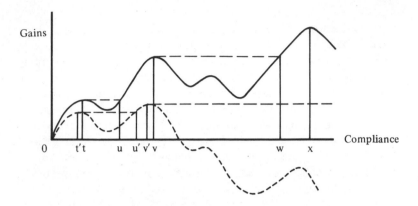

the probability of having to carry it out. These assumptions
need further exposition, which Barry provides, but the main
proposition is clear. The higher cost to A of carrying out
the threat, the less likely B is to believe him and, therefore,
the difference between gross gain and net gain becomes larger.
It is also reasonable to assume that threats, like rewards, are
lumpy and nothing effective may be available between one threat
and a much larger threat.

Various possible conceptions of power emerge from this model:
A's gross gain, B's gross loss, A's net gain, B's net loss and
the difference between A's gross gain and his net gain. This
is of little importance providing consistency is maintained but,
as Barry points out, there are various technical difficulties with
the model. There is a tendency to slide between subjective
and objective values and to consider actual costs, whereas in
practice they are estimated costs. It is often difficult to apply
the model to actual cases because, unless one is privy to the
calculations of the participants in the conflict, it is hard to
attach accurate data to the curves. Also, it is impossible to
identify definitely when someone has complied: '. . . compliance
is never observable; to say that a piece of behaviour is compliant
is always a theoretical statement involving a counter-factual
conditional.' (Barry, 1976, p. 74) Other difficulties and objections
could be mentioned but the attraction of the model is that
it has a basic simplicity which makes application of it possible,

at least in a rudimentary way. Any additional complexity might improve its theoretical coherence but would reduce its value as a tool of empirical enquiry.

The value of the Barry approach is that it permits a finer analysis than any general theory of power of the relations between governments and the monopolies capable of triggering an inflationary process. This is because, in the first place, it suggests that the exercise of power can be broken down into categories and different forms of analysis applied to each. There is, of course, much room for argument about the categories chosen, but the Barry–Parsons classification is plausible and departs little from the terms of ordinary language. In the second place, in the area of policy connected with inflation control, the manipulation of threats and promises is a frequently observed form of behaviour. The Barry model suggests ways of looking at the limitations of this form of power and the phenomenon of lumpiness when the size of threats and promises is increased. Perhaps the main weakness of the model in this area of policy is that, in looking at the exercise of power of A over B, it does not take account of attempts by B to alter A's behaviour by retaliatory action. Such attempts are very common in practice. Retaliatory action can, of course, be taken into account by regarding it as the beginning of the next round of the conflict between the parties. The issue of a threat or the making of a promise can be regarded as the starting point of a round and the response to them, or an escalation of them, as the end point.

Governments frequently use a mixture of the forms of power because they wish to mobilize whatever power resources they have available. As has already been remarked, physical constraint is a form of power which is usually not available to British governments in obtaining the compliance of workers pursuing wage claims by militant industrial action. Ministers often attempt to use persuasion in industrial disputes using various sorts of arguments about the consequences of large wage settlements on jobs, the future prospects of the industry and the likely reactions of other groups of workers. The activation of commitments of working people, in the sense of cashing in on norms they already have, involves appeals to obey the law, to the values of social harmony and to trade-union and working-class solidarity, and exhortations to consider the national interest.

Attempts to activate commitments are often mixed with threats. For example, Ray Gunter, speaking against an unofficial strike at London Airport in 1965, said:

> These men have flatly contradicted their own union and they pour spleen on ordinary folk. This is just irresponsibility. This is sheer viciousness. These men have the power to disrupt the lives of good people. These good people may, ere long, say they have had enough and are not going to be pushed around any longer, and they will have all my support. [quoted in Panitch, 1976, p. 86]

Here we have Gunter appealing to union solidarity, to decency and consideration for others, as well as threatening to support any sanctions that the rest of the working-class movement is willing to endorse.

In using persuasion and activation of commitments the government often tries to act through the Trades Union Congress. This has particularly been the case since the middle of the 1960s because appeals by non unionists have been received with increasing scepticism. Vic Feather, towards the end of the 1960s, remarked: 'Unions and work people have learned from experience that when the cry "the National Interest" goes up, it means everyone but them.' In government-TUC relations the manipulation of threats and promises has become the dominant form of the exercise of power when serious conflicts of interest have emerged. The request of Harold Wilson to Hugh Scanlon at the Chequers talks in 1969 on *In Place of Strife* to 'Get your tanks off my lawn', illustrates an awareness of this fact by the participants.

There are a large number of policy proposals which the government can use as threats and promises in its relations with the TUC but they can be grouped under a small number of general headings:

Promises
(i) Measures to promote the growth of the economy and increase real wages.
(ii) Tax concessions.
(iii) Redistributive measures, including transfer payments.
(iv) Measures to promote industrial democracy, giving the unions a major role.

(v) A return to free collective bargaining when the rate of inflation has been reduced.
(vi) Consultation with trade union leaders on all important policy matters ('a seat at the table').

Threats
(i) Policies allowing the level of unemployment to rise.
(ii) A reduction of trade-union influence on economic policy concerning wages and prices, training, industrial relations and industrial policy.
(iii) Limitation of trade-union rights and the right to strike.
(iv) A reduction of welfare payments, in particular of those available to striking workers and their families.

With the exception of threat (ii) and promise (vi), and marginally threat (iii) and promise (iv), these are directed towards the mass of trade-union members rather than the trade-union leadership. None the less, these are measures of inducement and coercion against the leadership because the union members can be expected to disobey the leadership, provoke leadership crises and, at the extreme, desert the union if they receive the punishments and do not receive the rewards.

A curious relationship is thus established. The government seeks to exercise power over the TUC by a mixture of threats and promises to the mass of union members, who can then be expected to put pressure on the leadership. The TUC, on the other hand, has no effective threats and promises with which to secure the compliance of the membership mainly, to borrow from a list from Barbash (1972, p. 140) because of:
(i) the previous lack of efficacy of incomes policies in stabilizing prices at a 'tolerable' level of unemployment;
(ii) the lack of a bargaining structure capable of making a binding commitment and enforcing it on the shop floor;
(iii) the rejection by the trade unions of state intervention in collective bargaining as a matter of principle; and
(iv) the existence of labour shortages which encourage employers to bid up wages beyond the agreed terms, that is, the phenomenon of wage drift.

The government has power over the TUC in terms of the three headings of Barry's paradigm of power: it has the opportunity, it has the motive and it has the incentive to get some form of compliance. But the TUC can only use persuasion and exhortation in its relations with trade union members and add its authority to government threats that things would be even worse in the absence of an incomes policy. George Woodcock's dictum that 'the TUC cannot become an agent of the government because the unions cannot be agents of the TUC' is strictly correct but the government can, in certain circumstances, get compliance from the TUC precisely because the union leaders cannot control the membership.

V

We can take one example of this sort of relationship as an illustration and apply the Barry model to it. The start point is the implementation of the Conservative government's Industrial Relations Act in February 1972, offering registered status to trade unions in return for legal advantages, various restrictions on the right to strike and the establishment of the National Industrial Relations Court. Within three months this legislation had been gravely undermined. The TUC adopted a policy of non-cooperation with the Act but this was only a contributory factor to its failure. The crucial conflict concerned an unofficial boycott by dockers of container work done outside the dock area. Their union, the TGWU, was fined £55,000 on the assumption that it was responsible for the dockers' action. The union then dropped its policy of total non-cooperation with the Act and agreed to put its case before the NIRC. The fine on the TGWU had no restraining effect on the dockers themselves who extended the boycott in defiance of the Court. The NIRC then applied the law directly to those organizing the boycott and five shop stewards were gaoled for defying the authority of the Court. Indignation at the grass roots was such that industrial action in sympathy with the gaoled men seemed likely to escalate spontaneously into a general strike. The TUC General Council then resolved that an official general strike would be called if the shop stewards were not released: they were released very quickly. The attempt to outlaw certain forms of union action which led to inflationary wage settlements had failed and this was the start point for the next round, which was the Heath government's attempt at agreement with the TUC on incomes policy. The Heath government was in a weaker position at the start of that round because it could not threaten to introduce legislation outlawing certain forms of industrial action if it failed to get agreement. Indeed, the Heath government finally abandoned its Industrial Relations Act as a concession to the TUC in order to get a co-operative incomes policy in 1972. The incident could be placed along the lines of a graph as shown in Chart IV.

There are, of course, difficult problems in applying such a graphical representation. First, arbitrary decisions have to be taken in dividing continuous relationships into rounds, with precise starting and end points. In the above example, the start is taken as the decision to bring a case against the TGWU and the end point is the release of the shop stewards. But a different interpretation of the motives of the participants could lead to the choice of other points. Secondly, different graphs can be drawn for the same round depending on the perspective adopted. In the example chosen, the government is using the threat of legal sanctions and it desisted when the cost of threats became too high: the round could be represented in another way, that is to say, to show compliance by the government to actions or retaliatory actions (not indicated in Chart IV) by trade unionists. Thirdly, there is often a divergence between estimated costs and actual costs. Miscalculation is represented as a form of loss of power. In the example given above, the Conservative government in implementing its legislation did so on the assumption that it was dealing with a minority of militant shop stewards and discovered that it was dealing with majorities of trade-union members. The estimated costs of dealing with the former were much smaller than the actual costs of dealing with the latter. In other words, the government in issuing a threat was mistaken about whom it was threatening. It is frequently the case that estimates of power resources of opponents turn out to be mistaken (in this case it was the estimate of numbers involved), because they cannot be precisely assessed until a conflict has been joined. The possible inaccuracy of estimates make it imprudent to rely too heavily on any shape of curve to predict the outcome of power exertion in practical situations.

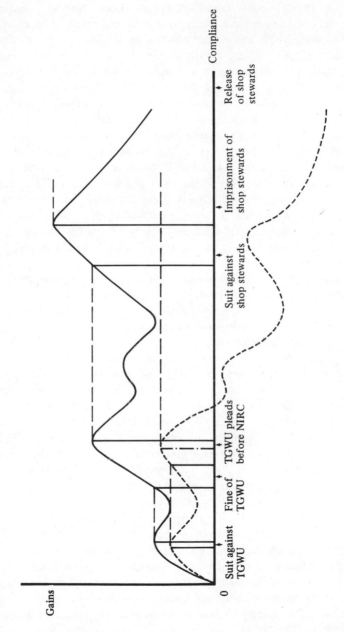

CHART IV

The model can be used only to reach general conclusions which are more or less likely to permit stable patterns of threats and promises from government and unions if the preference orders of the parties remain stable. Both the general objectives of economic management and the claims of trade unions may remain fairly constant but the preferences for particular policies can change when the costs of threats and promises are calculated. If the estimates of costs on both sides coincide, then this can lead to an agreement to abandon certain forms of action. This is roughly what happened in the so-called *Arbeitsfrieden* agreement of 1937 in the Swiss metal and machine industries, which effectively ruled out the strike as a weapon of collective bargaining: in return the employers had to surrender the lock-out, blackleg labour and non-recognition of trade unions. This example shows that there is no inevitability about the use of 'inducement/coercion' leading to a continuous escalation of threats and promises.

The model outlined above is furthermore appropriate only for big set-piece confrontations between the government and the trade unions. A subsidiary use of the model is therefore to arrive at a classification of different kinds of conflict. When the detailed operation of incomes policies is examined, the pattern of government–trade-union relations is much less sharply defined and a more complex exchange of threats and promises can be found. In the years of statutory incomes policy (1966–9, 1972–3) there was a large degree of compliance or various forms of loophole exploration, very different from the downright refusal of trade-unionists to obey the law, as in the aftermath of the industrial relations legislation of the Heath government. This point applies *a fortiori* to government relations with firms or producer groups because these latter rarely allow themselves to be manœuvred into a position of clear confrontation with the government. If this happens, unless there is an endemic weakness of the executive branch of government as under the Fourth French Republic or unless the government has already been gravely weakened by other factors, the government is almost certain to win. Producer groups seldom have the power resources of large numbers and solidarity, possessed by militant trade-unionists, necessary to beat governments in open and protracted conflicts. They have other resources, such as specialized information and easy access to decision makers, which can make them formidable opponents in private negotiations.

VI

Even when governments claim that price stability is a major objective of policy, it should not be assumed that they fail to achieve it because they lack the power to impose their will on recalcitrant groups. Beliefs, policy priorities and tactical considerations may influence policy makers not to use their power. For example, the policy makers may believe that neo-classical explanations of inflation are mistaken and that certain forms of credit expansion are not inflationary. In these circumstances, they could be charged with technical mismanagement. In terms of priorities, although they may appear firmly committed to price stability, policy makers may in fact regard it as less important than employment, regional balance, a certain distribution of income and wealth and so on. Tactical considerations are often related to calculations of electoral advantage and up to a certain point inflationary policies may win votes. The evidence for this, as Brittan notes (this volume), is not conclusive. But, at least in post Second World War Britain, the unpopularity of high levels of unemployment make it plausible to assume that governments have been encouraged to pursue inflationary policies in order to gain electoral advantage. The intellectual backing of Keynesian demand management theory has allowed them to do this in good faith. Beyond a certain point inflation is more likely to lose votes than a high level of unemployment and this point has been passed in the United Kingdom. Also, the major political parties have a strong interest in not undermining the existing political order which they dominate and, therefore, they are unlikely to continue competitive bidding in the field of employment, or in any other, to the point of catastrophic breakdown of institutions. Rarely are political leaders, parties and institutions totally at the mercy of blind clashes of interest or the short-sighted aspirations of sections of the electorate. They have resources of initiative, imagination and power which allow them to confront the inflationary demands of particular groups, although faced by a coalition they may lose. We have a great deal of information about the course and outcome of these confrontations but we need a tighter framework of explanation if we are to propose solutions to the problems of the British political economy.

NOTE

1. The main thrust of their argument is that incomes policies may serve to reduce inflationary expectations, but in a situation in which they have already been reduced they may provoke a series of wage settlements higher than they would otherwise be. Wage settlements become politicized and a numerically insignificant group may, for good market reasons, get a wage settlement which breaks the norm. Numerically large groups will then regard the norm, without any good market reason, as the minimum and refuse to settle for less. See a summary in the *Sunday Telegraph*, 6 March 1977.

CONCLUSION

The Ideological Underlay of Inflation*

Fred Hirsch

To understand and explain inflation, technical factors on the one hand and broad economic, political and social factors on the other hand need to be considered not as alternatives but as correlates. That general conclusion emerges strikingly from the previous chapters, for all their differences of methodological approach and of ideology. Inflation, a monetary phenomenon, is the end-product of the existing monetary instrumentalities and the use made of them. The instrumentalities represent the technique; their management or manipulation ultimately rests on political determination and on the social and economic forces that in turn underlie political decisions or confine them within a certain range. Economic factors, and they alone, can explain how inflation happens, but economic factors alone cannot explain why.

Inflation has been an endemic problem throughout the twentieth century. It kept its hold over the minds of policy makers even in the periods, such as the interwar depression, in which it was eradicated. Since the beginning of World War II inflation has been continuous, although from the early 1950s until the late 1960s it appeared tolerable. In the past decade, inflation has re-emerged as the central though still not exclusive concern of economic policy in the market economies of the industrial world; yet despite the more or less deliberate sacrifice of other economic objectives, involving the acceptance of higher unemploy-

* This chapter incorporates a number of suggestions made by John Goldthorpe on an earlier draft. It draws widely on the previous chapters and on discussions among the authors and others at the Warwick conference. But it is deliberately an individual interpretation, rather than an attempt at a consensus view.

ment and lower economic activity at least in the short term, inflation has not been eradicated or even rolled back very far. The achievement is essentially limited to breaking the spiral of inflationary acceleration.

The course and extent of inflation in the industrial market economies has clearly been influenced, and at times dominated, by real economic disturbances. By far the most important of these has been war. War has been an inflationary influence throughout history because it entails a sudden draft of resources by the state, which then finds it impossible or inexpedient to curtail competing demands for resources to the necessary extent. Both world wars of this century, as well as the Korean war at the beginning of the 1950s and the Vietnam war in the second half of the 1960s, generated inflation in this way. The other main potential source of inflation emanating in the real economy is a sharp deterioration in the terms of trade, such as that associated with the escalation of oil prices and other commodity prices in 1972–4. But that commodity boom, which was unique in modern experience in the absence of military escalation, had clear connections with earlier developments in the industrial economies; as noted by Flemming in chapter 1, it cannot therefore properly be regarded as an outside disturbance for the system as a whole. On this analysis, the recrudescence of inflation in the past decade of peace, on a scale previously associated only with major wars, suggests the presence of strong endogenous inflationary forces. Special factors and their coincidence can be identified as the source of particular inflationary episodes (McCracken, 1977). But the persistence and growth of the inflationary virus within the economic polity of the market economies point to more continuing influences. These are attributed in this chapter to both the monetary techniques and the socio-political element in their application, as well as to interaction between these. A convenient starting point is the profound change that has taken place in the monetary techniques.

I

The twentieth century has seen the coming of age of paper money. In the sixty years after 1914, paper money took the place of gold first in domestic monetary circulation; then as the domestic monetary base; and finally also as the international monetary base, when the last remaining link with gold was cut by the United States in August 1971.

The release of domestic and world money supplies from the metallic base to which they had been welded since the discovery of money has been the outstanding technical change. The change has been speeded along by the actions of governments and in this way has responded to political impulsions, but an autonomous dynamic towards an undiluted paper standard has operated on a purely technical level. The dynamic is essentially that of the banking process, which produces money more cheaply and more efficiently in the form of paper notes and book-keeping entries than in the alternative form of precious metals withdrawn from productive use.

The metallic link did serve an additional social function, in exerting an outside control on the monetary autonomy of the state. Yet the old gold standard kept its hold not because the managers of the state deliberately tied their hands; but predominantly because the attraction of paper money remained limited by the insecurity of the issuing banks. Full security could be provided only with the support of a public agency. This is the modern central bank, standing behind the commercial banks as insurer and ultimate guarantor. Establishment of a lender of last resort underpins the credit structure. In this way it is a natural technical banking development, even though collective action is needed to achieve it. The final step is extension of the central banking function internationally. This extension has developed in multiform, often inchoate ways, including informal co-operation between central banks and finance ministers as well as through the International Monetary Fund and other international financial agencies.

The natural outcome of this evolutionary process has been seen as a world central bank, in fact if not in name. This would again limit the monetary autonomy of individual states, but now by the discretionary action or automatic rules of the international agency rather than by the mechanism of gold supply and demand. The technical demands of the banking mechanism spilling across national frontiers undoubtedly create a functional demand for elevation of the central banking facility to the global level (Triffin, 1960 and 1964; Hirsch and Oppenheimer, 1976; Brittan, this volume).

But the opposing pull of political forces, towards increased
monetary autonomy of individual states, has checked the integrative process. The first premonitions of this political force may
be seen in the increasing difficulties of securing adherence to
the fixed-rate gold standard in the interwar years. Flexible
exchange rates, which had previously been an abandonment
of policy under *force majeure*, slowly became a more or less
deliberate policy option affording some cover for domestic objectives from a threatening international environment. The primacy
of domestic objectives was enshrined in distinctly qualified form
in the post World War II provision for fixed *but adjustable*
exchange rates in the Bretton Woods monetary order. The
break-up of that order in the early 1970s and its replacement
by a regime of flexible exchange rates, subject to national management and only the loosest international influence, can be seen
as a declaration of national independence in the monetary sphere.
The international order now allows a potentially limitless degree
of freedom for national monetary policies and national price
levels. At the same time, it still provides sufficient international
credit support to reduce greatly the risk of precipitous collapse
of currencies as the result of sudden pressures. In this way,
present international monetary arrangements go a long way
towards institutionalizing national monetary independence.

Yet this does not imply an equivalent extension of monetary
freedom of action for the state in the sense of its executive
agencies. One must beware in this context of an unduly state-
centred view of international relations in which nations are
seen as homogeneous or monolithic entities (Keohane and Nye,
1977). In practice the conflict between domestic interests makes
some of them concerned to limit the scope for state action
in the economic sphere. This has been true of bankers, leading
businessmen and other moneyed interests in an era in which
direct control of the state has been lost to the mass electorate.
The views and instincts of the financial community make themselves felt speedily and automatically through the condition of
financial markets. Thus a slump in the stock exchange dries
up the source of new capital funds for both industry and government. A panic in the foreign exchange market drains away
the country's gold or foreign exchange reserves (under fixed
exchange rates) or starts a downward spiral in the exchange

rate with the associated escalation of import costs and domestic prices (under flexible exchange rates). Since financial confidence will necessarily be affected by state actions that transgress the bounds considered safe by financial interests, a powerful indirect deterrent against such actions is constantly in play. The phenomenon is a part of the complex mixture of antagonism and mutual support characteristic of the modern relationship between bankers and nation-states. The banks cast critical eyes on state interventionism in all but its original and still most pervasive form, the support provided by the central bank to the banks themselves. Large and powerful banks provide at once a potential captive source of finance for the state, and a source of potential financial resistance to it. Such resistance can be curtailed by internal regulations requiring funds to be channelled in ways specified by the state. But the efficacy of such regulations is weakened by external financial connections. These provide an escape hatch for domestic capital and transmit important influence on the inflow and outflow of foreign capital.

Governments that have antagonized their business and financial communities have almost without exception encountered a "capital strike" in some degree. The ensuing economic difficulties have with equal regularity led to relaxations in the offending policies, with or without a change of government (Hirsch, 1965, ch. 5; Maier, 1975, chs. 7 and 8; Stein, 1969, chs. 5, 6 and 16). The essence of a capital strike is its unorganized, spontaneous character. This is rooted fundamentally in the requirements of an economy under mainly capitalist drive, as well as in the social cohesion and strong informal contacts among leaders of the business and financial communities.

Corporate financial interests, therefore, have been players in national and international finance in their own right. But while this has limited the significance that technical conditions of national monetary independence have for the freedom of manœuvre of governments, the counterforce no longer operates as a barrier against inflation. Pressures that previously led to gold outflows, deflating the money supply and the credit base, now manifest themselves in a fall in the exchange rate, giving an inflationary twist to prices and costs. Thus confrontation between financial markets and the state nowadays operate as much through as against the inflationary thrust.

This outcome on the international front provides a particularly clear illustration of the association and interaction of technical and socio-political factors in monetary affairs. The technical impulsion towards the replacement of metallic money by credit money and for financial integration at the global level proceeded to the point at which it encountered decisive political resistance; yet the technical developments themselves have limited the available political choices. The monetary options that were open at a less advanced stage of international financial integration are no longer technically available.

On the one side, technical developments have limited the financial protection potentially available to activist governments of the left. The feasibility of insulating the national finances from external influence has been greatly limited by the interpenetration of business and banking links, which make controls on flows of capital much more difficult to enforce without an almost equivalent control on trade and payments for current services. Insulation is available through flexible exchange rates, but only at the cost of additional inflation in the countries with depreciating currencies.

On the other side, financial protection for the *status quo*, traditionally sought by the right, has also become technically more elusive. The feasibility of limiting the state's effective freedom of monetary manœuvre through an automatic external constraint such as gold convertibility at an immutable exchange ratio has disappeared. A new and effective gold standard would require not only Brittan's impossibility of restoring punctured myths (p. 179 of this volume). It would also necessitate a comprehensive array of international controls to suppress the natural predilection of national monetary authorities, at this stage of the international banking process, to hold their reserves in interest-earning credit money rather than in gold metal. The automatic external monetary discipline is no longer technically available. An alternative proposal directed to a similar end, is for replacement of the state's monopoly in the issuance of money by free competition in currencies issued by commercial banks at home and abroad (Hayek, 1976). But this entails the prospect of recurrent monetary collapse on the pattern that historically called forth central banking and monopolization of note issue, so that this route also must be judged technically obsolescent. It follows that credible schemes to limit the state's room for monetary manœuvre have had to be openly directed to that end, as in the proposals for administrative or constitutional limits to the growth in money supply (Friedman, 1960; Jay, 1976).

A direct limitation of this kind, adopted as a matter of positive choice, lacks the automatic entrée of the gold standard as the compelling international norm. But in both cases, the technical instrument embodies a political function. This is essentially to confine the range of action by the state and within society by giving a silent veto to business and moneyed interests, which determine financial confidence and thereby hold a key to credit flows and attainment of financial targets. More generally, the range for discretionary action by political and administrative agencies is curtailed.

Renunciation of political weaponry is an unattractive option, above all for groups that look to political weapons to alter the economic and political *status quo* in their favour. (In the words of an old Labour Party slogan: 'The rich man has his money, the poor man has his politics'.) More generally, again, politicians as a professional class are wary of tying their own hands behind their backs. The domestic constitutional limits on money creation have therefore so far had no takers. Limits of an *ad hoc* kind have been introduced by monetary authorities in a number of countries in a pragmatic way, where and when political pressures have been containable. But this technical instrument has been clearly shown to be an adjunct of political consensus, rather than an unyielding environmental condition to which the political body must adapt. The outcome, compared with the traditional monetary constraint by external proxy, has been an extra degree of freedom for monetary inflation to accommodate political and social pressures. It is these pressures that provide the main explanation of why the additional technical degree of freedom to inflate has been so extensively used.

II

The role of inflation in reflecting and also mediating political struggles is a common theme of analysts in different disciplines and of different ideologies—witness Maier, Brittan and Crouch in this volume. Inflation is sometimes referred to as easing or accommodating political strife over income distribution. More generally, inflation has served as a vent for distributional strife, an escape hatch through which excess demands are automatically channelled. But the escape channel, besides providing an initial release, can also make its own contribution to the overload. Inflation has developed its own dynamic, political as well as monetary. As individuals and institutions adapt their behaviour increasingly to anticipation of inflation, the inflationary process becomes self-generating and perhaps accelerating. It then becomes difficult to stop inflation in a distributionally neutral way, so that even groups that do not gain from inflation itself are none the less fearful of measures to counter it. At the same time, the effects of inflation on the real economy, including the alleviating effects on distributional struggles, are progressively weakened with use, as money illusion fades with the experience of past inflation.

This progressive loss in efficacy of the inflationary drug has been seen in traditional analyses, focused on technical monetary effects, as both a rationale for the experience of inflationary acceleration (higher rates of inflation becoming necessary to achieve a given effect) and as providing on the same grounds the normative case for ending inflation. Inflation appears as straightforward monetary mismanagement, incapable of achieving even narrow objectives for more than transitional periods of diminishing duration. From the wider perspective of the politico-economic function of inflation, the policy inference is more ambivalent. Inflation is here seen as a palliative for underlying stresses on the polity which will become more exposed as the treatment falters.

A functional view of inflation as a vent for distributional conflict does not tell us very much in itself—it is perhaps the political economy equivalent of the monetarist characterization of inflation as too much money. Significance lies rather in different perceptions of the role of distributional conflict in the economy. A broad distinction can be made between two sets of approaches. The first sees such conflict as a political intrusion that destroys the harmony of implicit co-operation through individual pursuit of individual advantage in competitive markets. Deployment of political power by groups to further their economic aims is here seen as a diversion (and mostly as an avoidable diversion) from the royal road which leads to prosperity through adding to the resources available to all. A second set of approaches sees political organization of economic power, and the ensuing distributional conflict, as a natural outgrowth of market society. The associated disturbance to the smooth functioning of atomistic competition is here seen not as an extraneous political intrusion or excrescence, but rather as a fundamental and perhaps growing stress rooted in the core of the economic mechanism. The differing ideological bases of the two approaches lead on to differing and partly implicit assumptions of what elements are to be taken as fixtures— broadly, market capitalism in the first approach, and universalistic political legitimacy in the second. In this way, the contrasting normative interpretations arc inseparable from related positive analysis, with the different endogenous and exogenous elements.

The functional view of inflation in relation to distributional conflict will reflect or refract the same difference in approach and in underlying ideology. The connection is often indirect and unconscious.

Central to the first approach is the view of inflation as operational malfunction—not necessarily the source of malfunction but its reflection and consequence. More specifically in recent analysis, inflation is related to relapse or inadequacy in the rate of economic growth. Growth in this view has a central place because it is seen, implicitly or explicitly, as a surrogate for redistribution. It offers the one apparent means to square the circle between the demands of universal political and economic participation, and the constraint on egalitarianism imposed by the structure and needs of a capitalist or mixed economy. Through the painless and subtle process of equalization through time, growth and the prospect of growth avoid the need for economically risky and politically divisive attempts at direct redistribution (Hayek, 1960; Hirsch, 1977a, ch. 12). Continuing expansion in the size of the economic pie allows more to go to those with the smallest slice, and to communal use, without making anyone worse off than they were before: levelling up, not down.

This is what Maier aptly designates 'the great conservative idea of the last generation' (p. 70 above). In fact, its most pivotal place has been in the thinking of centrist social democrats and in the policies of progressive governments reaching for change by consensus (Crosland, 1956 and 1974). The strategy directly builds up future expectations; and if the rise in living standards is checked by a lapse in economic performance, a gap between aspirations and the means of fulfilling them will arise, which with unyielding demands will also be an inflationary gap. The concept of the aspirations gap has been extended to cover expectations based not only on the economy's own promise of growth based on its past performance, but more demandingly on an international demonstration effect set by the leaders in world living standards (Panić, 1976 and this volume).

The policy implications of analysis on these lines are fairly straightforward. The aspirations gap needs to be closed from one end or the other. Expectations need to be scaled down, except in so far as performance can be scaled up. The required combination of restraint, industry and efficiency on the part of the populace may be difficult to achieve, but since it provides a means (and perhaps the sole means) of adding to the welfare of all, it is seen as the technically dominant solution. The problem then reduces to the organizational issue of transmitting economic reality to individuals, above all in their political and social capacities. In practical terms, this involves finding a means of checking the tendency to excessive expectations perceived in democratic political institutions by a school of thought reaching back to Bagehot and Schumpeter; and of resisting the exertion of economic power through collective bodies, and notably trade unions, as a threat to the equilibrium and harmony of markets, which are in turn dependent on atomization of economic units. On this view it is the political and institutional surround of the market economy that has developed incompatible features and therefore tends to push the whole mechanism out of gear. Inflation here is a symptom essentially of this political and institutional diversion. For the economic mechanism itself, inflation represents mismanagement and misappropriation from outside, rather than fundamental internal defect.

The second set of approaches locates the malfunction within the economic process, and more specifically the market process, which is seen as generating internal political and social pressures in conflict with the economic requirements of equilibrium and growth. The most venerable such approach is of course the Marxist critique, its modern-dress variants incorporating the phenomenon of inflation and excess demands on government as part of the fiscal crisis of the state (O'Connor, 1973). The classical Marxist analysis of capitalist market economies is in one sense the mirror image of the idealized equilibrium model: both see the economy as governed by the imperatives of a closed system of abstract economic relationships, but where the one model programmes the variables for harmony, the other sets them for auto-destruct[1]. Fundamental weaknesses located within the economic core of market society are also identified in critiques drawing selectively on the Marxist tradition, but differing from it, as much as from the classical equilibrium model, in their rejection of deterministic economic imperatives. These critiques see the economy as a more open system governed by complex, variegated influences subject to internal change in alternative and therefore unpredictable ways. What are identified here, therefore, are continuing stresses rather than contradictions involving a preset cycle of emaciation, disintegration and replacement.

The most fruitful source of such critiques has been the attention directed by sociologists to the erosion of the social underlay of a stable capitalist order (and more generally of any market or contractual society) set in train by the value system of market society. This is matched by a concern with roles of class and status, and associated positions of subordination and dominance, which give central importance to both the structure of social relationships and the relative as distinct from the absolute economic position of the individual. The contribution by Goldthorpe in this volume is a pointed development of this theme in the particular context of inflation in mature capitalist society. There follows the traditionally greater emphasis by the sociologist on the rationale of conflictual roles, in contrast with the economist's emphasis on the scope for general betterment through positive-sum games with no losers.

Yet this traditionally sociological perspective can be given an economic dimension at important points. I have recently sought to demonstrate that even the archetypal economic man seeking to maximize his own welfare without concern for how this compares with the welfare of others, must none the less be concerned with how his *income* compares with that of others; for in the increasingly alluring sector of the economy in which consumption or styles of living and working are restricted to a minority by inherent limits of social scarcity, it is the individual's relative rather than absolute income that will predominantly determine his command over these positional goods. In parallel, an economic dimension can be given to the weakening of the social foundations of the market economy, by applying the economist's analysis of public goods. Provision of such goods involves costs for individuals, while the benefits accrue to all: contributors and non-contributors alike. If individuals' actions are determined entirely by maximization of personal advantage, such public goods therefore will be under-provided, and the existing 'stock' or legacy left over from the past will be eroded. Social patterns or standards of behaviour have the character of public goods. Elemental personal values of honesty, truthfulness, trust, restraint and obligation are all necessary inputs to an efficient (as well as pleasant) contractual society, but all are without significant direct pay-off to the individuals providing them. In this capacity as public goods—or more strictly, intermediate public goods providing part of the necessary input for desired final output—these influences on behaviour will not be forthcoming in the required form or magnitude through isolated decision-making at individual levels. As has now been well established in the economic literature, unconstrained individual maximization here makes actions that are rational for each individual irrational for all individuals together (Olson, 1965; Hirsch, 1977a and 1977b). The deficiencies therefore tend to be entrenched more deeply by the individualist orientation of the market system. And one facet of this is the deepening inflation scar.

III

The preceding section outlined two different and partly competing sets of interpretations of the aspirations gap in modern economies, broadly conceived as the tendency for economic demands to run continually ahead of capacity for delivery. This section turns more closely to the ensuing links with inflation. It suggests that the link operates on two levels. At the first level is the simple and direct link between the aspirations gap and the inflationary gap, a link that is established as soon as aspirations are expressed in monetary demands that the monetary authorities are prepared to fund. At this level, inflationary pressure is increased by any factor that augments expectations or detracts from performance, whatever the source. The same inflationary impulsion results whether increased demands reflect excess expectations generated by the processes of democracy or struggle to improve relative position, whether under primarily sociological or economic imperatives 'or simply because of more effective exploitation of collective bargaining. Thus elements from disparate forces combine together, with no necessary congruence or interconnection but exerting a cumulative impact.

The catalogue of effects operating at this level remains subject to the limitations of any partial analysis. It misses important general equilibrium elements determining the outcome in the system as a whole. These comprise both feedback between the several elements involved and responses induced by the flow of events in the policy actions of governments and of other entities with an influence on policy. For inflation, the policy responses are crucial, specifically of the monetary authorities. And these monetary policies, in a recurring theme of several authors in this volume, will respond to political and social forces not merely or necessarily in escape from responsibility or rationality, but to accommodate pressures that threaten or appear to threaten the broad political and constitutional fabric, and economic–financial stability in consequence. Thus even if no enduring gains are achieved by monetary accommodation of political or institutional pressures—which in its denial of any trade-off between inflation and unemployment is a strong assumption in the present state of economic knowledge—such accommodation may still have a powerful defensive rationale. Which is to say that there is no such thing as a dominant technical monetary policy outside the socio-political context.

On this second level of policy response, the contrast and partial conflict of approaches to inflation and the stresses that lie behind it, themselves tend to perpetuate and augment the inflationary force. This factor reflects at bottom the normative or ideological content of inflation. The point tends to be obscured by the evident difficulty in locating an ideology of inflation. Even the attribution of such an ideology to Lenin, as the best way to destroy the capitalist system, turns out to be a quotation rather of Keynes (Fetter, 1977); and empirical studies such as those of Maier and Piachaud above have found no group or class that has gained persistently and directly from inflation. Yet ideology and broad class interests may none the less play an important part, not in fomenting inflation as a chosen policy, but in acceptance of an inflationary outcome as less painful or less risky than a technically available alternative that appears ideologically threatening.

I am suggesting, therefore, that an implicit ideological underlay of inflation has been created by the confrontation or counterpoise of more direct ideological struggles. It is then no accident that inflation has been most entrenched in societies and periods in which the underlying ideological struggle has been most intense. Put another way, containment of the latent distributional struggle without financial instability requires either sufficient authority, or sufficient consensus, on the values or principles underlying the distribution of income and other aspects of welfare. If established authority weakens before a sufficient consensus or a new authority emerges, inflation results. The chapter by Portes above suggests strongly that this same influence operates in the non-market economies. Inflation in the Communist states has emerged either when state authority has been weakened by an unresolved ideological battle (post-revolutionary Russia and in minor key, Poland in the 1970s), or when established principles of distribution have been disturbed without consensus (Hungary after 1968). Thus inflation reflects the struggle of interests in broad as well as fragmented ways.

IV

Consider as a starting point the orthodox interpretations which see the basic impediment to the harmony of market society as the organization and exploitation of collective interests and the excessive demands made by mass participation on the political and consequentially the economic mechanism. The clear norma-

All such measures provoke popular resistance. The pain of
high rates of inflation makes them more palatable or less unthinkable, by wearing down resistance to alternative shocks. Accelerating inflation—though not steady-state inflation even at high
rates—eventually produces its catharsis in the form of a stabilization crisis. Its essential feature is the effective renegotiation
of the *modus vivendi* with organized labour, scaling down its
economic and political claims. The historical experience is presented by Maier in this volume. The theoretical basis of this
wider political function of financial stabilization was pointed
out by Kalecki in his pioneering exposition of the political
business cycle (Kalecki, 1943).

Kalecki foresaw that the decisive barrier to full employment
lay not in deficient demand but in the socio-political requirements
of an economy primarily dependent on capitalist drive and
capitalist values. Continuous full employment would undermine
both the discipline of factory workers and the confidence of
entrepreneurs, as the traditional limits on the boundaries of
state investment and welfare spending were eroded. The modern
revival of the pre-Keynesian doctrine of the natural rate of
unemployment rests on many of the same factors, but dresses
them up in technical constraints within a preset socio-political
system. But public acceptability of the old disciplines has been
eroded, not least by Keynesian doctrine. Experience after World
War II appeared to show that full employment was a feasible
policy option. Its abandonment required the public to be per-
suaded of greater evils. Inflation has been the central one.

This does not of course suggest that inflation has been a
preventive policy in a deliberate or conscious form. The suggestion
is that policy choice has operated in a negative way, through
the blocking of direct solutions by the counterpoise of opposing
ideologies and interests. Inflation then emerges by default as
the maximin strategy, the insurance against a still worse outcome.

International influences have tended in the same direction.
Too weak to impose price stability on national economies, they
have in effect served the second-best objective of the liberal
community, of maintaining an open international economy at
whatever inflation rate has to be accepted to attain this. This
ordering of priorities is openly visible in the lending policies
of the International Monetary Fund, which by giving primacy

The Ideological Underlay of Inflation   277

tive implication of this approach is that the offending intrusions
need to be rolled back. The key policy instruments include
limitations on the bargaining strength of trade unions, and
direct or indirect limitations on the power of executive and
legislative bodies over the money supply, and perhaps over
aggregate public expenditure as well. Within this broad approach
a conspectus of views exists on the feasibility of achieving the
necessary roll-back within existing institutional forms and on
the acceptability of various changes. The most sensitive issue
is whether it may be necessary or desirable to curtail political
democracy in order to preserve higher liberal values and the
market institutions which are seen as the necessary foundations
of such values.

The unifying theme which is relevant in our context is the
overriding need to avoid further collectivist inroads. Solutions
or accommodations that are in themselves collectivist in orientation are on this approach a cure worse than the disease.
The prime example is a comprehensive and continuing incomes
policy, in the form of state involvement in the specifics of
wage and salary differentials and in associated measures designed
to change (and in practice equalize) the distribution of income
and wealth. Such policies are condemned on the ground that
the logic of market forces can never be dammed up for long,
unless by progressively more severe extension of collective regulation, so that a positive incomes policy will be either futile
or dangerous (Brittan and Lilley, 1977).

Suppressed inflation is here seen as a greater evil than open
inflation, both because of the current distortion it involves in
the economy and because of the more enduring effect in encouraging non-market and anti-market policies. To the extent that
political and institutional pressures making for inflation cannot
be curbed, their release through the open inflation vent serves
a number of defensive purposes. Inflation in open guise, besides
avoiding the diversions of suppressed inflation, is more likely
eventually to mobilize the public support or tolerance needed
to eradicate or curtail the inflationary root. The necessary correc-
tives typically include higher unemployment, cutbacks in welfare
spending and perhaps also a direct weakening in the industrial
and political power of organized labour, which in turn may
require in some circumstances a more authoritarian regime.

to liberalization of trade and payments, typically require large devaluations and consequential domestic price rises. More generally, this choice ordering has been implicit in the post World War II international monetary regimes, in both the Bretton Woods system and its current successor regime of managed floating. Critics who see these international monetary arrangements as embodying a ratchet effect for world inflation are probably right. But the relevant question is whether a liberal international economy could have been purchased at any more acceptable price.

This international influence is essentially accommodative, opening the way to monetary accommodation domestically. It responds to the domestic tensions that produce inflation as the insurance against a still worse outcome. No conscious strategy is needed to produce this result, though it may sometimes be present. For where collectivist forces are sufficiently entrenched in the political body to resist attempts to roll them back, their continued strength imparts an inflationary bias to market forces themselves. Individual trade unions and other organizations exercising collective market power will maximize their own parochial group interests by jostling ahead of rival groups. In the end, all may lose from the higher inflation and/or higher unemployment that result from the chain of such leapfrogging, but at any point in the chain, a participant will lose more by standing still while others leapfrog over him. In brief, the presence of collective economic power creates a collective goods situation in which individual rationality no longer yields social rationality.

Where the solution of restoring harmony by cutting the collective down to size is blocked, the logical alternative reconciliation is to redirect the actions of the collective units to the collective interest—the incomes policy route. But the longer-term political implications of that accommodation encounter fierce resistance as a threat to the economic and perhaps also political *status quo*. There is no doubt that the internal logic of a continuing incomes policy involves progressive departures from market principles in regulation of the economy. In addition to this open ideological resistance to direct imposition of collective rationality to the determination of incomes, this course will tend to be resisted by groups looking solely to their parochial short-term interest. The ability of governments to impose social objectives on the actions of powerful groups is limited, as is the ability of group leaders to direct their members. In addition, the traditional emphasis of market liberalism on the pursuit of self-advantage may make collective organizations, or sub-groups of workers within them, instinctively hostile to the widening of group horizons. These points are discussed in the contributions of Anderson and Crouch to this volume.

There is, therefore, a range of ideological and pragmatic influences that tend to block the collectivist accommodation in turn. Does the resulting stand-off imply that the original collectivist intrusion or over-extension involves deadweight loss both for society and for the main organized groups themselves? This has become a standard interpretation in orthodox economic analysis, above all in the monetarist cast. The idea finds technical expression in the outward shift of the natural rate of unemployment and the less favourable shape of the Phillips curve. The limitation of this analysis lies in its restricted focus, fastening on a single economic dimension associated with real income and ignoring any connection with political influence, which is treated as exogenous.

A more rounded view can find at least four interconnected long-term benefits for workers and their families from the strengthening of organized labour, beyond the standard criterion of the level of the equilibrium wage. There is first the two-way connection between the industrial and the political strength of the working class—Hilferding's concept of the political wage (Maier in this volume): no trade unions, no Labour party. A second connection exists between labour's political–industrial leverage and the use of state power over the whole spectrum of social, political and economic life: indexed state pensions as part of the social contract. Thirdly, there are the benefits for those in the bottom half of the distribution of income and wealth derived from a narrowing of their relative disadvantage, benefits which as argued above can be given an economic as well as a sociological rationale. Fourthly, there is the gain in worker autonomy and the counter to the authority of management, which derive from the unions' basic function of job regulation at workplace level. To those who attach importance to these elements—and the first is admittedly dependent on a positive value attaching to at least one of the other three—the lack of statistical demonstration that trade unions have increased the real wage does not go to the heart of the issue. Resistance to a roll-back of industrial or political power of labour is fully explicable on grounds of collective self-interest, though a measure of social co-operation will as always be needed for the collective interest to be mobilized.

The fact that extension or defence of collective interests involves disruptions, such as inflation, is itself a double-edged consideration. It brings some self-inflicted damage on the perpetrators, and may also risk a public or political reaction against them; yet the additional nuisance value will often also have a positive pay-off. The marked success achieved by organized labour in battering its way into the formal and informal structures of governing establishments since World War II can be attributed in important part to the potential contribution that its co-operation has made to holding inflation at bay. Organized labour has thereby exerted a counterforce to the extra-parliamentary influence traditionally commanded by business and financial interests through both their market responses and their informal contacts with government ministers and officials. In addition, and more defensively, collectivist exertions that have inflationary results will often be in effect second-best strategies, warding off either alternative and more feared threats of a general policy nature, such as a roll-back of collective power, or the prospect of individual economic damage. Here too, the inflationary outcome is preferred, either ideologically or pragmatically, to the practically-available alternative.

That this implicit choice is common to opposing economic and ideological groups highlights the inadequacy of explaining the policies of different groups in connection with inflation by asking how much they gain or lose from it. That question is too narrow in frame. It misses not only the asymmetry arising from the dynamics of the inflationary process, which are now fairly familiar in the bandwagon and ratchet effects and the associated problems posed by deceleration. The more neglected omission, which is brought out by our analysis, is the connection with associated positive and negative policy actions—i.e. promotion of desired policies and vetoing or frustration of disfavoured ones—across a wide range of issues. This connection is implicit in the strategic or gaming considerations

which must be expected to influence behaviour in many situations
of social interdependence. Inflation is an instrument as well
as an outcome in the economic interdependence game. Opposing
groups, as well as individuals in isolated situations, will in
a number of circumstances each rationally choose the inflation
play, in the sense of action that results in more inflation than
the available alternative. One example is a bluffing play in
a game of chicken, in which players wield an instrument that
if used will harm themselves too, in the hope that their opponents
will be blustered into crying off their own threat. More straightforward is the maximin strategy adopted by individuals and uncoor-
dinated groups unable to mobilize the collective interest in an
outcome more beneficial to all.

V

Ideologies, as well as particularized interests, have contributed
to inflation through their confrontation and interaction. That
is the nub of the interpretation suggested in this chapter. As
stated, it is limited to a rather general hypothesis. Clearly,
it could be refined in various ways; whether it could then
be suitably tested I cannot judge at this stage. The statistical
examination by Peacock and Ricketts in this volume of the
correlation between public expenditure and inflation is a warning,
in its rejection of a simple association, of both the range of
influences and the complexity of the interactions involved. It
would clearly be technically far more difficult to test the association between inflation, the collective permeation of the economy
on a broader measure, and different intensities of ideological
confrontation. I venture the guess that if a general theory of
inflation is ever constructed it will incorporate broad socio-political interaction of this kind.

Meanwhile, attention to these general forces, even if they
cannot be precisely specified, at least suggests some explanation
of the conundrums left over by more rigorous but narrower
economic models. I would claim further that the need to widen
the analysis in this way can be derived from economic principles
themselves, notably by applying and extending the theory of

public goods. Constriction of the economic approach to a model of rationality appropriate only to private economic goods—a constriction that is operationally convenient but intellectually arbitrary and ideologically loaded—has the effect of expelling the interesting questions to Goldthorpe's 'residual categories', thereby opening the way for his neat counter-thrust in sociological imperialism. The present analysis seeks to recapture them by using economics to flank, rather than dominate, its neighbouring social sciences.

The interpretation raises a general question which remains to be considered. If inflation can be associated with ideologies and their confrontation in the ways suggested, how far is this association an enduring one, or rather to be ascribed to particular features of the time which themselves may be in process of internal change?

Three such features can be identified. The first is a technical monetary process, the maturation of paper money. This has proceeded to the point at which the old barriers against inflation, both domestic and international, have been broken, while new limitations serving similar purposes have not yet been agreed. The political response to the sweeping technical changes is still in flux. Secondly, the equally sweeping changes that have taken place in people's views on what is their proper economic station and how it should compare with other people's, are also clearly far from having worked themselves out. The decline of traditional authority and, in Goldthorpe's language, the decay of the status order, have not been succeeded by consensus on the distributional pattern. The resulting vacuum, providing the prime socio-political source of inflationary pressure, is hardly a stable condition of society, and could induce a reaction in either the consensual or authoritarian direction.

Thirdly, the age of inflation since World War I has coincided broadly with the rise and fall of the influences of John Maynard Keynes. From the early 1920s (Keynes, 1923), he made the case for discretionary monetary management in pursuit of macroeconomic stability. And while the Keynesian apparatus of demand management could in principle be used to counter inflationary excess as well as deflationary deficiency, it has been less effective in the former role for several reasons, discussed by Maier and by Peacock and Ricketts in earlier chapters. Keynes's opponents, from the beginning, have seen his system as an engine of inflation, above all because of its manipulability. The charge can now be seen to be basically correct, and yet misplaced, reflecting a blinkered vision. A striking example is the current hope that the discrediting of Keynesian management reopens the way to public acceptance of earlier financial disciplines. This approach passes over the broader aspect of the Keynesian contribution, which was to provide the missing legitimacy for a predominantly capitalist system in conditions of universal political participation. With neither the sustenance of full employment nor the promise of assured economic growth, the divisive questions both of distributional shares and of the moral validity of economic outcomes return to centre stage. Inflation itself helped fend them off. But experience of inflation makes it a weaker fender.

Both Keynesianism and inflation can be seen as defensive responses by capitalist societies challenged by the new political and economic imperatives of a democratic age. If these defences are now losing force, the underlying stresses will become more exposed. Does this mean that the Marxist contradictions of capitalism and the Schumpeterian contradictions of democracy are now finally upon us? Possibly. But that the convulsion of both systems has been held back for so long is a reminder of the fecundity of their defence mechanisms and their capacity for mutation. The changes involved may none the less bite deep into existing structures. The political economy of the death of Keynes ranges far wider than the limitation of a particular technical form of financial management. In a sense, it provides the unifying theme of the ideologically and methodologically diverse contributions in this book.

NOTE

1. I owe this formulation to a comment by John Goldthorpe.

Bibliography

AARON, HENRY J. (1976) *Inflation and the Income Tax*, Washington, D.C.: Brookings Institution.
ABRAMS, MARK (1973) 'Subjective Social Indicators', *Social Trends*, 4.
— (1974) 'Changing Values', *Encounter*, 43.
ADAMS, D. *et al.* (1975) 'Changes in Rural Purchasing Power in Taiwan, 1952–72', Ohio State University, *Food Research Institute Studies*, 14.
ADELMAN, I. and MORRIS, C. T. (1973) *Economic Growth and Social Equity in Developing Countries*, Stanford University Press.
AFTALION, ALBERT (1927) *Monnaie, prix et change*, Paris: Sirey.
AHLUWALIA, M. S. (1976) 'Inequality, Poverty and Development', *Journal of Development Economics*, 3.
ALEXANDER, K. J. W. (1974) 'The Politics of Inflation', *Political Quarterly*, 45.
ALLEN, R. G. D. (1958) 'Movements in Retail Prices since 1953', *Economica*, 25.
ALLEN, R. I. G. and SAVAGE, D. (1975) 'Indexing Personal Income Taxation', in T. Liesner and M. King (eds.) *Indexing and Inflation*, London: Heinemann.
ALLISON, L. (1974) 'The Nature of the Concept of Power', *European Journal of Political Research*, 2.
ARLT, ILSE (1925) 'Der Einzelhaushalt', in Julius Bunzel (ed.) *Geldentwertung und Stabilisierung in ihren Einflüssen auf die soziale Entwicklung in Österreich*, Schriften des Verein für Sozialpolitik. 169.
ATKINSON, A. B. (1972) *Unequal Shares—Wealth in Britain*, London: Allen Lane.
AUJAC, HENRI (1950) 'L'influence du comportement des groupes sociaux sur le développement d'une inflation', *Economie Appliqué*, 4.
AULD, D. A. L. and SOUTHEY, CLIVE (1977) 'The Simple Analytics of Tax-induced Inflation', *Public Finance*, 32.
BACH, G. L. and STEPHENSON, JAMES (1974) 'Inflation and the Redistribution of Wealth', *The Review of Economics and Statistics*, 56.
BACHRACH, P. and BARATZ, H. S. (1962) 'The Two Faces of Power', *American Political Science Review*, 56.
— (1970) *Power and Poverty: Theory and Practice*, New York: Cambridge University Press.
BARBASH, J. (1972) *Trade Unions and National Economic Policy*, Baltimore: Johns Hopkins.
BARRY, BRIAN (1970) *Economists, Sociologists and Democracy*, London: Collier-Macmillan.
— (1974) 'The Economic Approach to the Analysis of Power and Conflict', *Government and Opposition*, 9.
— (1976) 'Power: and Economic Analysis', in B. Barry (ed.) *Power and Political Theory*, London: Wiley.

286 *Bibliography*

BARUCCI, PIERO (1973) 'La Politica Economica Internazionale e le Scelte di Politica Economica dell'Italia', *Rassegna Economica*, 37.
BEACH, C. M. (1977) 'Cyclical Sensitivity of Aggregate Income Inequality', *Review of Economics and Statistics*, 59.
BEER, S. H. (1965) *Modern British Politics*, London: Faber.
— (1967) *British Politics in the Collectivist Age*, New York: Random.
BENDIX, REINHARD (1964) *Nation-Building and Citizenship*, New York: Wiley.
BIACABE, PIERRE (1962) *Analyses contemporaines de l'inflation*, Paris: Sirey.
BLINDER, ALAN S. and SOLOW, ROBERT M. (1974) 'Analytical Foundations of Fiscal Policy', in *The Economics of Public Finance*, Washington, D.C.: Brookings Institution.
BRANSON, WILLIAM H. (1972) *Macroeconomic Theory and Policy*, New York: Harper and Row.
BRAUN, ANNE ROMANIS (1976) 'Indexation of Wages and Salaries in Developed Economies', *International Monetary Fund Staff Papers*, 23.
BRESCIANI-TURRONI, COSTANTINO (1937) *The Economics of Inflation*, London: Allen and Unwin.
BRETON, A. (1974) *The Economic Theory of Representative Government*, London: Macmillan.
BRITTAIN, J. A. (1960) 'Some Neglected Features of Britain's Economic Levelling', *American Economic Review*, 50.
BRITTAN, SAMUEL (1973) *Capitalism and the Permissive Society*, London: Macmillan.
— (1975a) *Second Thoughts on Full Employment Policy*, London: Barry Rose and Chichester.
— (1975b) 'The Economic Contradictions of Democracy', *British Journal of Political Science*, 5.
BRITTAN, SAMUEL and LILLEY, PETER (1977) *The Delusion of Incomes Policy*, London: Temple Smith.
BRONFENBRENNER, M. and HOLZMAN, F. D. (1963) 'A Survey of Inflation Theory', *American Economic Review*, 53.
BROWN, A. J. (1955) *The Great Inflation, 1939–1951*, London: Oxford University Press.
BRUNNER, KARL (1975) 'Comment' [on Gordon (1975)], *Journal of Law and Economics*, 18.
BUCHANAN, JAMES (1972) 'Towards Analysis of Closed Behavioural Systems', in J. Buchanan and R. D. Tallison (eds.) *The Theory of Public Choice*, Ann Arbor: University of Michigan Press.
BULLOCK, LORD (1977) *Report of the Committee of Inquiry on Industrial Democracy*, Cmnd. 6706, London: HMSO.
BUTLER, D. and STOKES, D. (1974) *Political Change in Britain* (2nd edition), London: Macmillan.
CAGAN, PHILLIP (1956) 'The Monetary Dynamics of Hyperinflation', in Milton Friedman (ed.), *Studies in the Quantity Theory of Money*, Chicago University Press.
CAPLOVITZ, D. (1963) *The Poor Pay More*, Glencoe: Free Press.
CARR, E. H. (1952) *The Bolshevik Revolution, 1917–1923*, 2 vols., London: Macmillan.
CARRÉ, J. J., DUBOIS, P., and MALINVAUD, E. (1972) *La croissance française*, Paris: Seuil. (English translation, *French Economic Growth*, Stanford University Press, 1975.)
CASTELLS, M. (1975) 'Advanced Capitalism, Collective Consumption and Urban Contradictions', in L. Lindberg *et al.* (eds.) *Stress and Contradiction in Modern Capitalism*, Lexington, Mass.: D. C. Heath.

CASTLES, STEPHEN and KOSACK, GODULA (1973) *Immigrant Workers and Class Structure in Western Europe*, London: Oxford University Press.

CIPOLLA, C. M. (1976) *Before the Industrial Revolution: European Society and Economy, 1000–1700*, London: Methuen.

CLAASSEN, EMIL and SALIN, PASCAL (eds.) (1972) *Stabilization Policies in Interdependent Economies*, Amsterdam: North-Holland Publishing Co.

CLARK, COLIN (1977) 'The Scope for, and Limits of, Taxation', in *The State of Taxation*, Institute of Economic Affairs, Readings in Political Economy, 16, London.

CODDINGTON, ALAN (1976) 'Keynesian Economics: The Search for First Principles', *Journal of Economic Literature*, 14.

CONFEDERATION OF BRITISH INDUSTRY (1976) *The Road to Recovery*, London.

CONNOLLY, W. E. (1974) *The Terms of Political Discourse*, Lexington, Mass.: D. C. Heath.

CROSLAND, C. A. R. (1956) *The Future of Socialism*, London: Cape.

— (1974) 'A Social Democratic Britain', in *Socialism Now*, London: Cape.

CROUCH, C. J. (1975) 'The Drive for Equality', in L. Lindberg, *et al.* (eds.), *Stress and Contradiction in Modern Capitalism*, Lexington, Mass.: D. C. Heath.

— (1977a) 'The Place of Participation in the Study of Politics', in C. J. Crouch (ed.) *British Political Sociology Yearbook*, 3, *Participation in Politics*, London: Croom Helm.

— (1977b) *Class Conflict and the Industrial Relations Crisis*, London: Heinemann.

— (1978) 'The Changing Role of the State in Industrial Relations in Western Europe', in C. J. Crouch and A. Pizzorno (eds.) *The Resurgence of Class Conflict in Western Europe since 1968*, 2 vols., London: Macmillan.

CROUCH, C. J. and PIZZORNO, A. (eds.) (1978) *The Resurgence of Class Conflict in Western Europe since 1968*, 2 vols., London: Macmillan.

CUKIERMAN, A. (1973) 'A Study on the Formation of Inflationary Expectations in Israel', Tel Aviv University, Foerder Institute for Economic Research, Working Paper, No. 24.

DAHL, ROBERT A. (1961) *Who Governs?*, New Haven: Yale University Press.

DAHMÉN, E. (1973) 'Inflation—Economics or Politics?', *National Westminster Bank Quarterly Review*, November.

DANIEL, W. W. (1974) *A National Survey of the Unemployed*, London: Political and Economic Planning, Broadsheet 546.

— (1975) *The PEP Survey on Inflation*, London: Political and Economic Planning, Broadsheet 553.

DE CECCO, MARCELLO (1968) 'Sulla Politica di Stabilizzazione del 1947', *Saggi di Politica Monetaria*, Milan: Giuffre.

DEPARTMENT OF EMPLOYMENT (1976) *New Earnings Survey*, 1975, London: HMSO.

DIAZ-ALEJANDRO, CARLOS F. (1970) *Essays on the Economic History of the Argentine Republic*, New Haven: Yale University Press.

DONNITHORNE, A. (1974) 'China's Anti-Inflationary Policy', *Three Banks Review*, 103.

DORE, R. P. (1973) *British Factory—Japanese Factory*, London: Allen and Unwin.

DOWNS, A. (1957) *An Economic Theory of Democracy*, New York: Harper and Row.

— (1967) *Inside Bureaucracy*, Boston: Little, Brown & Co.

DUESENBERRY, J. S. (1949) *Income, Saving and the Theory of Consumer Behaviour*, Cambridge, Mass.: Harvard University Press.

DUPRIEZ, L. H. (1947) *Monetary Reconstruction in Belgium*, New York: King's Crown Press.

DURKHEIM, EMILE (1893)   *De la Division du Travail Social*, Paris: Alcan. (English translation, *The Division of Labour in Society*, New York: Macmillan, 1933.)

EASTERLIN, R. E. (1972)   'Does Economic Growth Improve the Human Lot?' in P. A. David and M. W. Reder (eds.) *Nations and Households in Economic Growth: Essays in Honor of Moses Abramovitz*, Stanford University Press.

The Economist (1974)   'Fair for All' and 'Learning to Love your Index', June 15.

ELLIS, HOWARD (1934)   *German Monetary Theory, 1905–1933*, Cambridge, Mass.: Harvard University Press.

ELSTER, J.   (1976)   'Some Conceptual Problems in Political Theory', in Brian Barry (ed.), *Power and Political Theory: Some European Perspectives*, London: Wiley.

ELSTER, KARL (1928)   *Von der Mark zur Reichsmark*, Jena: G. Fischer.

ERLICH, ALEXANDER (1967)   *The Soviet Industrialization Debate*, Cambridge, Mass.: Harvard University Press.

EULENBURG, FRANZ (1924)   'Die Sozialen Wirkungen der Währungsverhältnissen', *Jahrbücher für Nationalökonomie und Statistik*, 122.

EUROPEAN COOPERATION ADMINISTRATION (1950)   *Country Study (Italy)*, Washington, D.C.

FALLENBUCHL, Z. (1977)   'The Polish Economy in the 1970s', in Joint Economic Committee, U.S. Congress, *East European Economies Post-Helsinki*, Washington, D.C.: USGPO.

FALUSH, F. (1976)   'The Hungarian Hyperinflation of 1945–46', *National Westminster Bank Review*, August.

FELDMAN, GERALD D. (1977)   *Iron and Steel in the German Inflation, 1916–1923*, Princeton University Press.

FETTER, FRANK WHITSON (1977)   'Lenin, Keynes, and Inflation', *Economica*, 44.

FISHLOW, ALBERT (1974)   'Indexing Brazilian Style: Inflation Without Tears?', *Brookings Papers on Economic Activity*, 1.

FLEMMING, JOHN (1976)   *Inflation*, London: Oxford University Press.

FOA, BRUNO (1949)   *Monetary Reconstruction in Italy*, New York: King's Crown Press.

FORDE, C. D. (1934)   *Habitat, Economy and Society*, London: Methuen.

FOSTER, J. (1976a)   'The Redistributive Effects of Inflation—Questions and Answers', *Journal of Political Economy*, 84.

— (1976b)   'The Redistributive Effect of Inflation on Building Society Shares and Deposits: 1961–74', *Bulletin of Economic Research*, 28.

FOX, A. (1974)   *Beyond Contract: Work, Power and Trust Relations*, London: Faber.

FRANKFORT, H. *et al.* (1949)   *Before Philosophy*, London: Pelican Books.

FRIEDMAN, MILTON (1956)   'The Quantity Theory of Money—A Restatement', in Milton Friedman (ed.), *Studies in the Quantity Theory of Money*, Chicago University Press.

— (1960)   *A Program for Monetary Stability*, New York: Fordham University Press.

— (1966)   'Comment', in E. P. Shultz and R. Z. Aliber (eds.) *Guidelines*, Chicago University Press.

— (1968)   'The Role of Monetary Policy', *American Economic Review*, 58.

— (1971)   'Government Revenue from Inflation', *Journal of Political Economy*, 79.

— (1974a)   'Using Escalators to Help Fight Inflation', *Fortune*, 80.

— (1974b)   *Monetary Correction*, London: Institute of Economic Affairs.

— (1977a)   'Inflation and Unemployment', *Journal of Political Economy*, 85.

— (1977b) *From Galbraith to Economic Freedom*, London: Institute of Economic Affairs.

GALBRAITH, J. K. (1967) *The New Industrial State*, Harmondsworth: Penguin.

GELLNER, ERNEST (1975) 'A Social Contract in Search of an Idiom', *Political Quarterly*, 46.

GIDDENS, ANTHONY (1971) *Capitalism and Modern Social Theory*, Cambridge University Press.

GOLDEY, DAVID (1961) 'The Disintegration of the Cartel des Gauches and the Politics of French Government Finance, 1924–28' D.Phil. Thesis, University of Oxford.

GOLDSCHEID, RUDOLF (1917) 'Staatssozialismus oder Staatskapitalismus', in Rudolf Goldscheid and Joseph Schumpeter, *Die Finanzkrise des Steverstaates* (ed. R. Hickel), Frankfurt-am-Main: Suhrkamp Verlag, 1976.

— (1926) 'Staat, öffentlicher Haushalt und Gesellschaft', in *ibid.*

GOLDSTEIN, MORRIS (1975) 'Wage Indexation, Inflation, and the Labor Market', *International Monetary Fund Staff Papers*, 22.

GOLDTHORPE, JOHN H. (1974) 'Industrial Relations in Great Britain: a Critique of Reformism', *Politics and Society*, 4.

GOLDTHORPE, JOHN H. and BEVAN, PHILIPPA (1977) 'The Study of Social Stratification in Great Britain; 1946–1976', *Social Science Information*, 16.

GOLDTHORPE, JOHN H. and LLEWELLYN, CATRIONA (1977) 'Class Mobility in Modern Britain: Three Theses Examined', *Sociology*, 11.

GOLDTHORPE, JOHN H., LOCKWOOD, D., *et al.* (1968) *The Affluent Worker: Industrial Attitudes and Behaviour*, Cambridge University Press.

— (1969) *The Affluent Worker in the Class Structure*, Cambridge University Press.

GOLDTHORPE, JOHN H., PAYNE, CLIVE, and LLEWELLYN, CATRIONA (1978) 'Trends in Class Mobility', *Sociology*, 12.

GOODHART, C. A. E. (1975) *Money, Information, and Uncertainty*, London: Macmillan.

GOODHART, C. A. E. and BHANSALI, R. J. (1970) 'Political Economy', *Political Studies*, 18.

GORDON, ROBERT J. (1975) 'The Demand for and Supply of Inflation', *Journal of Law and Economics*, 18.

GOUGH, IAN (1975) 'State Expenditure in Advanced Capitalism', *New Left Review*, 92.

GOVERNMENT ACTUARY (1972) *Occupational Pension Schemes, 1971*, Fourth Survey, London: HMSO.

GRAHAM, FRANK D. (1930) *Exchange, Prices and Production in Hyper-inflation: Germany, 1920–1923*, Princeton University Press.

GROTIUS, FRITZ (1949) 'Die Europäischen Geldreformen nach dem 2. Weltkrieg', *Weltwirtschaftliches Archiv*, 63.

GULICK, CHARLES A. (1948) *Austria from Habsburg to Hitler* (2 vols.), Berkeley and Los Angeles: University of California Press.

GURLEY, J. C. (1953) 'Excess Liquidity and European Monetary Reforms', *American Economic Review*, 43.

HABERLER, GOTTFRIED (1966) *Inflation: Its Causes and Cures*, Washington, D.C.: American Enterprise Institute.

— (1972) 'Incomes Policy and Inflation', in *Inflation and the Unions*, Institute of Economic Affairs, Readings in Political Economy, 6, London.

HABERMAS, JÜRGEN (1973) *Legitimationsprobleme in Spätkapitalismus*, Frankfurt-am-Main: Suhrkamp Verlag. (English translation, *Legitimation Crisis*, London: Heinemann, 1976.)

HARBECK, KARL-HEINZ (ed.) (1968) *Das Kabinett Cuno 22. November 1922 bis 12. August 1923: Akten der Reichskanzlei, Weimarer Republik*, Boppard am Rhein: H. Boldt.

HARRIS, R. and SEWILL, B. (1975) *British Economic Policy, 1970–74: Two Views*, London: Institute of Economic Affairs.

HARTWICH, H. H. (1967) *Arbeitsmarkt, Verbände und Staat 1918–1933*, Berlin: de Gruyter.

HAYEK, F. A. (1958) 'Unions, Inflation, and Profits', in P. D. Bradley (ed.), *The Public Stake in Union Power*, Charlottesville: University of Virginia Press.

— (1960) *The Constitution of Liberty*, London: Routledge.

— (1976) *Choice in Currency*, London: Institute of Economic Affairs.

HICKS, J. R. (1946) *Value and Capital* (2nd Edition), Cambridge University Press.

— (1965) *Capital and Growth*, London: Oxford University Press.

— (1974) *The Crisis in Keynesian Economics*, Oxford: Blackwell.

HILDEBRAND, GEORGE H. (1965) *Growth and Structure in the Economy of Modern Italy*, Cambridge, Mass.: Harvard University Press.

HILFERDING, RUDOLF (1915) 'Arbeitsgemeinschaft der Klassen?', *Der Kampf*, 8.

— (1927) 'Die Aufgaben der Sozialdemokratie in der Republik', *Sozialdemokratischer Parteitag, Kiel 1927*, Berlin: Protokoll.

HIRSCH, FRED (1965) *The Pound Sterling: A Polemic*, London: Gollancz.

— (1977a) *Social Limits to Growth*, London: Routledge and Kegan Paul.

— (1977b) 'The Bagehot Problem', *The Manchester School*, September.

HIRSCH, FRED and GORDON, DAVID (1975) *Newspaper Money*, London: Hutchinson.

HIRSCH, FRED and OPPENHEIMER, PETER (1976) 'The Trial of Managed Money, 1920–1970', in Carlo M. Cipolla (ed.) *The Fontana Economic History of Europe: The Twentieth Century*, Glasgow: Collins.

HIRSCHMAN, ALBERT (1963) *Journeys Towards Progress*, New York: Twentieth Century Fund.

— (1973) 'The Changing Tolerance for Income Inequality in the Course of Economic Development', *Quarterly Journal of Economics*, 87.

HODGMAN, D. (1960) 'Soviet Monetary Controls through the Banking System', in G. Grossman (ed.), *Value and Plan*, Berkeley: University of California Press.

HOLLISTER, R. G. and PALMER, J. L. (1972) 'The Impact of Inflation on the Poor', in K. E. Boulding and M. Pfaff (eds.), *Redistribution to the Rich and the Poor: The Grants Economics of Income Distribution*, Belmont, Calif.: Wadsworth.

HOLZMAN, FRANKLYN D. (1950) 'Income Determination in Open Inflation', *The Review of Economics and Statistics*, 32.

— (1960) 'Soviet Inflationary Pressures, 1928–1957', *Quarterly Journal of Economics*, 74.

INSTITUTE OF ECONOMIC AFFAIRS (1972) *Inflation and the Unions*, Readings in Political Economy, 6, London.

— (1974) *Inflation: Causes, Consequences, Cures*, Readings in Political Economy, 14, London.

INTERNATIONAL LABOUR OFFICE (1972) *The Cost of Social Security: Seventh International Inquiry, 1964–1966*, Geneva.

JACKSON, DUDLEY, TURNER, H. A., and WILKINSON, FRANK (1972) *Do Trade Unions Cause Inflation?*, Cambridge University Press.

JAIN, S. (1975) *Size Distribution of Income: A Compilation of Data*, The World Bank, Washington, D.C.

JARVIE, I. C. (1972) *Concepts and Society*, London: Routledge and Kegan Paul.

JAY, PETER (1976) *Employment, Inflation and Politics*, London: Institute of Economic Affairs.

— (1977) 'The Workers' Co-operative Economy', unpublished paper to the Manchester Statistical Society.

JEFFERSON, MICHAEL (1977) 'A Record of Inflation', in *Inflation*, London: Platform Books.

JOHNSON, HARRY G. (1972) *Inflation and the Monetarist Controversy*, Amsterdam: North-Holland Publishing Co.

KAHN, LORD (1976) 'Thoughts on the Behaviour of Wages and Monetarism', *Lloyds Bank Review*, 119.

KALECKI, MICHAEL (1943) 'Political Aspects of Full Employment', *Political Quarterly*, 14.

— (1947) 'Three Ways to Full Employment', in Oxford University Institute of Statistics, *Studies in War Economics*, Oxford: Blackwell.

KATZENELLENBAUM, S. S. (1925) *Russian Currency and Banking, 1914–1924*, London: P. S. King.

KENDALL, WALTER (1975) *The Labour Movement in Europe*, London: Allen Lane.

KEOHANE, ROBERT O. (1977) 'Neo-Orthodox Economics, Inflation, and the Role of the State: Political Implications of the McCracken Report', forthcoming in *World Politics*.

KEOHANE, ROBERT O. and NYE, JOSEPH F. (1977) *Power and Interdependence*, Boston and Toronto: Little, Brown and Co.

KERR, CLARK, DUNLOP, JOHN T., HARBISON, FREDERICK H., and MYERS, CHARLES A. (1960) *Industrialism and Industrial Man*, Cambridge, Mass.: Harvard University Press.

KEYNES, JOHN MAYNARD (1923) *A Tract on Monetary Reform*, London: Macmillan.

— (1936) *The General Theory of Employment, Interest, and Money*, London: Macmillan.

— (1940) *How to Pay for the War*, London: Macmillan.

KNIGHT, FRANK (1947) *Freedom and Reform*, New York: Harper.

KOBLITZ, HORST GEORG (1971) *Einkommensverteilung und Inflation in kurzfristige Analyse*, Berlin and New York: de Gruyter.

KRAVIS, I. B., KENNESSY, Z., HESTON, A., and SUMMERS, R. (1975) *A System of International Comparisons of Gross Product and Purchasing Power*, London: Johns Hopkins Press.

KUZNETS, SIMON (1955) 'Economic Growth and Income Inequality', *American Economic Review*, 45.

— (1959) 'Quantitative Aspects of the Economic Growth of Nations, IV, Distribution of National Income by Factor Shares', *Economic Development and Cultural Change*, 7, 3, part ii.

— (1963) 'Quantitative Aspects of the Economic Growth of Nations: VIII, Distribution of Income by Size', *Economic Development and Cultural Change*, 11, 2, part ii.

LAIDLER, D. E. W. (1975) *Essays on Money and Inflation*, Manchester University Press.

— (1976) Comment on 'Why Stable Inflations Fail', in Parkin and Zis (eds.), *Inflation in the World Economy*, Manchester University Press.

LAIDLER, D. E. W. and PARKIN, J. M. (1975) 'Inflation—A Survey', *Economic Journal*, 85.

LAMBERT, DENIS (1959) *Les inflations suds-américaines: Inflation de sous-développement et inflation de croissance*, Paris: Institut des Hautes Études de l'Amérique Latine.

LANCASTER, K. (1973) 'The Dynamic Inefficiency of Capitalism', *Journal of Political Economy*, 81.

LAURSEN, K. and PEDERSON, J. (1964) *The German Inflation, 1918–1923*, Amsterdam: North-Holland Publishing Co.

LEMGRUBER, ANTONIO C. (1977) 'Inflation in Brazil', in Lawrence B. Krause and Walter S. Salant (eds.), *Worldwide Inflation: Theory and Recent Experience*, Washington: The Brookings Institution.

LEWIS, W. A. (1955) *The Theory of Economic Growth*, London: Allen and Unwin.

LIESNER, T. and KING, M. (eds.) (1975) *Indexation for Inflation*, London: Heinemann.

LINDER, S. (1961) *An Essay on Trade and Transformation*, New York: Wiley.

LIVELY, J. F. (1977) 'Wants and Needs, Interests and Welfare', unpublished paper, University of Warwick.

LLOYD, P. C. (1974) *Power and Independence: Urban Africans' Perception of Social Inequality*, London: Routledge and Kegan Paul.

LOCKWOOD, DAVID (1974) 'For T. H. Marshall', *Sociology*, 8.

LOCKWOOD, W. G. (1975) 'Social Status and Cultural Change in a Bosnian Moslem Village', *East European Quarterly*, 9.

LOWI, THEODORE J. (1969) *The End of Liberalism: Ideology, Policy, and the Crisis of Public Authority*, New York: Norton.

LUKES, S. (1974) *Power: A Radical View*, London: Macmillan.

LYNES, T. (1962) *National Assistance and National Prosperity*, Occasional Papers on Social Administration, No. 5, London: Codicote Press.

MCCONNELL, GRANT (1966) *Private Power and American Democracy*, New York: Knopf.

MCCRACKEN, PAUL et al. (1977) *Towards Full Employment and Price Stability*, Paris: OECD.

MAIER, CHARLES S. (1975) *Recasting Bourgeois Europe: Stabilization in France, Germany, and Italy in the Decade after World War I*, Princeton University Press.

MARRIS, STEPHEN (1972) 'World Inflation' contribution to Panel Discussion in Emil Claassen and Pascal Salin (eds.), *Stabilization Policies in Interdependent Economies*, Amsterdam: North-Holland Publishing Co.

MARSHALL, T. H. (1950) *Citizenship and Social Class*, Cambridge University Press.

MAYNARD, G. and VAN RYCKEGHEM, W. (1976) *A World of Inflation*, London: Batsford.

MEAD, M. (1937) *Cooperation and Competition Among Primitive Peoples*, New York: McGraw-Hill.

MELTZER, A. (1977) 'Anticipated Inflation and Unanticipated Price Change', *Journal of Money, Credit and Banking*, 9.

MILIBAND, R. (1969) *The State in Capitalist Society*, London: Weidenfeld and Nicolson.

MISHAN, E. J. (1967) *The Costs of Economic Growth*, London: Staples Press.

— (1974) 'The New Inflation', *Encounter*, 42.

— (1976) 'On the Road to Repression and Control', *Encounter*, 47.

MONTIAS, J. M. (1964) 'Inflation and Growth: The Experience of Eastern

Europe', in W. Baer and I. Kerstenetzky (eds.), *Inflation and Growth in Latin America*, Homewood, Ill.: Irwin.

MOREAU, EMILE (1954) *Souvenirs d'un Gouverneur de la Banque de France*, Paris: Génin.

MORTON, W. A. (1950) 'Trade Unions, Full Employment and Inflation', *American Economic Review*, 40.

MUELLBAUER, J. (1974) 'Prices and Inequality: the United Kingdom Experience', *Economic Journal*, 84.

— (1976) 'The Cost of Living', Evidence submitted to the Royal Commission on the Distribution of Income and Wealth.

NATIONAL FOOD SURVEY COMMITTEE (annual) *Household Food Consumption and Expenditure*, London: HMSO.

NICKELL, S. J. (1977) Personal communication and (with METCALF, D.) *The Plain Man's Guide to the Out-of-Work*, London School of Economics.

NISBET, ROBERT A. (1966) *The Sociological Tradition*, New York: Basic Books.

NISKANEN, W. A. (1971) *Bureaucracy and Representative Government*, New York: Aldine-Atherton.

NOGARO, BERTRAND (1948) 'Hungary's Recent Monetary Crisis and its Theoretical Meaning', *American Economic Review*, 38.

NORDHAUS, WILLIAM D. (1973) 'The Effect of Inflation on the Distribution of Economic Welfare', *Journal of Money, Credit, and Banking*, 5.

— (1974) 'The Falling Share of Profits', *Brookings Papers on Economic Activity*, 1.

— (1975) 'The Political Business Cycle', *Review of Economic Studies*, 42.

NOZICK, R. (1974) *Anarchy, State and Utopia*, Oxford: Blackwell.

O'CONNOR, J. (1973) *The Fiscal Crisis of the State*, New York: St Martin's Press.

OECD (1972) *Subjective Elements of Well-Being*, Paris.

— (1976) *Economic Outlook*, December.

OFFE, CLAUS (1970) *Leistungsprinzip und industrielle Arbeit*, Frankfurt-am-Main: Europaische Verlaganstalt. (English translation: *Inequality and Industry*, London: Edward Arnold, 1976.)

— (1975) 'Theses on the Theory of the State', *New German Critique*, 6.

OGBURN, WILLIAM F. and JAFFE, WILLIAM (1927) *The Economic Development of Postwar France*, New York: Columbia University Press.

OLSON, M. (1965) *The Logic of Collective Action*, Cambridge, Mass.: Harvard University Press.

PACKARD, V. (1957) *The Hidden Persuaders*, London: Longmans.

PANIĆ, M. (1976) 'The Inevitable Inflation', *Lloyds Bank Review*, 121.

PANITCH, L. (1976) *Social Democracy and Industrial Militancy*, Cambridge University Press.

PARKIN, M. (1975) 'The Politics of Inflation', *Government and Opposition*, 10.

PARODI, MAURICE (1971) *L'économie et la société française de 1945 à 1970*, Paris: A. Colin.

PARSONS, TALCOTT (1937) *The Structure of Social Action*, New York: McGraw-Hill.

— (1971) *The System of Modern Societies*, Englewood Cliffs: Prentice Hall.

PARSONS, TALCOTT and SMELSER, N. J. (1956) *Economy and Society*, London: Routledge and Kegan Paul.

PATINKIN, DON (1969) 'The Chicago Tradition, the Quantity Theory, and Friedman', *Journal of Money, Credit and Banking*, 1.

PAUKERT, F. (1973) 'Income Distribution at Different Levels of Development: A Survey of Evidence', *International Labour Review*, 108.

PAZOS, FELIPE (1972) *Chronic Inflation in Latin America*, New York: Praeger.

PEACOCK, ALAN T. and SHAW, G. K. 1976) *The Economic Theory of Fiscal Policy* (revised edition), London: Allen and Unwin.

PEACOCK, ALAN T. and WISEMAN, JACK (1967) *The Growth of Public Expenditure in the United Kingdom* (revised edition), London: Allen and Unwin.

PERETZ, PAUL (1976) 'The Political Economy of Inflation', Ph.D. thesis, University of Chicago.

PHELPS-BROWN, E. H. (1975) 'A Non-Monetarist View of the Pay Explosion', *Three Banks Review*, 105.

PIACHAUD, D. (1974) *Do the Poor Pay More?* Poverty Research Series, 3, London: Child Poverty Action Group.

— (1976) 'Prices and the Distribution of Incomes', Evidence submitted to the Royal Commission on the Distribution of Income and Wealth.

PIZZORNO, A. (1978) 'Political Exchange and Collective Identity in Industrial Conflict', in C. J. Crouch and A. Pizzorno (eds.), *The Resurgence of Class Conflict in Western Europe since 1968*, Vol. 2, London: Macmillan.

PLAMENATZ, JOHN (1954) 'Interests', *Political Studies*, 2.

PLOWMAN, D. E. G., MINCHINTON, W. E., and STACEY, M. (1962) 'Local Social Status in England and Wales', *Sociological Review*, n.s. 10.

POPPER, KARL (1945) *The Open Society and its Enemies*, London: Routledge.

— (1957) *The Poverty of Historicism*, London: Routledge.

— (1972) *Objective Knowledge*, London: Oxford University Press.

PORTES, RICHARD (1977a) 'The Control of Inflation: Lessons from East European Experience', *Economica*, 44.

— (1977b) 'Hungary: Economic Performance, Policy and Prospects', in Joint Economic Committee, U.S. Congress, *East European Economies post-Helsinki*, Washington, D.C.: USGPO.

PORTES, RICHARD and WINTER, D. (1977) 'The Supply of Consumption Goods in Centrally Planned Economies', *Journal of Comparative Economics*, 1.

— (1978) 'The Demand for Money and for Consumption Goods in Centrally Planned Economies', *Review of Economics and Statistics*, 60.

PRYBYLA, J. S. (1976) 'Work Incentives in the People's Republic of China', *Weltwirtschaftliches Archiv*, 4.

PRYOR, F. (1963) *The Communist Foreign Trade System*, London: Allen and Unwin.

ROBERTI, P. (1975) *The Impact of Economic Factors on the Distribution of Income in the U.K. 1957–1972*, London: Centre for Studies in Social Policy.

ROGERS, JAMES HARVEY (1929) *The Process of Inflation in France 1914–1927*, New York: Columbia University Press.

ROSS, ARTHUR M. and HARTMAN, PAUL T. (1960) *Changing Patterns of Industrial Conflict*, New York: Wiley.

ROSTOW, W. W. (1960) *The Stages of Economic Growth*, Cambridge University Press.

ROUTH, GUY (1965) *Occupation and Pay in Great Britain 1906–1960*, Cambridge University Press.

ROYAL COMMISSION ON THE DISTRIBUTION OF INCOME & WEALTH (1976) *Second Report on the Standing Reference*, Report No. 4, Cmnd. 6626, HMSO.

RUBIN, V. and SAVALLONI, M. (1966) *We Wish to Be Looked Upon: A Study of the Aspirations of Youth in a Developing Society*, New York: Institute of International Studies, Columbia University.

RUDCENKO, S. (1977) 'Household Money Income, Expenditure and Monetary Assets in Czechoslovakia, GDR, Hungary and Poland, 1956–1975', forthcoming in *Jahrbuch der Wirtschaft Osteuropas*.

RUFFOLO, UGO F. (1974) 'La Linea Einaudi', *Storia Contemporanea*, 5.

RUNCIMAN, W. G. (1966) *Relative Deprivation and Social Justice*, London: Routledge and Kegan Paul.

SARGENT, THOMAS J. and WALLACE, NEIL (1975) '"Rational" Expectations, the Optimal Money Instrument and the Optimal Money Supply Rule', *Journal of Political Economy*, 83.

SAUVY, ALFRED (1965) *Histoire économique de la France entre les deux guerres*, 2 vols, Paris: Fayard.

SAWYER, M. (1976) 'Income Distribution in OECD Countries', *OECD Occasional Studies*, July.

SCHUKER, STEPHEN A. (1976) *The End of French Predominance in Europe: The Financial Crisis of 1924 and the Negotiation of the Dawes Plan*, Chapel Hall, N.C.: University of North Carolina Press.

SCHUMPETER, J. A. (1942) *Capitalism, Socialism and Democracy*, London: Allen and Unwin.

SCHÜTZ, ALFRED (1967) *Collected Papers* (vols. 1 and 2), The Hague: Martinus Nijhoff.

SEERS, D. (1949) *Changes in the Cost-of-living and the Distribution of Income Since 1938*, Oxford: Blackwell.

SEN, A. (1973) *On Economic Inequality*, Oxford: Clarendon Press.

SKIDMORE, THOMAS (1976) 'The Politics of Economic Stabilization in Postwar Latin America', in James Malloy (ed.), *Authoritarianism and Corporatism in Latin America*, University of Pittsburgh Press.

SMITH, A. (1776) *An Inquiry into the Nature and Causes of the Wealth of Nations* (1976 ed.), Oxford: Clarendon Press.

SMITH, D. A. (1976) 'Labour Market Institutions and Inflation', *British Journal of Industrial Relations*, 14.

SMITH, H. (1976) *The Russians*, London: Sphere Books.

SSRC SURVEY UNIT (1976) *Subjective Social Indicators 1971–75*, Occasional Paper, 8.

SOLTOW, L. (1968) 'Long-run Changes in British Income Inequality', *Economic History Review*, 21.

STEIN, HERBERT (1969) *The Fiscal Revolution in America*, Chicago University Press.

SYLOS-LABINI, PAOLO (1974) *Trade Unions, Inflation, and Productivity*, Lexington, Mass.: Saxon House.

TAIT, A. A. (1967) 'A Simple Test of the Redistributive Nature of Price Changes for Wealth Owners in the U.S. and U.K.', *Review of Economics and Statistics*, 49.

TAYLOR, A. J. (1972) *Laissez-Faire and State Intervention in 19th Century Britain*, London: Macmillan.

TEIGEN, ROBERT L. (1972) 'A Critical Look at Monetarist Economics', *Federal Reserve Bank of St. Louis Review*, January.

THATCHER, A. R. (1968) 'The Distribution of Earnings of Employees in Great Britain', *Journal of the Royal Statistical Society*, Series A, 131.

TIPPING, D. G. (1970) 'Price Changes and Income Distribution', *Applied Statistics*, 19.

TOBIN, JAMES (1972) 'Inflation and Unemployment', *American Economic Review*, 62.

TREVITHICK, JAMES A. (1975) 'Keynes, Inflation, and Money Illusion', *Economic Journal*, 85.

TRIFFIN, ROBERT (1960) *Gold and the Dollar Crisis*, Yale University Press.

— (1964) *The Evolution of the International Monetary System: Historical Re-appraisal and Future Perspectives*, Princeton University Press.

TRINDER, C. (1975) 'Comment' on 'Indexing Personal Income Taxation', in T. Liesner and M. King (eds.) *Indexing and Inflation*, London: Heinemann.

TULLOCK, G. (1976) *The Vote Motive*, Institute of Economic Affairs, London.

TURVEY, RALPH (1951) 'Some Aspects of the Theory of Inflation in a Closed Economy', *Economic Journal*, 61.

USHER, D. (1968) *The Price Mechanism and the Meaning of National Income Statistics*, Oxford: Clarendon Press.

VANNEREAU, C. (1975) 'Comparability of Consumer Price Indices in OECD Countries', in OECD, *Economic Outlook*, July.

VOGEL, R. C. (1974) 'The Dynamics of Inflation in Latin America', *American Economic Review*, 64.

WACHTER, SUSAN M. (1976) *Latin-American Inflation*, Lexington, Mass.: Lexington Books.

WALRE DE BORDES, J. VAN (1924) *The Austrian Crown: Its Depreciation and Stabilization*, London: P. S. King.

WEBER, MAX (1903–6) 'Roscher und Knies und die Logischen Probleme der Historischen Nationaloekonomie', *Schmollers Jahrbuch*, 25, 29 and 30. (English translation, *Roscher and Knies: the Logical Problems of Historical Economics*, New York: Free Press, 1975.)

— (1922, 1925) *Wirtschaft und Gesellschaft*, Tubingen: J. C. B. Mohr. (English translation, *Economy and Society*, New York: Bedminster Press, 1968.)

WEINTRAUB, SIDNEY (1960) 'The Keynesian Theory of Inflation: The Two Faces of Janus', *International Economic Review*, 1.

WILENSKY, HAROLD L. (1975) *The Welfare State and Equality*, Berkeley: University of California Press.

— (1976) *The 'New Corporatism', Centralization and the Welfare State*, New York: Sage Publications.

WILES, PETER (1973) 'Cost Inflation and the State of Economic Theory' *Economic Journal*, 83.

— (1974) *Distribution of Income: East and West*, Amsterdam: North-Holland Publishing Co.

— (1977) *Economic Institutions Compared*, Oxford: Basil Blackwell.

WILLIAMSON, JEFFREY G. (1976a) 'American Prices and Urban Inequality since 1820', *Journal of Economic History*, 36.

— (1976b) 'The Sources of American Inequality, 1896–1948', *Review of Economics and Statistics*, 58.

WITT, PETER-CHRISTIAN (1974) 'Finanzpolitik und sozialer Wandel im Krieg und Inflation 1918–1924', in Hans Hommsen *et al.* (eds.) *Industrielles System und Politische Entwicklung in der Weimarer Republik*, Dusseldorf: Droste Verlag.

Woman's Own (1975) 'Housekeeping Survey', September 20.

YUROVSKY, L. M. (1925) *Currency Problems and Policy of the Soviet Union*, London: Leonard Parsons.

ZAWADZKI, K. K. F. (1965) *The Economics of Inflationary Processes*, London: Weidenfeld and Nicolson.

Index